To my early university mentors, the late Professor Rex and Mrs Margaret Knight; and my many friends in the Humanist Society Scotland and Humanists UK.

David Findlay Clark

AGAINST ALL GODS:
THE WAY TO HUMANISM

AUSTIN MACAULEY PUBLISHERS™
LONDON • CAMBRIDGE • NEW YORK • SHARJAH

Copyright © David Findlay Clark (2020)

The right of David Findlay Clark to be identified as author of this work has been asserted by him in accordance with section 77 and 78 of the Copyright, Designs and Patents Act 1988.

All rights reserved. No part of this publication may be reproduced, stored in a retrieval system, or transmitted in any form or by any means, electronic, mechanical, photocopying, recording, or otherwise, without the prior permission of the publishers.

Any person who commits any unauthorised act in relation to this publication may be liable to criminal prosecution and civil claims for damages.

A CIP catalogue record for this title is available from the British Library.

ISBN 9781528936149 (Paperback)
ISBN 9781528968577 (ePub e-book)

www.austinmacauley.com

First Published (2020)
Austin Macauley Publishers Ltd.
25 Canada Square
Canary Wharf
London
E14 5LQ

Acknowledgements

I wish to acknowledge the prompt agreement of Humanists UK to my quoting the Amsterdam Declaration in full and the helpfulness of the officers concerned.

I am especially grateful to Emeritus Professor P J Kodituwakku who took the trouble in a still very busy academic life both in USA and Sri Lanka, to provide me with the content of the back cover.

I should also like to thank the following who have assisted me by reading and commenting helpfully on early drafts of the book: Prof. P.J. Kodituwakku, Bob Sutton, Alan and Marion Richardson, Ralph Dutch, and Derek Burton.

It would be foolish of me not to acknowledge the contribution of many friends, students and professional colleagues for their contributions to my thinking through friendly discussion over many years. These discussions cemented many more friendships than they damaged and for that I am especially grateful.

AGAINST ALL GODS:
THE WAY TO HUMANISM

Sapere aude!
(Have the courage to use your own understanding!)

by
David Findlay Clark
OBE, DL, MA, PhD, C Psych, FBPsS, ARPS

Also by this author

Help, Hospitals and the Handicapped
One Boy's War
Stand by Your Beds! (1st and 2nd Editions)
Remember Who You Are!
Chancer!

Table of Contents

Preface — 9

Chapter 1 — 11
The Nurturing of a Sceptic

Chapter 2 — 24
The Faithful and the Sceptic

Chapter 3 — 30
Toward Answers

Chapter 4 — 36
Stardust to Skeletons and Skins

Chapter 5 — 51
A Closer Look at the Human Condition

Chapter 6 — 60
Speech, Language and Theory of Mind

Chapter 7 — 73
Morality, Gods and Religions

Chapter 8 — 103
Values

Chapter 9 121
Purpose in Life

Chapter 10 126
About Consciousness, Life and Death

Chapter 11 149
A Humanist Glance at the Wider World

Chapter 12 173
Humanism for All Humanity: A Background

Postscript 201

About the Author 204

Bibliography 206

Preface

In the mid-19th century, Cardinal John Henry Newman (1801-1890) might well have earned himself the term "religious extremist" in the sense that he had, after conversion from the Church of England to Roman Catholicism, devoted his life and writings to pointing out what were for him the gross doctrinal errors of Protestantism. Were we to rate the strength of a person's belief system on a 10-point scale (as we do in the assessment of pain, for example) then 10 would represent total, earnest and unshakable commitment to one's beliefs and 1 would represent no commitment to any belief system at all. In between would fall the descriptive 4, 5 and 6, average scores of most people who claim any systematic religious or other beliefs at all but who, in practice, vacillate between more or less firm commitments in the course of daily life. I am not sure whether in statistical terms one could claim that strength of beliefs could be, in Gaussian terms, normally distributed, but it pleases me to think that if I place Cardinal Newman and, say, the Pope or the Prophet Mohammed at the positive end of the distribution (+3 standard deviations above the mean score), at the "extremist" end of the distribution, then my life has seen me fitfully but progressively wandering down to the lower scores of such a distribution until I would, I guess, now be very close to -3 SD (standard deviations) below the mean at the negative end of the distribution—and, presumably, a different kind of "extremist".

There is a Latin phrase "apologia pro vita sua" which, apart from being the title of one of Newman's works, appeared in the notes of earlier prelates and sages. Strictly translated, it means "a defence of one's own life" but dictionaries translate it as "a written justification for his (the writer's) own beliefs or course of life". To that end, it could well have been my title for this book too. As the elder son of a Scottish Presbyterian minister, I was brought up and indoctrinated (inevitably, until I became old enough to think rationally for myself) in a rather austere Manse in a small northern Scottish town. Even at university, I was at first slow to cast about for ideas which might replace the religion with which, by the year, I was becoming increasingly dissatisfied, even disillusioned. Now, with senility beckoning with increasing insistence, I have decided to put down here the main ideational paths I have trodden in my search for a rational, humane, inclusive and evidence-based philosophy which has made, and looks like continuing to make, good sense of my life's rich store of experiences and ideas.

I set out to write, not a textbook, but a book, written in everyday language for the intelligent layman, students or simply for curious individuals who, like me, might be interested to find out whether humanism might offer some guiding principles, quite apart from religion, which would form the basis for living a satisfying, happy and morally principled. life. What follows are some of the considerations that ensured my steady progress along the way to humanism.

Inevitably, since I am not a trained philosopher but a clinical psychologist and neuroscientist, there may be some errors of logic, but, I trust, none of fact. If there are, the responsibility for them is mine. I have written very much as a common man who has, nearing the end of his life, reached a satisfying and reasonably comprehensive understanding of what it has all been about, so far as I, my species and the universe are concerned. Although the book draws from my professional background, it is written not so much as an academic text as an exposition of a basis for the humanist philosophic stance for students and the intelligent layman.

Chapter 1
The Nurturing of a Sceptic

A sudden flurry of hailstones blew in off the North Sea, stinging my cheeks as I stood, flanked by two Flight Sergeants, in front of a squad of shivering airmen on that Sunday morning Church parade in October 1952. A brand new and very junior Pilot Officer in the RAF, I had been designated as operational squadron commander by my CO—*just to test me out,* I thought. It was only months since Queen Elizabeth the Second had ascended the throne as a 25-year-old, and my thoughts had been wandering to my RAF colleagues who had been despatched to serve in the war in North Korea and, more recently, to the UK's exploding its own first atomic bomb on the Monte Bello Islands. However, tea had just come off rationing and I could look forward to a cuppa after the service. For me, no escape was permitted from that!

At a certain point in the proceedings, I had to intone a command, "Fall out, Roman Catholics and Jews!" Any Catholic and Jewish servicemen were then able to slink off to the gym or to their billets, where they would be spared what many of us thought the tedium of hearing the padre conduct a (Protestant) religious service. No account was ever taken of atheists, humanists, Buddhists, Theosophists, Taoists or Hindus. None of us who fell into any of these categories—and there was at least one of each of these in my Officers' Mess at that time, and probably more in the station as a whole—was ever excused. We had to line up with the Protestants. Even at the time I thought that that was odd, since those of us in the categories other than the RCs and Jews were really more protesting than the Protestants!

As the decades passed, I was often asked, sometimes on official forms, what was my religion. As soon as I said, "None. I'm a humanist", the inevitable next question would be either, "Are you a Protestant humanist or a Catholic humanist?" or "What's a humanist anyway?" Several sections of the many answers I have tried to supply have been the starting point of this book.

Ever since I can remember, scepticism seemed to come as second nature to me. Very early in my childhood, perhaps at about the age of four or five, I was occasionally troubled by bad dreams in which various devils from my unconscious would come and leer at me in my sleep. Waking did not always put paid to them immediately, though when one of my parents, or the maid—for I grew up in a bourgeois Scottish household, a manse—came in and went through the fairly lengthy ritual of lighting a candle before fumbling with the gas lamp with its delicate mantle, the grotesque intruders would inevitably disappear back into the Rorschach patterns of the wallpaper. No doubt they were tamed by the very ordinariness of my football, my piggy bank or my wooden fort with its nasty looking lead soldiers. It was explained to me that these demons were the product of my imagination and without substance. Even then, I found this hard to square with the fact that an hour or so earlier I had been asked by these adults to say my prayers to similarly unreal creations of what seemed to be of their imaginations—and equally insubstantial ones at that! No doubt the demons that had wakened me were hellish enough, but I did wonder how they could be written off so easily when the angels in heaven were so patently of the same order, and I was not, by any means, to doubt *their* reality.

Even from our pre-school years, my brother Tom and I had to fall into the ritual of attending church every Sunday; sometimes twice, morning and evening. We were attired in full dress Highland rigouts, which were 'for best' and seldom worn on any other occasion. We would be marched down to my father's kirk, St Mary's Parish Church in Banff, and led by my mother down the central aisle all the way to the very front seat—the manse pew—before what I inevitably felt must be the careful and even rather censorious gaze of the waiting, and in those days relatively large, congregation. This was generally fully assembled before our entrance because of my mother's habitual penchant for leaving everything to the last minute and sometimes later. She had many fine qualities but, somehow, punctuality was not one of them.

Then followed the ritual appearance of the beadle solemnly carrying in the great Bible from the vestry to its place on the pulpit lectern. He retraced his steps with solemn dignity, never a glance to right nor left, before reappearing to lead in the fairly imposing figure of my father in black gown and the purple and ermine-trimmed B.D. hood of Edinburgh University. (Later, he sported a red Edinburgh Doctoral robe.) Not many children in those days got to see their dads at work, for that was what it was. Only it went further than that. The scene was set by the solemn organ music, the expectant silence that followed as he mounted the pulpit steps, the sun casting odd-coloured patterns from the stained glass in the chancel windows and his dramatically raised hands as he opened the service with the time-honoured phrase, "Let us worship God!" Even then, I used to wonder why.

There were parts of the service which offended my rational understanding less than others. Some of the hymns allowed me to mouth the words without paying much attention to them while enjoying the musical harmonies and rich chords of the organ and choir. Later, in the sermon, though, in the traditions of the "Auld Kirk" (the Church of Scotland) there were included some matters of high theology. There would from time to time be elements which dwelt on the potentials of man's humanity to man. At the time that these sonorous phrases were being uttered—in 1939—it seemed to me that it was man's *in*humanity that seemed to be most in evidence. Nevertheless, my father had a high regard for his fellow humans' capacity to rise above adversity, to formulate some sort of humane ethics in relation to others, to consider the merits of ideas such as "From those who have to those who need" and to commend the notion of cooperation rather than competition in the achievement of the greater good. He was very strong on human rights but always stressed that they were not absolute and had to be conditional, earned by our meeting equally fundamental duties and obligations toward our fellow humans. So far as he was concerned, these came first. I have never found it difficult to disagree with that view and still support it.

Ever since, I have retained an adherence to several of these Christian principles; not, however, because they were in any way, God-given or written in the "good book" but because they seemed, even to my largely unformed mind, a valuable basis for people to share in the lives of others. I have also tended to have more than a sneaking sympathy for the underdog.

Never, however, can I remember my father or my mother revealing in so many words what might have been their political leanings. They held firmly to the view that these were matters which were secret to themselves. Even when, as a teenager, I was brash enough simply to ask them directly, they would firmly remind me that every person cast his or her vote at the ballot box as he or she chose, and it was no one else's business. I even doubt whether they vouchsafed to each other how their votes might have been cast at a national or even local election. With the benefit of hindsight and a keen awareness of the socio-political values they personally embraced, I have little doubt that my father was socialist, or at worst—from my perspective, at least—voted Liberal, whereas my mother was probably as Conservative in her voting as she was conservative in her views. She certainly aspired to that!

As a child, my problems were always with the discipline exerted on me to distinguish between the products of my imagination and the outcomes of systematic and logical thought. It was not hard to grasp that these were different categories of mental activity. I suppose that, at that stage, I tended to associate the latter with work and school and the former with pleasure and great chunks of my day-dreaming inner life. Yet as soon as I was carted off to church and Sunday school there seemed to be a demand that all these distinctions should be muddied and that I should engage in a willing suspension of disbelief. When it came to solving problems in daily life, however, prayer, even in my experience, did no good at all. For a short time, I thought that it was because I was not really very good at it. On the other hand, it was apparent to me that structured and planned activity of body and brain seemed to achieve an awful lot more. The love of God seemed to me to be little more than a meaningless phrase, something I could neither experience nor understand in the least, and therefore, like the calculus or the elements of quantum physics to a young child, irrelevant for the moment. Both heaven and hell sounded pretty nasty: fire and brimstone in the latter and pious goody-goodies permanently smarming their way around the former—and worse, doing so eternally!

Every Sunday, as the family would, in ones, twos, threes or, occasionally, fours, walk down to the kirk, we would pass a few dozen pious Roman Catholics heading up the same street in the opposite direction to attend Mass in the Chapel. My father had always schooled Tom and me to be properly respectful toward all of these. Theologically, he would say, they were inclined to be idolaters and had some odd ideas; but, still, they worshipped the same God. At the time, there were nine active churches of different Christian denomination in the small town of 4,000 people and again I would wonder whether they would have different cubicles in hell or heaven in due course. For an omniscient, all-powerful and allegedly beneficent being, God did seem to be a bit of a ditherer when it came to getting His organisation right. My father and his ilk would be inclined to ascribe these difficulties to man rather than God, but if the latter was such a great creator and designer, surely the blame should rest with Him? As they said in Her Majesty's Services when I was a bit older, it sounded as if He couldn't organise a booze-up in a brewery! It always seemed to me to be a bit of a cop-out to say that while God was omnipotent and omniscient, He deliberately arranged for his creation, including mankind, to be so brimming over with 'original sin' as to make such a mess of the beautiful earth with war, pestilence, madness and mayhem of weird and wonderful sorts. And why he should complicate matters by even allowing the possibility of 'false' gods, prophets and sages, such as the Buddha, Mohammed, Shiva or Vishnu and their pals, struck me as improbably incompetent. No wonder that Einstein questioned whether God had had any choice as to whether He created the universe or not. Perhaps He hadn't. Or there may have been other omniscient, omnipotent and equally incompetent but competitive Creators or Designers messing up God's work that neither we, nor He, had formerly noticed.

My father, however, was ecumenical enough in his own way. He and three others made up a four for golf every Monday morning, including the priest from the Roman Catholic Chapel. He still would have his little dig, though. One day I overheard him tell my mother that the Monsignor had not been able to get to the first tee in time. "I'm sorry, Clark," he said, "but I've just been away helping an old man to die." The Reverend, not to be outdone in the theological stakes, replied that when he went to see his parishioners, he preferred to help them to live. Privately, I think he thought Roman Catholics were, as I remarked earlier, idolaters at heart: not nearly astringent and rigorous enough philosophically for his brand of Protestantism, though, at the same time, not as liberal either. Some of my father's ecumenical sentiments were fuelled by the scarcely conscious thought that sooner or later all the "faiths" would have to unite if they were to survive the onslaught of the scientific way of thinking. Having been, until he was thirty, a teacher at Hillhead High School in Glasgow, he had gone off to Edinburgh University to do a Bachelor of Divinity degree and become a minister of religion. This he saw as a matter of conviction rather than as a reasoned position. Discussing it with him on his deathbed in 1966, I could see that what he called faith overcame any need to be wholly rational in analysing the human situation. He recognised that he was insufficiently educated in the sciences to do otherwise. He was, however, an open and tolerant man and he understood that for me, holding a "faith" was an unsatisfactory position. He knew that the philosopher Søren Kierkegaard considered that faith was a total renunciation of the habits of being bound by evidence and experiment. Mark Twain put it more colloquially: "Faith is believing what you know just ain't so."

My early questionings of the nature and value of religious belief were usually palmed off with the explanation that, in some strange way as yet unrevealed to me, I would understand it all better when I had grown up a bit more. Eight decades on, such revelation seems to have eluded me. At school, there was an institution known as the Watt Bible Prize. Naturally, it was always assumed that the sons of the manse would be there or thereabouts when the examination results for that prize were announced. I think, for the record, that I did win the thing a couple of years though it could have been attributed more to the unconscious assimilation of knowledge that came simply from living in the manse than to any special conviction or knowledge vouchsafed to me by dint of some direct line to the Almighty—as others seemed to assume. I was patently unenthusiastic about the whole affair. Unlike much of what I was learning at the time—and not all of it in school—I found it hard to relate any Biblical studies to my experience or to see them having any direct relevance to daily life.

It struck me as odd that when I overheard adult conversations between my parents, they were often analytical to the point of paranoia about the motives and behaviour of others, and yet they set much store by this curious non-analytical process called "faith" in matters of religion. Both my parents used to describe Roman Catholicism as an authoritarian religion, and yet they were themselves quite authoritarian in their declarations about what one should believe. Such adjurations always sat uncomfortably with their insistence that as a pupil and later, student, I should be critical, analytical and self-sufficient. "Think for yourself, boy. Take nothing for granted!" they would say in the context of a lesson in Mathematics, Geography or English Literature. Perhaps the key difference lay in the fact that many adults seemed to be very aware of life's temporary nature, its many frustrations, difficulties and sorrows. Children and youths are so full of burgeoning life that the notion of death is of an event so distant that it has little impact or even reality in one's day to day life. Sometimes children will wonder what might happen to them should a parent die, but it would never occur to them that they themselves might do so. And life was so hard for many in the past, and even now in our less favoured streets and in the less developed world that it might have been unbearable were it not for the prospect of some sort of life after death. The details of and conditions of entry to that life seemed to me to take up an inordinate amount of time and attention—especially for something the existence of which could only be affirmed rather than empirically demonstrated.

In later years, and especially when I was at home during the university vacations, my father and I would argue and discuss philosophic viewpoints and theological concepts long into the night. My mother would get quite anxious about this and would often scuttle away to bed alone with some such parting shot as "I can't see why you don't just accept that there are some things you'll never know and will have to have faith!" What actually happened as I grew up was that I did, indeed, recognise that there are things that I would never know, but, fortunately, I was happy to live with my ignorance and to make inroads into my ignorance when I could. I suspect that at the time of her declaration, she wanted to be well away from the site of the falling thunderbolt which would eventually rid me of my errant views.

My father had greater faith in the heavenly marksmanship and sat around while we considered the imponderables of multiple translations from Aramaic to Hebrew, to Greek, to Latin, and to English as the "Great Story", as he called it, was passed down the generations. His knowledge of the ancient languages (Latin, Greek and Hebrew, all of which he could read comfortably) made him much more sensitive to the use of metaphor in the transmission of both a written and an oral culture or history of ideas. He was also deeply interested himself in the transmission of an oral culture to a written one and was always open to the realistic notion that scribes and Pharisees, just like us, could become bored and get writer's cramp halfway through their chores, fill in their own little bits and miss out some of the difficult paragraphs. And he applied that liberal view of the written word to other religions as well. He had copies of the Talmud and the Koran on his bookshelves and he insisted that I read texts on several of the world religions before I ventured to be too critical of what they were alleged to have written. So, I did—and became perhaps even more critical. Thus, it was that I began to read huge chunks of the Bible, especially, some of the Koran and the Talmud and outline texts about Shintoism and Hinduism. Freedom of speech and thought is not a notable feature of any of the main religious writings and tolerance of other ways of construing the world is low or non-existent. "They wish that you should disbelieve as they disbelieve, and then you would be equal; therefore take not to yourselves friends of them, until they emigrate in the way of God; then, if they turn their backs, take them, and slay them wherever you find them; take not to yourselves any one of them as friend or helper." (Quran, 4:89)

This sentiment applies to all Muslims, not just extremists. Several religions, of which Islam is the most obvious, also fail to allow that women are as worthy citizens as men. Nor do they see homosexuality in either sex as allowable. It is not too hard to see how far such precepts clash with liberal Western cultures. Sam Harris, the American philosopher and neuroscientist, declared in *The End of Faith* (2004) that he considers Islam to be the greatest threat to modern civilisation.

After my early readings of the texts of several religions, the conclusions I came to were that charismatic figures no doubt lived—mostly in subtropical climes where they were less concerned with simply fighting the elements to survive (Woden and Thor were notable exceptions from above the 60th parallel)—and, in some cases, were wise enough to create systems of thought and attitudes which endowed them with certain powers and potencies. These figures might no doubt have declared a number of general moral precepts which might underpin a more benign social organisation. Wisely, none of the great prophets suggested that following their precepts would be easy, and, just to keep the punters on their toes, they would, like some more modern philosophers, often speak in riddles.

Perhaps because of my protracted and vigorous, though usually interesting, discussions with my father on the relationship between ethics and religious systems, I yielded to the strong social pressure from within the family and became a reluctant communicant within the Church of Scotland. For a year or two at the end of my school career and into my first year at Aberdeen University, I attended church and the university chapel at Kings College in, as it turned out, a vain attempt to see whether a formal commitment to the rituals of religion would afford any more "spiritual" insights or accesses of faith than my previous more casual or incidental associations with the church had afforded. Certainly, the content of the sermons of, for example, Professor Sir Thomas Taylor or Professor Donald MacKinnon at the Chapel of Kings College was intellectually stimulating and replete with knowledge of a variety of forms of theism, the history of philosophy, comparative religion and literary reference. At the end of the day, however, the notion of worship—of anything—and especially of a god (a concept which is so ill-defined in empirically testable terms as to be meaningless) left me cold. Indeed, it puzzled me then, and for years subsequently, why so many sharp intellects in university and elsewhere did not more seriously and vigorously challenge the nature of the "God concept".

At the time, my explorations into the mainsprings of human and animal behaviour, the philosophy of the logical positivists and the deterministic position inevitable for any scientist, natural, behavioural or otherwise, who might be concerned to explore the understanding and control of behaviour and experience, left no room for capricious "acts of God", the concept of faith or the relevance of worship. For me, in the 1950s, Wittgenstein, Bertrand Russell, Ayer and Ryle and, of course, Charles Darwin made potent reading, especially when their ideas were linked to those of Watson and the neo-Behaviourists, Skinner, Hull and Eysenck. Since then I have moved a bit away, as most cognitive psychologists have, from what might be called 'hard-nosed behaviourism'. Most of all, however, was I influenced by the clarity, cogency and confirmability of the arguments put before me by Rex and Margaret Knight. Rex was Anderson Professor of Psychology at the University and his wife a reader there. They were both self-declared scientific humanists, a breed of thinker which, with the exception of Julian Huxley and H J Blackham, I had not much heard of until then. Half a century on, however, the detailed discovery of the human genome, and the publications of many scientists and philosophers–Richard Dawkins' *The Selfish Gene* (1976) and his many other works, including *The God Delusion* (2006), the work of Steven Rose, Michael Shermer (*The Believing Brain* (2011) and Sam Harris' *The End of Faith* (2005), the work of Daniel Dennett, primarily a philosopher, on his particular neuroscientific understanding of consciousness, A C Grayling's output, especially his *The God Argument* (2013) and Steven Pinker's *How the Mind Works* (1998)—have updated my views substantially, though confirming what was becoming my fundamentally humanist position.

During my third and fourth years at university, the consequence of many an hour's formal and informal laboratory experimentation, debate and discussion with other students and with Rex and Margaret Knight themselves was that any religious notions that I had attempted to harbour in the past became totally untenable in terms of logic and evidence and indeed utterly at variance with a great deal of the experimental work and theories of learning, perception and behaviour I was then studying in the psychology and physiology labs. That view does not, however, contradict Mick Power (2012), a clinical psychologist like myself, in his demonstration of how the adherents of many religions cling to their beliefs motivated and supported by many psychological processes and mechanisms that he has dealt with and explained.

So it was that I felt constrained to hand back my Communicant's card (signifying my formal membership of the church) to my father and to tell him, as gently as I could, that his, or anyone else's, religion was not for me. To me, the concept of God was far too indeterminate and vague. For others, the properties of a god, with or without an initial capital, were affirmed rather than empirically demonstrated, historically primitive and essentially supernatural—which in itself takes it beyond meaning or rational examination. The concept served simply to complicate rather than to simplify an understanding of the human situation. In my experience there had never been any glimmer of what others called faith. Indeed, to this day I have never experienced anything that could not be more accurately and parsimoniously explained by a scientific rationale than by what others call faith. Anthony Grayling, in *The Meaning of Things* (2001) is blunt about faith. "Faith is a negation of reason. Reason is the faculty of proportioning judgment to evidence, after first weighing the evidence. Faith is belief even in the face of contrary evidence" (p117). Kierkegaard defined faith as "the leap taken despite everything, despite the very absurdity of what one is asked to believe." Where and in what circumstances such a "leap" (beyond logic, we are to presume) might be taken is not specified.

As it turned out, my father's understanding of my position was much clearer and more sympathetic than was my mother's. He himself was able to acknowledge that his beliefs rested on faith—a faith which he hung on to, even tenuously at times, till his death. He recognised that if that element were missing, then the catechism and other bases of his theology were pointless and could have little personal meaning. My mother, by contrast, was shocked and distressed. She could not conceive of anyone daring *not* to believe. To her, there were no other rationales of existence and I am sure that she felt that my unbelief would bring down the lethal thunderbolt not only on my head but also on those of the whole family—and right quickly too. As time passed and the thunderbolt, or even plagues of locusts, boils or floods and famine seemed to bypass our little town—with the exception of the Episcopal Church which was hit by lightning that year—she became reconciled to the fact that I was a lost soul.

The only occasion on which I came anywhere near to recanting was my wedding to Janet in October 1954. By that time, my father was in his seventies and had set his mind on officiating at my marriage in church. To mitigate what would have been a terrible sadness for my parents, I was happy to go along with their wishes, given that my father recognised that whenever he mentioned God, it would mean nothing to me. For me, it was a solemn vow I was to take, one which I took with happiness and seriousness and which had a solemnity wherever it was spoken. If my parents thought the marriage was made in heaven, that was fine by me and Janet. For me, it was made on earth, has been enjoyed on earth (for more than 63 years at the time of writing) and will, in due course, end on earth. That has not reduced its quality for me in the slightest.

One of my main pleas in this book is that belief is fundamentally dangerous and even destructive, even if it holds talismanic qualities for some, protecting them from the slings and arrows of outrageous fortune and supporting them in times of stress. An early definition of what I mean by belief is therefore important. From three contemporary dictionaries, including the Oxford, I have extracted a definition combining the key elements in their definitions. A belief, they declare, is "an idea or principle which is held to be true in the absence of any empirical evidence for it." That is why I am not a believer—in anything. Some challenge this by saying that I must believe in the scientific method. My reply is that that method is constantly updating itself and validating its content. There is too much evidence of the success of the scientific method for me to discard it; it is a system of thought which allows for uncertainty and is always ready to modify its propositions in the light of changing evidence. I do not *believe* in it: as a pragmatist, I simply use the scientific method because I observe that it works. Religions, by contrast, are always declaring great "truths" that are given and unchanging. Some of the latter may well be worth hanging on to because, by chance or otherwise, they can be evidentially supported and have had some evolutionarily worthwhile features. Others—often declared by prophets wandering about the deserts of the Middle East more than one or two thousand years ago, and whose store of knowledge and experience of other peoples and cultures must have been relatively limited—are now irrelevant to or clash with modern knowledge and lifestyles. This dissonance has generated conflict and antagonisms which, unless reconciled over the next few hundred years, may lead to the extinction of our species.

When I was a young student, and thinking about systems of belief, I read a volume of essays by anthropologist, Robert Briffault, *Reasons for Anger* (1937) in one of which he writes: "One of the most stupid principles, and certainly the most pernicious, of our current tradition is the doctrine that all beliefs that are held sincerely are equally entitled to respect. Nine-tenths of the atrocities which convert the human world from a glorious achievement to a ghastly horror are the result of sincere beliefs of good men and women. Those sincere beliefs have plunged the world into misery and deluged it with blood. I have no respect for them. The principle is, of course, merely a device for the protection of traditional stupidity. Were it once admitted that the only criterion of the respectability of a belief is its validity on rational grounds, the difficult task of safeguarding irrational traditions would become hopeless." It is worth noting, incidentally, that this passage was written two years before the outbreak of the Second World War.

While my general thesis is that a steady increase in (scientific) knowledge will gradually erode all kinds of beliefs, even stricter intellectual disciplines will be required as new beliefs about how knowledge should be applied and used will, at first, tend to spring, Phoenix-like, from the ashes of older discarded beliefs. As I have noted above, Mick Power (2012) has closely examined what psychological underpinnings prevent the steady erosion of many religious beliefs in the face of contrary evidence dealing with their content. Daniel Dennett (2006) is of the opinion that, in spite of the rapid advancement of the sciences, religions will persist for several centuries to come, basically because of the support and solace they afford peoples deprived of higher levels of education and understanding.

Is there then any alternative world view or philosophic stance which might usefully replace religion but which eschews gods, irrationality and superstition? The intention of this book is to suggest that humanism is such a philosophy.

Chapter 2
The Faithful and the Sceptic

Even as a young man I had been able to see the considerable emotional support that many people derived from the religious beliefs they held. From a psychologist's point of view, this support strongly reinforced their faith and religious practices. For that very reason, however, the faithful are reluctant to engage in much argument or discussion about their religion's content or foundations. This was brought home to me relatively unexpectedly, but quite forcibly, during a series of lectures and seminars which NHS England invited me to give alongside Dr Cunningham, a consultant psychiatrist from nearby Lancaster Moor Hospital. Our audience was a large group – 'group' will have to do, as I am unsure whether there is a suitable collective noun – consisting of all the hospital chaplains of all Christian denominations in psychiatric hospitals throughout England. Dr Cunningham and I were to guide these chaplains on how to communicate better with 'difficult' patients, how to keep themselves safe from assault by disturbed patients, how to exercise their pastoral skills in a threatening or confused environment and how to communicate effectively with often very uncommunicative or disturbed patients.

The seminars were held in the historic Whalley Abbey near Clitheroe, once a Cistercian institution but now semi-ruined in places and endlessly draughty. I, as the only resident lecturer, was afforded the luxury/penance of a six-by-five-foot cell with bare stone walls and floor, a simple bed with a straw paillasse, an upright chair, a green baize curtain for a door and a share of the monks' communal toilets and showers 60 or more metres away along the stone flagged corridors of the abbey. Dr Cunningham, being a local, knew about the abbey and wisely decided to drive home to Lancaster every night of the colloquium. My home at the time, in Leicester, was just too far for escape to be practical. The reader will understand my ready acceptance of a kind invitation from four Jesuit priests for me to join them for a slap-up private dinner with appropriate libations at a fine pub and restaurant within walking distance of my cell. They genially suggested that they would dearly like to have some prolonged discussion of my humanist – or, as they then thought, atheist – views.

It was a convivial evening with dinner served in a private room which ran well into the next morning. It soon became clear that they were surprisingly unused to discussing their religious beliefs and the theology associated with them with someone who held no beliefs at all but simply declared that he knew things and did not know some things yet who would not fill in the gaps in his knowledge with superstitions and fantasies. To me, belief in gods was like belief in fairies. I had experience of or empirical evidence for neither. For that reason, I saw no merit at all in studying theology when there is no theos (god) in the first place. Since, as far as I was concerned, 'god' is just a noise we make – an idea or a name, which for the irreligious carries no fixed definition, locus, mode of operation or physical properties – I suggested that if they were to read the Bible, replacing every occurrence of the word 'God' with the word 'fairies', then the ludicrousness of their beliefs would become obvious. For example, the Old Testament in the Bible would then say that Moses was called by 'the fairies' to climb up to the top of Mount Sinai, talk with 'fairies' and bring down their commandments on two hefty tablets of stone. If Moses, or anyone else, spoke like that anywhere in a western culture now, doctors would offer him a course of chlorpromazine, perhaps a hernia truss and a warning that if he continued to speak in these terms in the UK, the men with white coats would have him 'sectioned' under the Mental Health Act.

To the humanist, theology is a discipline about nothing of substance or reality, a game for philosophers playing with words, or, at best, the discussion of an **idea** created by their brains which can be endlessly elaborated but which represents no clearly identifiable natural phenomenon. Often in our lives we may create, from bits of remembered experience, brain activity which my early teachers in psychology used to call 'constructed images'. Never, however, did we confuse such images with actual perceptions or memories, even if we did recognise that such cerebral activities could serve as a bank of creativity for designers, artists, musicians, poets and other kinds of writers.

At one point in my discussion with the Jesuits, I remember asking them what they thought their God was for. That seemed to give rise to some more than brief debate amongst themselves, but in the end, they averred that (a) God was the creator of the world and universe, (b) God was the source of all morality, (c) God afforded humans a purpose in life, and (d) God offered his believers (but apparently no Buddhists, Muslims, Confucians, Humanists or Hindus) eternal life after death, having promised rewards and punishments, via heaven and hell as something to look forward to.

Since they were all hospital chaplains, it surprised me that none of them offered the idea that God was a source of comfort and succour to people in distress. Doctrine appeared to be taking precedence over pastoral practice and simple human sympathy. Perhaps if my question had been, "What is religion, as distinct from God, for?" they might have answered differently.

As this book progresses, I hope to present a humanist rebuttal of those four propositions that they did enunciate and to elaborate the alternative humanist world view. At my personal statement of unbelief, the priests all spluttered into their brandy and gingers.

"But you must believe something, Dr Clark!"

"Why?" I replied. "I can observe, evaluate, weigh evidence and conclude what significance any object, person, event, idea or experience may hold for me as I seek to assimilate it into the store of knowledge I have accumulated so far. Some issues may, of course, need time for further evidence and scrutiny, but I would prefer to work and wait until the information and experience I needed would augment my knowledge rather than accept, as a kind of intellectual stopgap, any belief as the word is defined in the dictionary."

We all departed to our cells in the Abbey at some early hour of the morning, apparently still in friendship. As we parted, one of them said, "But what happens to *you* when you die?" I suspect they were all quite relieved when I said that I would be burned and that all the atoms that formerly comprised me would be redistributed about the universe(s), all fulfilling an infinity of other necessary functions. They probably thought that that was as good a way as any to dispose of the diabolical iconoclast for whom they had generously bought dinner and wine.

For my part, a few good liqueurs could not atone for the way in which the priests had dwelt on dogma and trodden some strange byways of Christian theology. Their discussions so offended my scientific understanding of the human condition that I began to consider the subject in detail, continuing to think about it for several years until at last I took to writing this. With every year it becomes more important that the humanist view is propagated as fully and as widely as possible, simply because the threat to our present civilisation is sustained more by the real or threatened conflicts between the organised religions of the world than by non-religious groups, rather fewer of which initiate conflict. History comprehensively illustrates the unnecessary suffering, the destruction of whole cultures, the restrictions and embargoes on scientific research and freedoms of speech and writing which organised religions have wrought.

Much of the above polemic may suggest that, while the observations reported are all too apparent, the writer has largely ignored the benefits that the organised religions imparted to several populations during the past two millennia. Much moral teaching, writing and other cultural pursuits like painting, literature, music and styles of family care were part of the more valuable legacy of religion. There are examples like the paintings in the Sistine Chapel, the music of, for example, the *St Matthew Passion* or the rich vocal harmonies of Handel's *Messiah* oratorio that will enrich the cultural heritage of religious and non-religious people alike for centuries yet. That is acknowledged and that legacy will be referred to again from time to time. The writer's view is, however, that, on balance, civilisation and human progress have been better served by the humanist/scientific understandings and knowledge free of the cramping effects of religious thinking. Further detailed elaboration of this point has been undertaken by the psychologist and explorer of the nature of language Steven Pinker (2018) in his book *Enlightenment Now*; this will be referred to by myself later in this book.

In spite of any cultural legacy, however, poorly educated but religious peoples living in arid regions will still be encouraged, for example, to pray to their gods (with little or no effect) for rain. Humanists would prefer to teach them how to bore artesian wells, build dams, aqueducts and storage tanks, or even seed suitable clouds from the air with silver iodide crystals as a less superstitious and much more rational way to solve their problem.

That is but one example among many. Unfortunately, the costs of such practical interventions are often just too high. Humanists should consider it their responsibility to help with these more rational methods in any reasonable way. Individual humanists as members of other clubs such as Rotary International, the United Nations and, to its credit, Christian Aid, have already contributed substantially in this way.

Too often, the religions and their gods and theologies are described, resourced and protected, even by governments, to a degree unwarranted by their own self-declared status and significance. That is why a major aim of this book is to present a non-religious but rational and potentially unifying philosophic standpoint which is all too often ignored as a valuable and viable alternative to any of the current world religions.

So where does someone like me, rejecting belief in general as an unsatisfactory principle, start to rationalise his existence? Perhaps, earlier in my life, the key areas of knowledge, principles or ideas while at university were those of relativity, natural selection and evolution, cognitive and abnormal psychology and new findings in cosmology and neuroscience (this last largely taught as physiological psychology at that time). Wider discussion with fellow students doing philosophy, natural sciences and medicine introduced me to new ideas and an appreciation of the multi-layered nature of knowledge. Names like Einstein, Newton and Darwin in the natural sciences, and Wittgenstein, Ayer, Bertrand Russell and Gilbert Ryle in philosophy tripped from our lips. Some of that was mere post-adolescent showing off, but some useful gleanings stuck. Much more recently, Sam Harris, Daniel Dennett and A C Grayling in philosophy and the psychologists B F Skinner, G A Kelly, Carl Rogers, Abraham Maslow and H J Eysenck have shouldered Jung, Freud and Adler out of the way. Now the bibliography will reveal other significant influences on my more recent thinking. Jim Baggott, Colin Blakemore, Antonio Damasio, Mick Power, Steven Pinker, Michael Shermer and Nick Humphrey in psychology and neuroscience have been significant in moulding how I think of religion, the human condition and my own place in it. More recently still, of course, influences not only from psychology but from biology and neuroscience such as Richard Dawkins, Jonathan Haidt, Joshua Greene and, again, Michael Shermer have all played their part. I acknowledge a great debt to them, their thinking and the clarity of their expositions of it. The extent of my debt to them will become more apparent as you read on—should you choose to do so!

Chapter 3
Toward Answers

Egocentrically, I start from the position that, like other life forms on this planet, I am a bundle of organic molecules, growing in an environment which I have come to relate to, depend upon and be influenced by. It seems to me from observation that there are strong similarities between the creature I call 'me' and all of the other creatures of my species around me. However, it is also apparent that we differ from other animals in this way: our capacity to communicate with each other in a variety of languages, verbal, numerical, symbolic, musical and graphic, far outstrips the capacity of other species. Moreover, the internalisation of speech provides a strong positive feedback loop whereby we enhance our capacity to think and by so doing, manipulate our environment and develop our capacity to think and communicate even more extensively, intensively and with increasing complexity.

It has been the pursuit of such thinking brain activity by others that has rationalised the observations of man throughout his existence into some systematic understanding of what we call our environment, the world and indeed the cosmos. The evolution of thought about what we see as our world has moved from the primitive animism, the earliest civilisations and stone age man to our present, more subtle and complex understandings of natural phenomena. These have progressed to the point of enabling us to explore the surface of the moon and to circumnavigate and place apparatus and space vehicles on some of the nearer planets. So far, we have no hard evidence of life in any way similar to any of the life forms we know of on our own blue planet. This is, of course, a long way from ruling out any other life forms having evolved on other planets elsewhere in the cosmos.

Scientific thinking has also allowed us to probe not only the nature of space/time and its dimensionality but to recognise the structure, particles and wavelengths of the tiniest components of the atom and even to consider the role of 'black holes', uncertainty and anti-matter in the nature of the universe that we see ourselves as inhabiting. For, ultimately, it all depends on the understanding and perception of individual humans or, put in other terms, the micro-neural electro-chemical activities of sundry human brains duly communicated to others and validated by the observations of similar living humans to form a corpus of knowledge. That corpus of knowledge must satisfy the following conditions: to be subject to confirmation or disconfirmation by observation and experiment; to be communicable by symbolic logic and language; to allow predictions to be made which, when confirmed, revalidate the theories which gave rise to them. In this way the hypothetico-deductive method has in itself become, for scientists, almost a 'neural habit' which underlies all systematic, empirical thinking and experiment.

The human brain—easily the most wonderful functioning biological structure so far known in the universe—has taught itself to allow us to adapt with increasing competence and survival value to an increasingly complex and changing micro- and macro-environment (Eagleman, David (2015)). Our autoimmune systems fight off assaults by viruses and we learn to cope with earthquakes and landslips. Human brains, for all our wonderment at their complexity and power, are not by any means infallible. Like all computers, they have to be programmed and each of us will spend about 90% of our lives endlessly doing just that, as well as updating every second. Every day we learn new skills: to type, play golf, speak another language, to change our political allegiances or circle of friends. We remember and forget, study or daydream and all the time our brains and bodies are interacting—almost feeding off each other to keep us in touch with those around us and our changing environment. All of these operations involve billions of brain cell interactions for each of them.

For readers who may not be familiar with nerve impulses and the like, a brief digression might be helpful. The average human brain weighs around 1.4 kgs of a soft jelly-like tissue made up of 10^{11} neurons or cells all interconnected with each other so as to make at least 10^{15} storage processing and linking possibilities for every adult. Human brain weight can vary, but only when it drops to 1,000g or less would the casual observer notice serious differences in the owner's behaviour. For example, two famous writers whose brains found their way to the pathologist's bench were those of French novelist Anatole France (just over 1200g, as was Einstein's) and of Russian novelist Ivan Turgenev (2021 g). The structural integrity and functionality of the brain matters far more than sheer brain weight. The right and left hemispheres of the brain are linked physically and functionally by a mass of neurons, the corpus callosum, which appear white in colour. There are two further small central bodies, each just a few millimetres in diameter. The first is the pineal gland, found deep between the hemispheres and once thought (wrongly) by Descartes and others to be the probable centre of the 'soul' or 'mind'. The other small central body is the nucleus accumbens, variously described as the orgiastic or pleasure centre of the brain. Experimental rats, trained to press a lever which rewarded them with a tiny pulse to this small organ, had to be removed from the experiment before they killed themselves by irresistible repeated pressings of the lever. The huge numbers of neurons available to the brain is, literally, astronomic—more than the visible stars of our galaxy (the Milky Way) on a clear night sky, and although age takes its toll as some brain cells die, it is possible for remaining nuclei to grow more or longer dendrites to allow more compensatory interconnections. Neuroscientists are now aware that the efficient functioning of dendrites, leading to their proliferation, is now due to increased usage, whereas some shrivel and die if not kept busy.

Each neuron consists of a nucleus which keeps it alive and an axon (or main stem) consisting of a porous tubular membrane protected and insulated by a myelin (fatty) sheath. Sensory or afferent neurons carrying signals to and within the brain may vary greatly in length. There are also huge numbers of other neurons. Some are called internuncial neurons, while there are other cells with little or no axon called glial cells. These cells are generally much smaller but carry very many dendrites in order to facilitate the all-important signals between all the brain's nerves and the rest of the body. The so-called 'grey matter' of the brain is largely made up of neuron cells and all are held in position by glial cells. 'γλοία' is the Greek word for glue and as a result, glia are commonly known as the glue of the nervous system. However, this is not fully accurate as neuroscientists have currently identified that glial cells, as well as insulating one neuron from another, surround them, hold them in place and protect them; the neurons supply the glial cells with oxygen and nutrients and protect them from pathogens

When a neuron is stimulated by another (or by some interfering neuroscientist), the nerve becomes depolarised. The interior of the nerve contains potassium, negatively charged, whereas the outside, the permeable membrane, is mostly sodium with a positive charge. At the point of origination of the stimulus, the resting potential of the neuron may drop from perhaps up to 30 mV or even 70 mV to 0 mV or, depending on the type of neuron, may drop to a low negative value. This is because the function of some neurons is to inhibit the activity of the nerve rather than to stimulate the nerve to positive action. The depolarised area then travels along the axon of the neuron toward the terminal dendrites (at about 300 feet per second in a large neuron, much slower than a purely electric current) where the nerve impulse is passed on, via the synapses, to one or many more neurons.

Every neuron has at each end of long axons, or all over and in all directions in internuncial neurons, glial cells and others, tiny (even microscopic) twig- or finger-like bunches of extensions called dendrites (from the Greek 'dendron'—a tree). These are the parts of neurons which pass nerve impulses to one or more alternative neurons. No dendrite tips ever actually touch others, but they form what have been described as 'spark-gap' type connections, the synapses. Between dendrites are what are called neurotransmitter chemicals such as dopamine, epinephrine, norepinephrine, serotonin, acetylcholine or oxytocin which are mono-amine molecules manufactured by the body almost instantaneously as required. You will now appreciate that the brain is an incredibly busy organ, simultaneously fulfilling a variety of electro-chemical functions. Some of this overall brain activity can be, as a general level, revealed by electroencephalographic or scanning techniques.

Some critics of my approach will be inclined to decry as utterly 'reductionist' because it seems that tracing everything back to electro-chemical changes in neurons in our brains and elsewhere removes all the mystery and wonderment of life to bio-chemistry. For myself, on the contrary, it richly enhances my wonder and sense of the glory of the evolution of man, his intellect and where that may yet lead us. The fact that our brains and bodies alike have evolved from the tiniest of single cells, over a small proportion of the time that the universe—or even our world—has existed, is a fascinating narrative and wonder enough for me.

The Danish philosopher Kierkegaard found himself compelled to remark that life could only be understood backwards even if it had to be lived forwards, and even that depends on a conventional view of time. Stephen Hawking, in *The Grand Design* and *A Brief History of Time* (2010) has commented on how arbitrary our notion of time only running 'forwards' is. It can be construed by contemporary theoretical physicists as running in several directions. The evolution of our brains has, however, forced most of us into sequencing our perceptions and activities on a single time vector in such a way that we predicate our understanding of objects, their movements, our experiences and events on a sequenced and progressive continuum of what we differentiate as past, present and future. In that sense we are time-trapped by our own brain's structure and functioning.

The triumph of the intellect lies in its capacity to tread lightly over the centuries, cutting the shackles of our captivity within the present limits of our finite lives. It has the freedom to pick the finest flowers from the rich gardens of observations, ideas and discourse cultivated and nourished by the most distinguished thinkers of humankind. The legacy of the intellect is that we are freed from the limits of our 'three score years and ten'—or whatever time we may have—even if our biology and awareness of other lives compels us to construe all things as following a similar linear sequence with a beginning, middle and an end. Stephen Hawking (2010) was comfortable with the view that we can construct and use more than one model of understanding, employing new mathematical and philosophic approaches as we work our way towards the model that finally works best. The development of several models about thinking and behaviour has certainly been the case in psychology; there will be occasion for further remarks on this later.

It is a standard joke by after-dinner speakers that in two days' time, tomorrow will be yesterday. In one sense, only the present has reality in our heads for it contains both the 'future' and the 'past', as we call them. For all of us, awareness and scrutiny of all of these depend on current firings of electro-chemical neural impulses, measurable as micro-voltages, within our nervous systems, especially within the brain. The longer view, however, shows us that it all has evolved from stardust, and for all that we know, the process may be continuing at different stages in our planet or elsewhere in other galaxies and other universes.

Chapter 4
Stardust to Skeletons and Skins

The intention underlying this chapter is not to divert the reader from my central thesis—that gods are unnecessary for the understanding of the human condition—but more to illustrate my secondary thesis that one or more universes have always existed, continually regenerating themselves in the infinite curvilinearity of space/time which has no beginning and no end. We are compelled by the biology of our brains to search for a beginning, for origins and consequently 'creators' within a linear concept of time.

This chapter will look at the understanding of astronomers and cosmologists of the recurrent cycles of events which not only gave rise to the formation of our planet, but also predict its eventual demise and replacement by new structures through entropy. Astronomers' observations so far indicate that we live on the edge of a spiral galaxy pulsating with the light of 100 billion stars and stretching 100,000 light years through space/time. Through the rotation of the galaxy over a period of about 12 billion years, the region where new stars are born has been flattened into a disc. Our sun rotates within the galaxy, about 28,000 light years from its centre. We see the galaxy compressed, like a plate, edge-on, and we call it the Milky Way. Hundreds of thousands of other galaxies in our universe are pulsing out their light long after their deaths and others again are being born, their light not likely to reach earth for millions of light years—perhaps long after earth ceases to exist. In that setting, we humans have little to get conceited about.

Hubble, in the latter part of the twentieth century, has shown that the other known galaxies are moving away from us at a speed which accelerates the further they get away from us. Correspondingly, the further back in time we go, the closer together all these galaxies must have been. Probably about 13.8 to 14 billion years ago, by current best calculations, all the matter of these galaxies must have occupied a single point: the singularity, the moment/place of what we currently describe as the Big Bang. But whether the increasing expansion of the universe will continue until it becomes infinitely inflated or diffuse—a return to entropy, some stars dying because their nuclear fuel will be burned up and others sucked into the enormously powerful gravitational sink holes of 'black holes' at which point the universe will have broken down—or whether it will collapse again into its own gravity and become yet again a single point with no dimensions is an open question. My own ideas about the singularity is that, if space/time is curvilinear, then it is possible to think of space/time as being represented as a circle, like a ring of soft wire. Gravitational waves and other random forces can constantly distort that circular curvilinearity into a sort of 'dumbbell' outline. Then, similar random forces give one end of the 'dumbbell' a 180 degree twist so that the formerly opposed and separated space/time lines cross and touch each other. That point could represent the singularity, 'the Big Bang', and the result is not one new expanding universe but two, one of which we have recognised as ours and each having its own space/time circle, so to speak. A small diagram might illustrate what I am thinking, which can be found on the following page.

- A linear time vector with a beginning, middle and end. (Fig. 1)

- That 'line' becoming curvilinear until it becomes totally curvilinear, a circle, with no beginning or end. (Figs. 2 and 3)

- The time line circle is twisted so the separate parts of the time line touch to form a singularity. (Figs. 4 and 5)

- And two new closed timelines result. (Fig. 6)

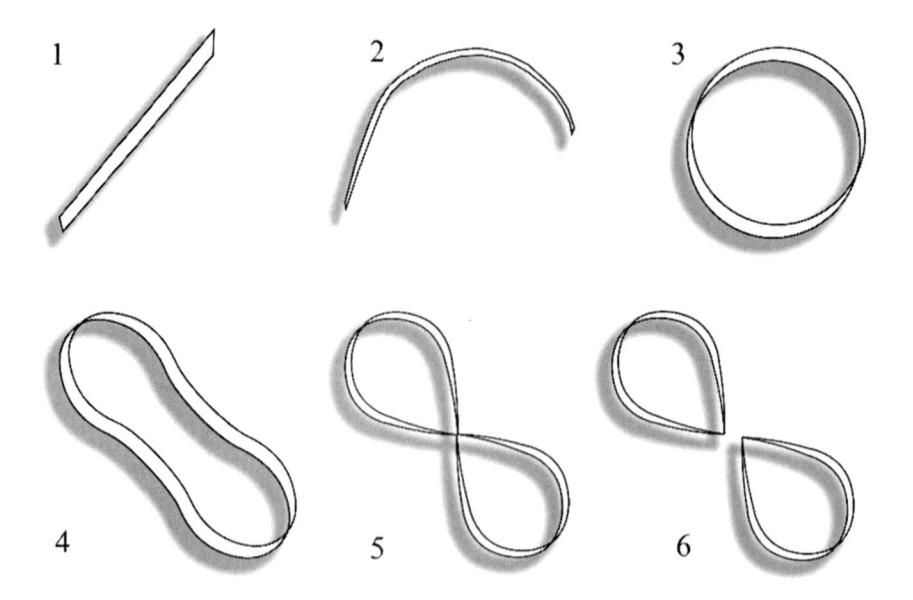

Space/Time never ends.

The astrophysicists have certainly shown that, because our universe supplies us with energy, evidence of matter (and anti-matter) at different stages of its evolution in space/time, there is a kind of reiterating cycle possible at a scale slightly less than that to which I have been referring. The universe appears, therefore, to be regenerating or replacing itself perpetually.

That cycle goes something like this. At some point in the universe, a cold, dense cloud of gas may be impacted by the edge of a galaxy at which point it becomes broken into fragments. In each of these fragments, the gas clumps by its own gravity into a dense core. This is surrounded by a halo-like structure of gas all falling in on itself to form the beginnings of a star perhaps 60 times more massive than our sun. After about 50,000 years, the centre of such a mass becomes so hot that nuclear burning begins, and the body of the star is a mass of convecting gas currents from the edge of which stray gasses are blown off into space. After another 50,000 years or so, this massive star reaches stability, a hot maturity in which the outward pressure of the light from the nuclear fusion of hydrogen into helium is exactly counterbalanced by the pull of the star's own gravity. Our sun is at about this stage in its development now.

Only in conditions of reasonably constant warmth and light can any life, as we know it, form, develop and evolve. The prospects for our sun are those of any other mature star. After at least 10,000,000 years, all the hydrogen in the core of a star becomes exhausted. With no outward thrusting force to counteract the pull of gravity, the core contracts and heats up. Hydrogen continues to fuse into helium in an outer shell and the star expands into what has been called a red giant. Eventually the star's core becomes hot enough to fuse helium into carbon, which in due course is fused into heavier elements.

Finally, when iron has been produced by this successive fusion process in the core, there is a stage when no more energy can be produced by nuclear fusion and the middle of the star then collapses catastrophically under its own gravity. The collapse releases energy into the outer parts of the star and produces the most violent type of explosion in the universe, a supernova. The supernova sends shock waves and new clouds of gas into space from which new generations of stars will form, enriched by elements from the supernova. As has happened in the case of our sun, this may give rise to planets on which life forms may evolve.

Since the universe is full of these recurring cycles of growth and decay, the need to consider whether there is ever a beginning or an end is superfluous. So many processes of regeneration in both inanimate objects like stars and animate things like viruses, animals and man are continually happening that the perpetuation of universes seems to be the inevitable condition. The context of all our observations, then, is this eternal continuity of the universe(s) which has been studied, allowing man to develop a wide and coherent understanding which breaks no physical laws and has never been gratuitously interfered with by gods, fairies or anything else. There seems to be no good reason for vainly talking about a designer or creator at all.

Like lost children crying for their daddy, religious people, theologians and some philosophers seem to need to posit some sort of god, designer or creator to account for there being a universe or universes at all. Even Descartes was keen on the idea of a First Cause. It seems to me, however, that whether there was one or not is immaterial so long as he/she/it continues not to interfere with our scientific activities and understanding in the meantime. The scientific literature has not so far recorded any such interference or force. In any event, if you have to postulate 'a creator', then that simply leads to a totally unproductive and endless regression of postulating the creator of the creator…. of the creator of the creator and so on. The same argument disposes of the notion of an 'Intelligent Designer', though the literature never seems to clarify whether the god(s) made the 'designer' as their creative agent or vice versa, or which of the 36,000 historically reported gods was the one that mattered! In either event the design turned out to be neither intelligent nor efficient. Half of the allegedly intelligently designed living creatures of many species ever known to inhabit the earth have not survived. The earth itself took an inordinately long 9 billion years to get going and is predicted to last only for a further 4.9 billion years when the Andromeda nebula is due to collide with the Milky Way galaxy. If the great designer/god decided to make man 'in his image', why are we not all clones? Individual differences are what make evolution work—but that all takes time. In fact, one could go so far as to suggest that evolution has, for millennia, gone about trying to repair the damage wrought by the original 'designer'.

More than 200 years ago, when William Paley, walking on the beach, found the much reported, wonderfully designed watch, he failed to stress that it was clearly a humanly designed and man-made object. Its design sprang from a watchmaker's brain. Indeed, the concept of design is a very human one and entirely in keeping with the brain's inexhaustible propensity to hunt for patterns in everything. For example, if an image of a dozen randomly positioned dots is flashed briefly from a tachistoscope, a human observer will report "A group of dots!" But if this group of dots is equally briefly exposed, but the dots positioned to form the number five, the observer will invariably report "Five!" Both presentations contain the same number of similar stimulus items, but pattern-seeking or the tendency to see or create designs is a key human brain function which has driven much of humanity's ability to discover and use what we call the laws of nature (not those of any supernatural agency).

As far as the Cartesian First Cause which itself is not caused is concerned, then why not simply declare that all the universes, ours included, are themselves uncaused first causes? The creator or first cause argument also seems to assume that the concept of time is linear—like a line drawn on a page which starts here, the beginning, and ends over there, the end. However, modern physicists such as Stephen Hawking (2010) work in a multi-dimensional time/space universe beyond the four dimensions of length, breadth, height and time. That formerly sufficed (and still does for many of us); however, modern theoretical physicists, space vehicle engineers and cosmologists think of space/time not as a straight line but as curvilinear or circular. Calculations for planning the course and power parameters of inter-stellar and inter-planetary space vehicles have to take account of curvilinear time/space. Space/time being therefore curvilinear, time has no beginning and no end. It is continuous. Looking at a circle, it makes no sense to ask where the line depicting it begins. It can begin anywhere, just as it can end anywhere or nowhere. (See diagram on p.38.)

Some philosophers and theologians seem to require an explanation of how something (the universe) could be created from nothing. But the whole idea of 'nothing' is more bizarre than the idea of eternal continuity of universes. It cannot be recognised even as present or absent, by any human; you cannot have bottles of 'nothing' or even half bottles of 'nothing' on the laboratory or kitchen shelf, for 'nothing' has no properties that can be observed or otherwise described. 'Nothing' is not the symbol zero. That has some value in mathematics as, for example, the midpoint of a series e.g. -3 -2 -1 0 +1 +2 +3. Nothing is a concept which has no exemplars—like god, which could perhaps be used as a synonym for nothing! Anyway, when all is said and done, why do we have to persist in thinking that in the beginning, there was nothing? It seems no less reasonable to suggest that in the beginning was a universe, and not necessarily the presently observed one.

If the notion of space/time as a composite dimension seems difficult, you can think that the two dimensions of space and time have always been closely interrelated.

Try a little practical science. Fill something like a flat seedling box with sand. Level and smooth the surface before sticking a pencil or other piece of wood or pencil vertically in the middle. On a fine sunny day, take it to a spot where the sun will catch it all day. From dawn to dusk the sun will cast a line of shadow from the pencil on to the sand. Remember the sundial? Starting as soon as the sun comes up to cast an early shadow, place a small pebble (say, 5 mm in diameter) on the sand where the tip of the shadow lies. Repeat this with more pebbles at intervals of, say, 30 to 60 minutes until the last long shadow of sundown can be seen. You will then see an arc of pebbles created by the changing length of the pencil's shadow as the day progressed—the distances of the first and last pebbles from the base of the pencil being the farthest and the shadow at or near midday being the shortest. The arc of stones is thus a spatial representation of time.

Unravelling space from time (or converting from time to a position in space) is known to every navigator. Knowing the earth to be (nearly) a globe, navigators and geographers required a datum or fixed reference point or line which was eventually settled as an imaginary line drawn from North Pole to South Pole, passing through Greenwich—the Greenwich Meridian. Were I to start walking due west from Greenwich at, say, 3 mph, then, given that I know my speed of travel and that I possessed an excellent watch or chronometer, I might look at it six hours later and calculate that I am now in a position 18 miles west of Greenwich. In this little exercise I have thus represented my position in space by measuring time. For navigational purposes, of course, there is no need to start all journeys from the line of the Greenwich meridian. Other meridian lines are now drawn at 1-degree intervals (equivalent to 69.2 miles) through the poles but at equal distances from each other at the equator. These lines form a grid with lines of latitude—but that's another story!

Einstein's famous equation, $E=Mc^2$, states that energy equals mass multiplied by a constant which is the square of the speed of light. The first of the Laws of Thermodynamics is that energy and matter are conserved, and we need not seek to explain a beginning. The 'Big Bang' is currently and conveniently seen as a useful starting point for calculation in our current understanding of the history of our continually expanding universe (inflation), but that is simply because it defines an arbitrary point from which observations and measurements can and have been made, all of which cohere sufficiently to sustain our present understanding of the expanding cosmos. There is no good reason why the Big Bang was itself not a culmination of a continuing universal process that we are not yet able to measure and describe but eventually will. The Big Bang is more a useful concept than a phenomenon. Metaphysics has gradually been supplanted by physics, chemistry and biology in explaining the universe, its characteristics, its contents, and especially the emergence of life, the evolution of the human brain and the electrochemical magic of neural complexity and function. It is important to remember that the human brain is still evolving, and that levels of explanation and different kinds of observation will evolve with it. As I never tire of saying, the growth of knowledge and understanding is iterative and incremental and often dependent on novel instrumentation.

My own view as to how mankind's scientific understanding of the universe(s) and the early preoccupation with beginnings and ends have so persisted in philosophic and scientific writings is intrinsically bound up in the nature and functioning of the human organism and brain in particular. Unlike the constant regenerative processes we can observe in the cosmos and in more detail within the various evolutionary developments and deaths on our own small planet, each human brain has its own unique beginning, growth to maturity and increasing complexity before it finally dies and decays. Every human brain is unique: it has its beginning in the embryo, then the foetus as cells differentiate; it will in due course function broadly as do other human brains but may also scale the heights of originality, creativity and understanding of what surrounds it far beyond the simple bony shell that contains it.

Because the brain has had a clear beginning and will have an equally clear end and because it is also known to possess the reflexive capacity to record and act upon what it is doing, it is not altogether surprising that, because of its very nature, its structure and patterns of functioning will tend to adopt a linear conformity with time in the first instance and will also tend to operate and understand causes and effects in the same way. (In time, event A > event B > event C > etc., and we have come to see event A as causing event B and so on.) You will recognise this as a gross oversimplification. The sophistication of working with the curvilinearity of the space/time model will come later, but at this point, I feel that the superfluity of thinking up some supernatural being to 'create' and 'design' universes, man and all the rest will be obvious.

When I was first an undergraduate at my own ancient university, scientists were trained and instructed in a department of 'Natural Philosophy', but by the time I did my doctorate in the Medical School at that same university, that department had become the Department of Physics, then under the aegis of the great and to me, at least, very charming Professor R V Jones, one of Sir Winston Churchill's key scientific advisors during World War 2. For some, Jones was (in spite of his proficiency on the harmonica) not the easiest of men to get along with. Nevertheless, I and others in other disciplines than physics enjoyed many a conversation in the senior common room with him on topics crossing several disciplines. That department now occupies physicists who tread warily along theoretical pathways that once might themselves have been considered metaphysical. Now its considerations of space/time being multidimensional and time being curvilinear rather than linear are backed by solid experiment, observations and mathematics that are all open to potential falsification and are in the public domain. Even if, as I have already hinted, the 'Big Bang' is but a punctuation mark at the end of a sentence we have not yet uttered or read, it merely marks the beginning of a new sentence in the book of the universe which we have begun now to write and to read with some attention to detail.

While very large stars, perhaps more than 15 times the mass of our sun, may end in a supernova, some may end less dramatically if their own gravity becomes so strong that all possible structures upon it are smashed by gravitational pressure, as it were, feeding on itself. The very building blocks of matter disintegrate. Since the velocity required for matter to escape the gravitational field exceeds the speed of light, even light cannot escape the field. Thus, nothing can emerge from the resultant 'black hole' and matter has retreated elsewhere—into the universe of the singularity, where space and time are bent into a tight circle and eventually crushed to a single point.

The universe is full of such 'black holes', perhaps keeping a balance with the new matter apparently created in the course of other 'big bangs', perhaps not. Though 'black holes' can of course never be seen directly though in recent weeks an image of one has been created from data collected by large radio telescopes synchronised from many world positions, the matter 'falling into' any one of them releases large amounts of energy, with x-rays forming a large component of that energy. It is probably this energy source that may lie at the heart of quasars and help to explain how the brightest and the most distant objects known, though only a few times bigger than the solar system, can emit more energy than a whole galaxy. We also know that after the explosion of a supernova, only the very central core of the original star survives, a very, very dense object of relatively tiny dimensions (a few miles across) in which the vast gravitational pressures crush everything into neutrons packed very tightly together. This neutron star spins at about thirty times a second, pushing out strong radio beams concentrated at the magnetic poles. As the neutron star sweeps through space, the radio pulses are recorded by astronomers on earth and have been likened to the beams from a lighthouse. These neutron stars, first recorded in 1967, are called pulsars for this reason.

If the known universe is in a state of change and flux like this, it does at least supply information which allows inferences to be drawn about its nature and its rate of change. One of these inferences is that it is highly probable that our solar system is not unique. The irregular but still structured motion of several relatively nearby stars, such as Barnard's star (5.9 light years away) suggests that there are gravitational forces at work best explained by the presence of planetary companions. Astrophysicists reckon that in around probably 20 billion of the stars in our galaxy, there is likely to be at least one planet at the right distance from its star and enjoying the other conditions to allow the emergence of life.

In the course of the physical evolution of our planet (something that we know took rather longer than the Biblical seven days), the main building blocks of life, starting with hydrogen and continuing with helium, oxygen, nitrogen and carbon, were generated early in the process but depended on the light and heat of the sun to create the construction of molecules combining these elements in a way which could in turn allow the development of organic life. But, additional to the amino-acids and forms of stardust falling on us from comets in outer space, a liquid medium, water, with a large temperature range, was also required to promote chemical reactions; an ambient atmospheric temperature was also required in a range which fitted with the sustaining of the chemical reactions to facilitate the bonding and the breakdown of molecules.

While the sun provides a source of energy to produce these fine variations of temperature and other radiations, the earth also has to be shielded by an atmosphere to protect new organic development from cosmic radiation. Our earth is the only planet in the solar system which provides all these favourable conditions and it may be that, for all that there are many, many other planets surrounding their own stars elsewhere in the universe, relatively fewer of them are likely to have just that appropriate combination of prerequisite energetic/chemical conditions to produce life forms cognate with our own.

Even in the very primitive environment of the emerging earth, these first molecular combinations were occurring in random ways with little significance except for inorganic chemistry. However, some were of greater significance: that is, those occurring in warm water bombarded with ultraviolet light and played on by lightning from massive thunderstorms. Electrical power was, and is, abundant and not just happening as remotely spaced incidents. Contemporary NASA scientists photographing lightning activity over earth from the International Space Station report that across Earth's atmosphere, lightning flashes around 50 times per second, 4.3 million times a day and roughly 1.5 billion times a year. Early in the life of the earth, the resultant amino-acids and nucleic acids formed the first structures leading to the emergence of microbes and bacteria. We know that that stage has happened elsewhere because astronomers have detected amino-acids floating in areas between the stars. On earth, however, these basic structures became differentiated into many and varied life forms; some of these, often unicellular, did not have what it took to survive, whereas others did. Bacteria, structurally simple though they are, prospered in some credible and many incredible habitats. They can be found a kilometre down in the rock of the ocean floor even in the Mariana Trench which is the deepest known part of all the oceans. They can be found in hot springs water under Yellowstone National Park in USA surviving in water at 140^0 Celsius, and of course, they can be found in their billions in the gut of all of us (in less extreme temperatures, of course). It has been calculated that the biomass of all the bacteria on earth outweigh all other animal and plant life, including man. We have been lucky to survive amid that sort of competition—so far!

The transition from inorganic stardust floating everywhere in our galaxy to organic amino-acids (required to form DNA) was notably and successfully experimented on by Miller and Urey (1953) from the universities of California at San Diego and at Chicago. These scientists examined the hypothesis that was first adumbrated by Darwin and others that life emerged from what has been called a primal soup of water and chemicals at the right temperature and sparked by lightning to give molecular combinations a sort of starting kick, like cardioversion.

Miller and Urey's apparatus was not unduly complicated, and diagrams and drawings are easily available. What they started with were inorganic chemicals and what was created by the experiment was a set of about twenty or so different amino-acids, or organic chemicals. These are the building blocks of all life. Much more recently, some of the original vials of amino-acid left by the original researchers have been opened. They revealed many more amino-acids now than were reported by Miller and Urey—so organic chemical 'work' must have gone on in the interim. Current researchers are now strongly of the view that the jump from amino-acid formation to life as we understand it is most likely to be found in the membranous structure within deep submarine funnels releasing warm gas on the ocean beds. The proton/electron exchanges across these membrane-like surfaces is reminiscent of or analogous to the sodium/potassium imbalance across the neural membranes which produce the all-important electro-chemical pulses, action potentials, which power our brains and nervous systems.

From the first amino-acids to bacteria and then to more complex life forms, the genetic pool was formed which was to grow into the 10,000,000 or so different microscopic organisms, plants and animals alive on earth today. At one time, there may have been as many as twice that number. The interaction with the changing environment, however, has whittled away those that could not adapt to the conditions prevalent at the time and perished. Because of the tremendous variety that exists in the earthly

Extant —

environment in terms of its conditions, topography, climate and the important interactions between different life forms, a huge variety of forms still persists, some symbiotic with each other, some seriously antagonistic to each other. The tick bird with the African buffalo is in the former category, the AIDS virus and human beings in the latter. Even today there are living organisms that can exist and even proliferate in blocks of ice and others which breed in very hot oil.

Among all of these organisms, man is indubitably the one who has evolved beyond all other species. If the first life forms, bacteria, were extant about 3.5 to 4 billion years ago, this is still recent in terms of the growth and flux of the wider universe. And the emergence of man is even more recent. His story begins about 65 million years ago in the tropical forests of the world (very likely in central Africa) where the very first of the primates, the order of mammals to which man belongs, had appeared. A mere 5 million years ago, these primates, the gorilla, the chimpanzee, the bonobo, the orangutan and the man-like hominids seem to have shared a common ancestor even if various 'branches' of the species may have emerged at different times, some perhaps co-existing. It is, therefore, clear that all this took more than the Biblical seven days. Even if the story of that busy week had been written as a metaphor, it is so far removed from the available and recorded geological and anthropological data as to be laughable. Now that we know better, it is time to scrap such misleading metaphors.

What did happen about that time was a drop in global temperature which led to the primates coming down from the trees to seek new pastures, literally, in the then flourishing grasslands. Ancient footprints found in volcanic ash in Tanzania have been placed by carbon dating at about 3.75 million years old and they suggest that by that time, 'Australopithecus' was walking upright. Subsequently, further evidence pointed to the development in our species of sensitive finger pads, a larger brain than that in other animals and a pincer grip in the fingers and thumb allowing many more subtle manipulative skills.

From 100,000 to 35,000 years ago, Neanderthal man had established the erect habit, the use of tools and fire, the beginnings of the use of animal skins for bedding, clothing and possibly the first use of ceremony and ritual. Only in the last 10,000 years—a blink of an eye in terms of geological or evolutionary time—has man settled to an agricultural style with attempts to manage and control natural growth and breeding of plants and animals. That was the time when the so-called Ice Age relented and thawed, thus allowing more plant growth and a gentler environment. That left time for the species to begin to organise itself socially, over time, into settlements and towns. In the scale and immensity of time and the universe, *Homo Sapiens* (and we are flattered by such a denomination) is a relatively novel and perhaps transient phenomenon.

The growth and development of the higher cortex of the brain in the primates, and especially in man, has, however, led to an ever-accelerating development of the species, rushing beyond its competitors by dint of having mastered the trick of speech. Among other things, this has facilitated the development of the capacity to problem-solve vicariously, in words and pictures rather than in deeds to be copied, to communicate in increasingly complex ways among ourselves and with the environment, and, crucially, by the internalisation of speech, to think.

But we live in a demanding and hugely varied environment, one which in the twentieth and twenty-first centuries, by means of modern travel and communication, can encompass the whole world. Only 100 years ago, very few humans might have expected to travel more than a few hundred miles from their home bases. Oddly, it is possible that some 3,000 years ago the nomadic habits of humans in certain harsh environments might have had them trudging or sailing rather further in the quest for fresh lands, woods and water sources. By the end of the first millennium of the Christian era, Vikings from Scandinavia had marched and sailed to the edge of the Black Sea. Explorations ranging that widely across varying climatic zones meant that clothing progressed from rough animal skins to woven materials from spun wool. By the end of the second millennium, however, a high proportion of the advanced peoples of the world may travel to work or on holiday to almost any part of the globe within several hours, may like what they see and may settle amid a strange people with unfamiliar languages and habits and have to adapt to a different climate and pattern of life. This is as true for a Hebridean crofter deciding to make a new life among the finance houses of greater London as it is for an Australian aborigine leaving his territory to earn a living among the oil wells of Brunei, an Indian peasant from the Deccan Plateau settling into a living selling rugs in Johannesburg or an Afghan Muslim settling down to sell hardware in Camden Town or Glasgow.

The increasing demands which this potentially world-wide environment makes on man are constantly interacting with our understanding of it in sociological and ecological terms to bring about a new evolutionary pattern in our behaviour. We fight to enhance earthly living conditions for ourselves by inventing antibiotics, but bacteria and viruses themselves constantly evolve, much faster than we do (because of a shorter lifespan and breeding cycle), into resistant strains which our drugs fail to control .It is true that just as we can attempt to conquer disease on the one hand, so also we can self-destruct in our attempts to achieve certain goals by war or conflict. The very variety of acts which is now open to humans and the variety of environmental settings which will precipitate or inhibit these acts are the very stuff of continuing evolution. We either learn to respect and cope with the world and its resources as they are and with our fellow creatures on earth, men and beasts, or we extinguish the species in our failure to do so. As the deliberate breeding of animals increased world-wide over the last millennium, so also did our use of animal by-products—finer wools, softer leather from skins, as well as fats and glues for waterproofing and jointing.

One of the key adaptations to all this complexity is our capacity to extend our knowledge and hence our range of ways of manipulating the environment, ourselves and others. Knowledge is power, and the past hundred years have seen an exponential development of knowledge in all areas of human endeavour. This knowledge, in turn, leads to changes in behaviour of the species not only in relation to each other but also in relation to other animals. The harsh and unremitting challenges which the environment and man set for the dodo, eventually driving it to extinction, and the ravages currently being wrought on many other land and sea animals, show no signs of lessening. Humanists must rally to the call to preserve remaining species. I shall return to this in Chapter 11. When our capacity to store information within ourselves, supposedly in our brains, becomes overloaded, we now can use computers, books, films and tapes—and an appropriate retrieval system! There is no excuse therefore for not being aware of our responsibilities for maintaining diversity Our success as a species is still in the balance.

epiphenomena,

Chapter 5
A Closer Look at the Human Condition

As a clinical psychologist trying to rationalise my own existence after more than eighty-seven years of a happy and satisfying life, rich in experience and including a certain amount of adventure and achievement, I am compelled to start from a relatively simple, perhaps even banal or simplistic, viewpoint. It is the observation that all knowledge, all understanding, all art, all science and technology, all medicine, philosophy, religions, theology and all writings and other productions in various media are, in the first instance, the products of healthy human brains. This general principle has also been voiced by Sir Francis Crick, the co-discoverer of the structure of DNA, who wrote, "You, your joys and your sorrows, your memories and your ambitions, your sense of personal identity and free will are in fact no more than the behaviour of a vast assembly of nerve cells and their attendant molecules." Personally, I would have left out the 'no more than' and replaced it with 'the epiphenomena of', but Crick is, of course, correct. At the same time, however, we are all intensely aware of our own consciousness, its privacy and its richness. That awareness is what persuaded the philosopher Mary Midgley to write a whole book, *Are You an Illusion?*, in an attempt to rebut Crick's position. Midgley claimed that she was 'shocked and bloody horrified' at Crick's pronouncement; then again, like a decreasing number of other philosophers, she apparently has scant regard for modern science. She should understand that she cannot rebut Crick's position by simply saying how 'bloody horrified' she is to be in any way convincing, she would need to present a reasoned argument backed by a ruthless empiricism and appropriate data.

→ *and Algorithms?*

Whatever Plato, Aristotle, Pythagoras, Newton, Shakespeare, Einstein, Genghis Khan, Gandhi, Mozart, Robert Burns, Nicola Sturgeon, Paul McCartney, Mohammed, Alex Ferguson, Jesus Christ or Julius Caesar or possibly 'old Uncle Tom Cobley and all' have thought, done, said or written, they have all depended on the possession of a healthy and properly functioning central and peripheral nervous system (at least in the case of most of them). Sensing, doing, saying and writing, after all, are the human activities which allow us to infer states of consciousness in others and enable us to be the transmitters of knowledge and our culture. Thinking, planning, calculating and, particularly, remembering and communicating give us all a chance to develop a sense of our own identity and, further, an awareness that other members of our species appear also to share that sense of their own and others' identity. (See Chapter 10 for further discussion of consciousness.)

Because of its capacity to develop language, followed by writing and the use of symbols, the human species has been able to generate, compile and transmit to their own time and later generations the products of yet other human brains. Dogs, horses, elephants and especially the great apes and cetaceans can show the rudiments of problem-solving, communication and social adaptation, but man, mainly by having developed more complex and flexible languages than any other species, has so far outstripped them all.

In the evolutionary progression from the chance impact on our planet of amino-acid molecules from stardust and comets (Gribbin, 2000) from our own or other universes, to the development of the carbon atom and the transition from inorganic to organic chemistry, to rudimentary cell division and the proliferation of multiple lifeforms, the capacity of our particular species to begin to make sense of how we all interact with each other, with other life forms and with our physical environment and adapt to it, culminates in, for example, among myriad other human achievements, my writing and your reading or listening to this essay. The awareness of all this is also what compels the humanist not only to respect and foster the development of his fellow humans but also to respect and conserve, in all its rich variety, the whole of our natural environment and everything that lives in it.

Each of us begins not from nothing but as a natural biological development following the intrusion of a male sperm into a female ovum.

The subsequent multiplication of progressively differentiated cells in our mother's uterus progresses to an embryo, to a foetus, to a baby whose nervous system will continue to grow for some months after birth. More complex growth processes produce the child and eventually, an adult. In due course, all our biological systems will run down and wear out as we become old men and women. Some of us, however, will, by then, have added value to the development of the species and to our environment. Others will simply have just sustained it and themselves. Some, wittingly or unwittingly, will have destroyed or attempted to destroy or damage it. Others, in less destructive ways, will continue to undermine that progression by a lack of capacity to appreciate and use the human heritage of reason, knowledge and wisdom. Not to use our brains to evaluate and to discriminate to those brains' highest capacity must be the ultimate crime against our species.

In spite of a currently popular view that it is in some way politically correct for us to be neither 'judgmental' nor 'discriminating', the ability to discriminate subtle differences and to make accurate judgments are indicative of the higher levels of intelligence. These are abilities fundamental to our understanding of each other and the control of our world. They should be enhanced rather than scorned and our educational systems should be adjusted to enhance them. In contemporary life, the notion of our being 'judgmental' is often used pejoratively as if it automatically has the adverb 'morally' before it. But there are a thousand ways other than that when we are judgmental—about whether Kane had a good game for England, whether a Dell is a better computer than Sony, whether Acker Bilk was as good a clarinettist as Benny Goodman or whether a new picture is hanging straight on the wall. If we are free to exercise our judgment in such matters, why then should we not be judgmental in matters of human behaviour such as morality, politics or religion? The fear that our judgment might be prejudiced and not evidence-based is understandable, but that is where good education comes in. Most developed educational systems, especially in the Western world, are in fact geared to teaching pupils and students to make fine discriminations and to exercise sound judgment, whether of literary merit, logical precision or elegance of design. This is not to say that wrong judgments are to go uncorrected if the available evidence goes against the pronounced judgment.

All of us have a duty carefully to weigh the evidence and background of an opinion or proposition before expressing any judgment on it. All our lives will be punctuated by occasions when we have to make fine and often important discriminations of widely differing kinds and often be challenged by the possible outcomes whether they be correct or mistaken. I remember when, in managing certain airborne situations during my time in the RAF, I was expected to discriminate the angle subtended by one luminous dot on a screen to two other plots (forming as it were the base of a triangle) and, by eye alone, to get the angle right to within 2 degrees. If we could not make such discriminations within a few seconds, we could not do the job. Later in my life, I sat on the Sheriff Court bench in Scotland as an honorary sheriff (judge) during summary cases (when there was no jury) and again had to learn to be extremely discriminating as I heard the evidence and arguments put by the (Crown) prosecution and the defence before having to pronounce a verdict. The content of these two kinds of discrimination could hardly be greater, but both illustrate the plasticity of the human brain and its capacity to guide our judgment in many contexts.

As children, we begin by learning to sort out what William James (1890) described as the 'blooming, buzzing confusion' of disorganised sensory input. "The baby, assailed by eyes, ears, nose, skin, and entrails at once, feels it all as one great blooming, buzzing confusion; and to the very end of life, our location of all things in one space is due to the fact that the original extents or sizes of all the sensations which came to our notice at once, coalesced together into one and the same space. There is no other reason than this why 'the hand I touch and see' coincides spatially with 'the hand I immediately feel' (William James, *Principles of Psychology*, 1890). More than a century on, we know much more about the nature and further development of the child and adult human brain.

The child further resolves this mystifying experience by living through a variety of 'separation' experiences which serve to distinguish between what is her/him and what is not. For example, the baby grabs his or her own toe and feels both the experience of grabbing and being grabbed, and they usually see this happening. However, if someone else grabs their toe, they only have the experience of being grabbed but none of grabbing. After many repetitions of this and like experiences, they will begin to establish what is 'me' and what is 'not me' in terms of their body parts and internal body image. There can be no 'me' without a body. Similarly, every time they baby throws their toy out of the cot, it disappears and is 'not me'; indeed, initially, it does not even exist, whereas the hand and arm that flung it are always there and must be 'me'. There are of course many cognate experiences which taken together progressively define a notion of the 'self'—essentially the body with its brain and the sensory inputs and internal processing of these (to which we attach the word 'consciousness') and the motor outputs it can achieve.

Now, the further development of digital memory storage and retrieval gives humans the added advantage of a near exponential growth of information and understanding. Our body image, or notion of what we are as sentient objects in space/time, will be formed through childhood and adolescence as we grow; and it will be relatively fixed (even if inaccurately in many cases) by early adulthood. Skin, nails and hair form the boundaries between the self and the environment. How we evaluate and understand that body image is more complex, depending on all sensory inputs from the external environment as well as proprioceptive inputs and emotional arousal from within our bodies. (Clark, D. F. (1974).

This is not a treatise on human development but just an indicator of how we all first form a sense of identity and subsequently, or even in parallel, begin to use language and communicate with others. That occurs alongside our making distinctions between the self and the environment. What we often fail to note is that, while most of us progressively define our body and identity more and more accurately, other 'selves' become part of our environment. There is, too, room for debate about where, under certain conditions, the individual organism starts and finishes and where the environment starts and finishes. We have no difficulty recognising the wind as it blows across our cheeks as part of our environment, but if we take a deep breath of it, it suddenly becomes part of our selves. Parts of our self can also be discarded and become elements in the environment—hair, teeth, excreta. Words and other noises that we express and what we paint or write were all 'inside' our brains/bodies but then became part of the environment for ourselves and others to interact with and evaluate. All the written material within this book, originating from inside my head will, as likely as not, end up in a waste paper basket of some philosophically innocent but curious citizen. Or it may last long enough just to influence the thinking and behaviour of some other modestly literate humans.

And, of course, all other members of our species, all with their own peculiar conceptions and understanding of their perceived worlds, and indeed all other life forms, are all themselves part of our environment. Physicists working with subatomic particles such as electrons, positrons, neutrinos and muons in multiple dimensions may well find the distinction between 'self' and 'other' even harder to sustain in the theoretical terms of quantum mechanics—even though they will manage it quite well in practice. In the world of particle physics, everything is constructed of atoms and the subatomic particles they comprise. The fact that those atoms which make up our bodies and brains are organised to make distinctions between self and not-self is not only fortunate but also a credit to how our brains have evolved to facilitate such distinctions.

We are all aware, too, that the specimen of our kind that each of us turns out to be is determined in part by biological and hereditary factors transmitted by the genes in our DNA. How we perceive and react to our environment is determined by how our bodies and brains are set up to react and how complex or well-understood our current environment happens to be, as well as by what and how we have been taught formally or informally earlier in our lives. Over time, cultural patterns develop—Richard Dawkins (1989) calls them memes—which will determine much of what we might call the routinised features of our personal and social behaviour. The disciplines of psychology and neuroscience have themselves developed as means of structuring and understanding these. Popularly, however, there has grown an expectation that these disciplines should, along with neurophysiology and biochemistry, examine the less routinised and more stimulus-specific behaviours of individuals and groups of humans. In recent years, brain scans of normal humans acting in specific ways, or even just thinking of acting in particular ways, have greatly facilitated this process.

As I have noted earlier, there has always been a fascinating interaction between the growth of knowledge and the development of new technology or instrumentation. In our remote past, men may have watched as a great fallen log rolled down a slope. "Aha!" So they (or more likely, he or she) thought that placing a very heavy stone or log lengthwise on top of two or three such round rollers could convey the object further and more easily than they themselves could carry or drag it. To this day, many coastal boatmen still use that method for rolling heavy boats up or down a shingle or soft sand beach. Then one day, a man, centuries later, with flints as tools to cut wood, cut a very short end of a big, round-sectioned log and—lo and behold—on its edge, and with a thick rod of wood through a hole in the middle of its diameter, it became a wheel on an axle. Simple mechanics was born. That technology allowed more substantial and easier manipulation of the environment and in due course more wide-ranging travel and exploration. As a consequence, the study of geography was born. Much more recently, in the 16th and 17th centuries, optical microscopes allowed us to explore the smallest of objects; however, this allowed only limited exploration of the tiny until the electron microscope vastly increased our knowledge of particles, such as viruses, well beyond our unaided visual capacity. The telescope in the early 17th century and then the spectroscope led to the exploration of space, the stars and planets and their composition as well as further exploration of our own planet. Our knowledge and understanding of our place on this planet and its place in the solar system as well as its place in the known universe expanded almost logarithmically in consequence. Scientific knowledge, in particular, grows incrementally and at varying rates, each new chunk of knowledge having to be tested and fitted into the wider frame of reference as it emerges.

New means of measurement and novel apparatus often give impetus to this process. Even as I wrote the first draft of this work, we were told that the Hadron Collider near Geneva had revealed the Higgs boson, a subatomic particle whose existence had been predicted but not, until then, recorded. New understandings in physics will follow. The development of lasers and fibre optics has also revolutionised measurement in engineering and internal anatomy as well as in ophthalmology and intestinal surgery. New instrumentation and tools derive from well-informed practice just as the latter drives the development of better and more sophisticated tools.

An article by James Le Fanu in the August 2010 issue of the journal *Prospect* proposed the general theme that, for all the immense amount of activity and money poured into all kinds of scientific research in recent years, it seemed to him that surprisingly little advance in knowledge had been achieved, compared to the surge in the early last century. In particular, he noted how, in the first decades of the 20th century, Planck's quantum theory, Einstein's special theory of relativity, Rutherford's work on the structure of the atom and Sherrington's description of the integrative action of the nervous system had emerged. Since then, in spite of a huge amount of published scientific work, knowledge seemed to him not to have expanded at a comparable rate.

In my view, however, this is a rather superficial analysis. It fails to take sufficient account of the incremental and iterative nature of scientific endeavour and knowledge remarked on earlier in this paper. New knowledge, especially now that teams of scientists rather than brilliant individuals work on it, is an accretion on existing knowledge. As more and more detailed aspects of scientific knowledge in an expanding range of disciplines and subjects are tested and assimilated into the canon, or rejected from it, each of these new developments leads to a further proliferation of hypotheses still to be tested and experimented on. When the body of knowledge is slight, then any significant development signifies a relatively large advance, but when more and more has been discovered, then more and more work is necessary to validate the preceding experiments, propositions and hypotheses. That work, too, may require the development of even more sophisticated apparatus to be invented (e.g. the Hadron collider, the Hubble space telescope, or the CAT scanner) to enable the observations and measurements necessary.

The analogy or model which I currently adopt to assist in the understanding of the growth of scientific, or indeed, of all knowledge is that of a huge, circular jigsaw puzzle of infinite size which has no initial guiding picture or illustration for the puzzler (representing our researcher attempting to reduce our ignorance); the first few, quite large, pieces which are successfully put together near its centre (inspired guesses) to create the beginnings of a coherent image, represent a relatively major increment of knowledge compared to what was there before. As our expanding jigsaw of knowledge, like our expanding universe, grows out to become an ever-larger circle, more and more of the jigsaw pieces have to be put together for significant change to be noticed in the whole image represented. Each new piece fitted represents a progressively smaller proportion of the knowledge represented by the existing state or number of pieces of the puzzle—but as the image of the puzzle expands, then we begin to see the larger picture and our tentative earlier moves can be validated and our next moves are hinted at. As the picture grows bigger, then more and more pieces need to be placed for any significant overall change to be noticed. Sudden huge leaps forward, therefore, become less and less probable but the general coherence of all kinds of scientific knowledge becomes more and more apparent, integrated and structured as more and more often little pieces are added to the growing picture of our understanding. It is therefore not surprising that every new increment (discovery) will seem smaller proportionately in relation to the whole accumulation of the body of knowledge.

The periphery of the jigsaw will take ever longer to show its significant extensions. Good examples of this process can be seen in pharmacology where, for example, the discovery of a new drug for an illness not formerly treatable shows initially good results, only for wider use to bring out damaging side effects that demand more research to correct them. That new research may often be as painstaking and detailed as was demanded by the original discovery, but it will inevitably draw less attention and kudos than did the original discovery. The great jigsaw of knowledge will show only a very small increment but one that is necessary and worthwhile.

Another factor not taken account of by Le Fanu's article was that it ignored the many, many hours, days or months spent by scientists researching a new topic which may end in the expected outcome not being supported. Back in the 1970s, the author collaborated with a consultant psychiatric colleague at the behest of the pharmaceutical company which wished to test one of their drugs (already widely and successfully used in another context) for a new therapeutic purpose. After months of devising tests, apparatus, procedures for a double-blind test of the expected effect on patients, we were forced by the results to conclude that the drug could not be successfully and safely used for the purpose that the manufacturer had proposed. All our research had done was to prevent a drug being used improperly, and such researches very seldom are reported either in the press or in the scientific literature. The great jigsaw of knowledge depends as much on that sort of evidence-seeking work as it does on the occasional massive leap forward if the growing area covered by the jigsaw is, little by little, to be expanded. The designation *Homo sapiens* can be justified only in so far as we see ignorance as a spur to understand more and not as a gaping void to be filled with speculation and fantasies.

Chapter 6
Speech, Language and Theory of Mind

The reader may wonder why this chapter, and a later one on consciousness, should fit into a polemic against the gods—or against anything for that matter. It is because the book has to be more than just a polemic; it needs to be an exploration of ideas which humanists are likely to ponder in consolidating their philosophic stance. Speech and language are what has set *Homo sapiens* above almost all other living things on our planet. The fact that man has been able to debate and explore ideas including the need for gods, ghosts or gremlins at various junctures through all these centuries (including periods remote from the present) and presenting vicissitudes of all kinds, natural and personal, is a remarkable phenomenon. The cognitive resilience required could not have happened had not man been physically and mentally able to develop speech and language, and, importantly, a sense of his own identity and capacity to plan and pursue intentions.

After the previous chapter's little digression into a simple philosophy of science, I shall return to these important developments of *Homo sapiens*. About 3.5 million years ago, Australopithecus, having come down from the trees on to the flat grassy African plains, gradually developed bipedalism (i.e. standing on only the two hind legs rather than the more usual all four), due to a need to see further and leave limbs free to hold tools or to use in self-defence. Bears indulge in this stance from time to time, to express dominance or to improve range of vision; meerkats also do it regularly to keep a better lookout for predators. In other words, man's early predecessors began to walk and run in a nearly erect position. For early *Homo sapiens* (2.5 to 0.8 million years ago), going from moving on four limbs to two would have brought developmental changes to the angle of the skull, spine and skeleton. This allowed the vocal tract to become more L-shaped with the larynx positioned relatively low in the neck, a necessary prerequisite for making many of the sounds that these early humans were thought to utter both as a means of warning or alerting, and for more elaborate communication, all in the interests of survival. There is room for debate about the relevance of these changes to all the sounds made but with the proliferation of phonemes, there would have been a further parallel development of the brain to support control and interpretation of the sounds.

In contemporary brains, Broca's (speech) and Wernicke's (language) areas of the left side of the temporo-parietal cerebral cortex bear testimony to such a development. Charles Darwin (1871) wrote, "Later in the human story, and offering higher survival value, these early and rudimentary noises, largely concerned with warning, bonding and aggression, evolved into new noises, for social communication. Then the noises had to be differentiated for fuller communication. Words had to be invented to describe objects and actions. I cannot doubt that language owes its origin to the imitation and modification, aided by signs and gestures, of various natural sounds, the voices of other animals, and man's own instinctive cries." Plausibly, therefore, a vocabulary developed from a variety of grunts, moans, screams, clicking noises and so on; this allowed the good news to be spread, if not from Ghent to Aix, at least to the next family group nearby. This rewarding habit still persists several tens of thousands of years on. Other species have signally failed to develop beyond the pre-speech stage to achieve communicative skills such as those man achieved. The cetaceans (the species which includes dolphins and whales) are probably the nearest to ourselves in this regard. Well-developed speech and language are particularly human attributes. The processes involved in this have been nicely commented on by Steven Pinker, director of MIT's Center of Cognitive Neuroscience, in his book *The Language Instinct: The New Science* (2015):

Pinker at one point in his text remarks that the reader is exemplifying "one of the wonders of the natural world." Most of us take speech for granted – even the ability to speak several languages. Speech and language are a gift our species has developed beyond all other species to the extent that our brains have evolved in two particular areas to facilitate this. This valuable capacity to convey, frequently with great precision and accuracy, ideas, instructions, intentions and emotions from one of us to one or many others has given man the ability to create thoughts, express intentions and moods or emotions, all involving changes in another brain. Simply by making very particular noises with our mouth and larynx, we can influence others to respond, positively or negatively either in thought or behaviour. We do this so easily, even casually, that, as Pinker reminds us just what a miracle of evolution this is.

It is hard to overestimate the importance of the ability to communicate with fellow members of our species in this complex way. It strengthens social bonds, passes on information, communicates intention and allows future planning—to name but a few of the advantages of language. Many authorities describe such development of our species as 'modern behaviour', that is, behaviours which rapidly develop to allow future intentions, to be realised and supported by technological innovation. The range of these skills and behaviours as they emerged over the centuries from how to make fire to inventing the telephone was substantial. "Modern behaviours", coupled to the wider geographic dispersal of human groups included adapting to changing environments or living conditions going on to elaborate symbolic behaviours such as cave painting, constructing artefacts like beads and ornaments from a variety of materials to show status and even to finding ways of safely and respectfully disposing of dead bodies. The further and more widespread development of this so-called 'modern behaviour' led to the invention of different languages.

Estimates of when and where such languages were first formed vary quite widely. The written languages of early Sumerian and Semitic cultures are thought to date from around 3,300 BCE to 3,000 BCE, but spoken languages may have originated much earlier: for example, Sanskrit – which perhaps should have been spelled Sans Script as there seems to be no record of any written form of the language – and Tamil. At the other end of the historic scale, Norwegian only became recognised as a language in the early 20th century.

Archaeological evidence can help with recorded written languages, but spoken languages defy researchers simply because they change dynamically in use and may also be spread inaccurately by relatively small populations. For example, as a boy, I would always have said, "Thank you" but now young people say "Cheers" with the same meaning. Asked how I was feeling, I would have said, "Well" whereas most young people now say, "Good".

In *Homo sapiens,* some language may have been used around 70,000 to 50,000 years ago; this would not have been shared by earlier Neanderthal man. Researches show that, for the first time, more sophisticated tools, made out of different materials, were then being used to make a variety of arrow and spear heads, drilling, cutting and piercing tools. Some authorities consider that, concomitantly, more sophisticated language skills must have developed so that others might be taught how to make all these items by more than just mechanical copying of the toolmaker's actions. Imitative skills can be developed by some birds and animals though only the apes demonstrate this at a higher level. None of them, however, can replace mechanical and instrumental copying with instruction by speech.

While in the museum at Les Eyzies de Tayac in the French Dordogne, I was greatly impressed to see petrified brushes made with small fibres and bound with a kind of string to wooden handles. These, along with vegetable tubes, were the tools used between 35,000 and 17,000 years ago to paint the great pictures in the Lascaux grotto in that area. The cooperative effort necessary to have achieved these art works, in near total darkness and using small vegetable oil lamps, must have necessitated significant communication and more than rudimentary language and artistic skills.

Gradually, probably in east and north-east Africa and broadly within the timescale noted above, a rather stilted, simple early language seems to have developed into something more complicated, with a grammar and syntax allowing more intricate communication styles; as always, there would have been a parallel development of language and thinking. Debate continues as to whether this development took place over thousands of years as it depended on the existing, very slow evolution of general anatomical, and in particular, brain structure and function, or whether it occurred over a shorter term as a result of relatively sudden biological change in the brain, possibly as a mutation of a gene such as FOXP2. Areas like Broca's and Wernicke's areas in the left temporo-parietal lobes of the human brain occur also in the primate brain, the first area being involved in the motor, cognitive and perceptual aspects of speech, the latter lending to language and interpretive skills. Brain scans of chimpanzees when they are communicating by sign language (which they can learn quite well) show that the same Broca's and Wernicke's cortical convolutions are implicated as are the same areas in the human communicator. It is important to bear in mind that fMRI scans show only patterns of blood flow about the brain; from these, one may begin to infer specific and local electro-chemical neural activity. The same circuits discussed in the primates' brain stem and limbic system control non-verbal sounds in humans (laughing, groaning, crying, etc.), which suggests that the human language centre is a modification of neural circuits common to all primates.

In parenthesis, may I be indulged by my quoting from my own clinical experience? I remember treating a young man with a severe stutter who could, nevertheless, hum or whistle a tune without error or hesitation. I asked him to 'sing' his sentences. He started to do this by using a strong melody quite loudly; subsequently, he tried it less loudly and with progressively less modulated or defined melodies. The procedure worked well although weekly 'refresher courses' were at first necessary. The bundles of neurons of the 'music centre' of the brain were making new synaptic connections aiding the rhythms and flow of his speech. A CAT scan was not available to me at that time, but I would have confidently expected it to show increased activity linking the small area a few centimetres away from Broca's and Wernicke's areas.

This modification and the skill it affords for linguistic communication seem to be unique to humans, which implies that the 'language organ' developed after the human lineage split from the primate (chimpanzees and bonobos) lineage. Plainly stated, spoken language depends on both a modification of the larynx that is unique to humans and on one form or another, slow evolution or fast genetic mutation of the human brain.

As already noted, the earliest of the species *Homo* probably used grunts, other calls and gestures—not unlike the various but differentiated calls of, for example, vervet monkeys reported above. These use quite different cries to warn of, say, snakes, as against those warning of eagles or larger predators such as leopards. These cries are consistent even if limited in number and should probably be classed as signals rather than speech. Nevertheless—and I have observed this at quite close range of a few metres in the wild in Kenya—they are recognised and responded to in the same way by all vervet monkeys and therefore have evolutionary survival value. Some more recent research by ethologists suggests that other animals sharing their habitat have learned to respond appropriately to these warning calls. They also, as did the early human equivalents, impress on other individuals of the same species the notion that they are all not only similar to each other in appearance but that they all perceive the world in broadly the same way. Thus, in more recent years, behavioural scientists have described this recognition as another aspect of 'theory of mind'. By using this phrase, contemporary psychologists are not slipping unobtrusively into the old Cartesian dualism of 'mind' and 'body'. They regard it as a kind of shorthand to express the intuitive awareness that one human comes to understand that others share broadly the same perception of the world as they do.

While we use the term 'mind', it is not directly observable—only inferred—from observing the behaviour of other humans, just like 'consciousness'. In my past professional life, I would occasionally remind my students that if they sat still, never asked a question or offered a comment, then I might have doubts about their being conscious at all. They had to take the risk of moving, changing their expressions and speaking for me and others to ascertain whether they were geniuses or idiots. (Most, of course, were neither.)

There are, at our present state of technology, relatively few methods of gaining direct access to the 'mind' or brain of another. Electroencephalography can show wave forms indicative of states of arousal or somnolence or indicators of malfunction such as epilepsy in the subject but that simply shows the overall electrochemical status of the brain at the time of examination. Wilder Penfield (1975), an experimentally minded neurosurgeon several decades ago, was more interested in the detail of cerebral activity and was able to elicit, in the conscious subject, long lost but genuine memories by stimulating specific parts of the cerebral cortex with very low voltage DC electrical impulses. Penfield could lift his instrument and, by fractionally changing the micro-voltage or the instrument's position by even a millimetre, elicit different experiences or memories from his conscious subject. Such experiments were (and are) possible because the brain itself has no sensory nerve endings and the preliminary surgery (i.e. opening the skull) can be done using local anaesthesia.

New ways of discovering what is going on in the brain when it is activated by action or thoughts are becoming increasingly sophisticated and detailed. Computer aided tomographic (CAT) and functional nuclear magnetic resonance (fNMR) scanning, while having been originally developed primarily for clinical medical purposes, are now being used by clinical psychologists and neuroscientists to study the role and function of specific parts of the brain and to correlate the findings with the conscious experience and behaviour of the subject. Once again, the invention of new instrumentation has generated important new information to be added to the great jigsaw of knowledge.

Among other things, these developments and the extensive constant observation of others does cement the idea that there is some general correspondence between what each human experiences of the environment and what I or another observer experience in the same environment. This has allowed psychologists to develop what is referred to above as 'theory of mind'. Having a theory of mind allows one to attribute thoughts, desires, attitudes and intentions to others, to predict or explain their actions and to figure out their intentions. As originally defined, it enables one to understand that mental states, the epiphenomena of brain activity, can be the cause of, and thus be used to explain and predict, the behaviour of others. Being able to attribute mental states to others and understanding them as causes of behaviour implies, in part, that one must be able to conceive of the brain as a 'generator of representations'. There is some debate as to whether theory of mind is 'hard-wired' into human brains or whether it is mainly the product of serially reinforced observations by the growing animal, human or otherwise. Even were it the former, it seems to require social and other experience over several years to come to a useful level.

Simon Baron-Cohen (1999) argued that theory of mind must have preceded language use. He bases this on evidence of use of the following elemental 'speech' characteristics as much as 40,000 years ago. In early days, they would have been rudimentary, gradually becoming more structured and sophisticated as social groupings became larger and more diverse. Theory of mind is reinforced by intentional communication, clearing up former misunderstandings, following previously failed communication, teaching old and new skills to other members of the species, intentional persuasion, intentional deception, building shared plans and goals, intentional sharing of focus or topic and pretending. Moreover, Baron-Cohen argues that many primates show some, but not all, of these abilities. Tomasello and Call's (1997) research on chimpanzees supports this, in that individual chimps seem to understand that other chimps have awareness, knowledge, and intention but do not seem, rather touchingly, to understand false beliefs or cheating. Many primates show some tendencies toward a theory of mind, though this is not as developed as in humans. Ultimately, there is some consensus within this field of research that a theory of mind is necessary for language to be constructed. There is little point in attempting to communicate by sound or other signals unless there is the tacit understanding that the others in the scene are like the speaker/signaller in many respects. Thus, the development of a full theory of mind in humans was a necessary precursor to language.

Not only in thinking about the development of language but in reviewing other aspects of the nature of *Homo sapiens*, psychologists and other neuroscientists find themselves having to develop different models of understanding. Normal healthy functioning of the brain is necessary for effective and efficient interaction with the environment and other beings. As remarked earlier, various methods of CAT and fNMR scanning of the brain in action, together with observations from molecular biology and pharmacology, have led to the growing awareness of the secret skills of the human brain not only to create needed chemicals like noradrenaline, serotonin, dopamine, oxytocin and endorphins, but also to create and facilitate new dendritic connections between nuclei. This can continue even if the actual number of active nerve cells in the brain is continually diminishing with each passing year—and with each passing hangover! These are the processes which, for example, enable us to experience wellbeing rather than depression, to recover partially or wholly from a stroke, to experience love and affection and even to enable us to have the occasional original thought or flash of insight. Ian McEwan (2005), in his fine novel *Saturday*, expresses in richer language his fascination with developing knowledge of the brain/mind relationship:

A contributor to much of the dialogue in the book is Henry, a neurosurgeon, who is constantly and wonderingly, even for a scientist, aware of how the kilogram of damp tissue that is the human brain can have succeeded in coding and decoding the trillions of neural cells' electrochemistry into the constant flux of multisensory consciousness. Henry is confident that, just as the digital codes held within our DNA are now known and used, so also will these deep secrets of the brain be understood with increasing clarity, a clarity which will long be a source of wonder and meaning. Like many of us, McEwan marvels at how some few pounds of uninspiring tissue can maintain so many skills while the whole cinema of multisensory awareness keeps a continuous present running in which we maintain our being. Memories, dreams, intentions and feelings are the stuff of that present. He wonders how this material base becomes conscious. The neurosurgeon is confident that though the answers have not all been found so far, we humans will keep the institutions for research filled with clever and cautious scientists who will foster the incremental expansion of knowledge that has taken mankind thus far. This, says McEwan, is the only sort of faith Henry has. McEwan admits that there is "a grandeur in this view of life".

Developing motor skills in, for example, the use of tools has gone hand in hand with the incredibly rapid (in evolutionary terms) development of speech and languages throughout several civilisations in the historic world. Some languages have become more elaborate and adapted to the level of civilisation around them. Modern English, more than perhaps Gaelic or Inuit, has a vocabulary and syntax more suited to the expression of abstract and technological thinking, and is, of course, still developing in this way. Greek and Latin in their time endowed the language of science with 'muons', 'electrons', 'asymptote', 'transients' and so forth and ancient Greek letters like alpha, beta and sigma keep cropping up in mathematics as symbols in equations. Further expansions in language and symbolic expression will almost certainly occur in the course of this 21st century. New words and new ideas develop and interact with each other constantly. Some, like 'atom', will survive because they are supported by empirical knowledge. Others, like 'phlogiston' (related to the theory that fire was an element), have faded from use simply because they have not been validated by our increasing knowledge. In passing, it might be noted that a major difference between a scientific understanding of the world and its occupants and a theological or religious one is that the so-called 'truths' of the former are constantly being annulled, confirmed, or revised in the light of modern experiment and observation, whereas those of the latter tend to be institutionalised, unchanging and static as the 'given word', not to be challenged or contradicted—in some religions, on pain of death. "I Am The Word," saith the Lord, presumably in Aramaic, out of courtesy to his original listeners, and that rigidity seems to have stuck with most of the theologians.

In the early days of speech and language, however, such distinctions would not have been sustained. Communication would likely have been largely utilitarian and task-specific in nature. With the advent and progressive development of reproducing speech by writing, painting and eventually, printing and electronic recording, speech could be stored, studied and thought about at leisure. Runes and hieroglyphs led to better differentiated alphabets, symbols and numbers. Parchments, carved messages on wood and stone, traced letters in wax in the case of the ancient Romans and Greeks and, in due course, the almost overwhelming proliferation of books, all demonstrated the varied ways of storing and transmitting information. It is a matter of simple observation, however, that some of that information has been and will be superseded, discarded or refined. As a student, I read Davidson's *Textbook of Medicine* in, I think, its third edition, but thirty years later, I needed to buy the 18th edition, so outmoded and inadequate had the earlier edition become because of huge advances both in medicine and in the associated sciences.

It is equally apparent that knowledge written down or recorded in other ways can be of widely different kinds and reliability. There is no need to discard the words of a beautifully worded and evocative poem just because it makes statements that are unreliable when put to empirical test. For example, we do not take Shelley to task for describing the skylark as "Hail to thee, blithe spirit, bird thou never wert!"—though a bird it always was, of course. When, however, an astrologer states that, for example, people born under the sign of Gemini are quicker at learning languages, this is open to empirical examination and may be rejected as a lie. Many religious pronouncements are of a sort which conflate both these kinds of statement and for this reason, it can be discursively awkward to separate the wheat from the chaff, so to speak.

The early grunts, chants, whistles and moans of prehistoric man have evolved into poetry, mathematical equations, musical scores and other elaborated and creative codes. Some of these codes were interpretable only by certain subgroups of our species. From my childhood I have remembered that "Hail to thee, blithe spirit, bird thou never wert" was not the usual way I called to my girlfriend. The sentence *"Ich weiss nicht was soll es bedeuten dass ich so traurig bin"* is understood only by German speakers, while Sin2A=2SinACosA has significance for mathematicians, navigators and school pupils or students studying trigonometry. This pattern of the dots and lines *Dot dot dot, dash dash dash, dot dot dot* means SOS, an internationally recognised call for help from persons in mortal danger, to those who know Morse code. And so on. As a number of civilisations emerged and began to talk, write and record, so those civilisations imposed themselves on population groups which had not matched their development. Extended and increasingly specialised knowledge had, and still has, significant survival value for those who know the code or language. Words became the fundamental tools of thought, creating as they were accumulated more and more complex patterns of cerebral neural structures and electrochemical activity.

Thus *Homo sapiens* began to move into the world of ideas. As languages developed, so did ways of giving permanence to the more important messages. As already noted, chipping or scoring shapes in stone, runes, hieroglyphs and alphabets made these messages more precise and put them in a form which could be passed down through the generations.

Much, much later came the invention of writing and printing. The Gutenberg Bible and myriad other books—hand written, in the first instance, largely by members of religious orders—led to the proliferation of papers and books from the 15th to the 21st centuries, which have for long carried the essence of many cultures as part of the human heritage. The almost incomprehensible expansion of 'knowledge' contained in books (and now in microchips and other artificial memory media) led to some demand that those bearing great 'truths' should be separated from the others.

It became apparent, however, that there were several kinds of 'great truths' to be found in books and journals. One broad division is between the truth of evidence-based, empirically testable, scientific findings—in particular, mathematical truths—and philosophic and metaphysical propositions, such as religious 'truths', declared as such by those with a vested interest in promoting a religious understanding of how the universe, this planet and the world's peoples came to be and worked.

In our modern world, a clear distinction can now be made between at least two general principles of thought and endeavour—the scientific and the non-scientific. Included in the latter would be all knowledge which is accepted without question as true because it is, in the eyes of those who wish to assimilate and apply it, 'the given word', pronounced by a god, a prophet or a poet, by a seer, a priest, a politician or a charlatan. It is believed to be true rather than being recognised as demonstrably true by observation and experiment which can be checked, validated and is in the public domain. Examples of such 'given truths' or truths emerging from personal revelation as many religious truths are said to be, would be found as quotations from the Koran of the Muslims, the Bible of the Christians, the Talmud or the Torah of the Jews. Prophets, priests and proselytisers down the ages have hastened to declare that sayings and scripts from gods, kings and a fair share of charlatans are rich with 'truths' which we lesser mortals ignore at our peril. It is also a characteristic of such 'truths' that they are generally deemed to be immutable and remain unmodified by newer evidence, or even by some re-thinking about them by their more knowledgeable exponents. For example, sections of the contemporary Christian churches are wrestling with the problem of condoning homosexuality by allowing gay marriages in church or not discriminating against gay people who wish to become priests, despite the fact that the Bible condemns homosexuality out of hand.

This is, of course, not to say that all these 'truths' are false or without value. Much modern law and morality have been derived from some of them even if many of them were extracted from ancient writings rather than being developed from rational argument and evidence at the time of their application. As I shall attempt to explain later, however, such declarations are by no means the only sound bases for moral systems. Why these *ex cathedra* declarations have persisted into the present is, however, not because they were spoken by prophets but because they are consonant with what is a rational guide towards rules for human interaction which have evolutionary value for the species. For example, if we cooperate, we shall live longer and happier lives than if we wage war and compete remorselessly. We shall survive hardship better by sharing food as well as weapons (though not, so far in Europe, by sharing wives) rather than selfishly hoarding, while our young, and their genes, will survive better if we rear them with care, affection and in security. We shall gain more allies and friends if we are just and kind than if we thoughtlessly cheat and lie. The fact that some of these principles just quoted have been incorporated into the books and teachings of some religions is fortunate for our species but must not blind us to the fact that the latter also contain much which is sheer rubbish; often misleading, even false and sometimes dangerous. Moreover, some of the moral and legal principles adopted directly from the readings of 'the given word' such as the Bible or the Koran are conflicting, in spite of their having been transmitted, through their respective prophets, by what each of these two religions describe as the same God or Allah.

Chapter 7
Morality, Gods and Religions

It is important to note that scientists do not themselves operate within a moral vacuum. The Frankenstein story remains a warning to all. Scientists, as well as those who fund their research and those who use their ideas and products—be these atom bombs, washing powders or genetic modifications of other living things—need to give careful thought to the human implications and consequences of what they do and discover. The responsibility for this belongs not only to the scientists but must be shared with the whole of society. The latter, however, needs both to be educated in the principles of scientific endeavour and to be trained and ready to engage willingly and thoroughly in all forms of wide public discourse on present, past and future moral issues.

Even the most cursory glance at our contemporary world demonstrates that there are societies and cultures in which the prevailing moral infrastructures and attitudes can be difficult to reconcile with each other. One need only compare the moral tone of, say, the Bible Belt dogmatism and rigidity of central, southern USA, the new rise of Orthodox Christianity in Russia, the rituals and rites of remote groups of Hindus and even stranger moral habits and attitudes of some Central American and South American peoples to appreciate the huge task of general and scientifically based education which will be required to promote long-term openness to understanding and even thinking about moral principles and judgment.

This is not a new burden. The flint arrowhead could be aimed at a deer to feed a family or at a fellow human to gain some petty victory, for example by putting down a rival to gain goods or love. Millennia ago there were always some wiser tribal leaders, priests, kings or counsellors who would offer guidance to those who felt concern about such matters. Christianity and Islam in particular tend to forget that the beginnings of moral behaviour did not derive only from the word of their Lord but from a repertory of moral behaviours initiated and maintained by groups of animals and humans for centuries before the moral dictates of various gods were expressed. Evolution has ensured that men and women of wisdom and balanced judgment have survived down the millennia, often against the odds. I have tended to suspect that such survival has resulted from certain gene mixes, some more directly biological determining brain and body complexity and efficiency and others determining the kinds of neural functioning which favour the learning and persistence of rudimentary pro-social attitudes and possibly some of Dawkins' social memes.

Matt Ridley (1996) in *The Origins of Virtue* has drawn attention to how both man and other animals could, by their skills and behavioural characteristics, make gains which afforded them dominance among peers—a reputation, a recognition of status—which could serve them well in evolutionary terms. Common examples are of smaller 'cleaner' fish, wrasse, which gain a reputation amongst their larger host fish deriving from how well and diligently they clean off parasites. In very early human groups, a comparable reputation might have been gained by a powerful guardian male who defeated potential usurpers so frequently that the number of challengers diminished simply because of his reputation. I have often observed this effect amongst red deer in the Scottish Highlands. Once a dominant stag has defeated two or three rival stags for his harem, his 'reputation' is made.

While there is no doubt that, in the small groups which characterised several social animals which preceded man, a principle of reciprocal altruism formed the basis for a simple moral system, the main purpose of this would have been to maintain bonding and mutual support within a species. Some apparently pro-social and cooperative behaviours are found to have existed in animals other than man and still occur regularly. African hunting dogs will, for example, always leave one mature member of the thirty-strong pack, not necessarily the mother, to guard pups in their den while the rest of the pack hunts. The pack, too, will always bring back food after a kill not only for the pups but also for the guard dog. Mature members of the pack, of either sex, share the guard dog duties from day to day. This altruistic behaviour may be interpreted anthropomorphically but is clearly attuned to the survival of the species. It is less obvious how the unrestrained and noisily expressed joy of the pack's reunion with pups and sentry dog can equally protect the pack, although it might also be consonant with survival in the wild. It is most likely that such behaviour enhances bonding within the pack, thus enabling future coordinated pack behaviour in hunting and caring for the young. These wild dogs are still, consequently, a successful species amid many fiercer and larger predators. Here is reciprocal altruism in practice. Since their morphology and behaviour patterns do not appear to have changed much, if at all, for a very long period, it has to be assumed that the species has, to date, reached a symbiotic relationship with what, for the dogs, must be a compatible environment. Would that man might, even for a time, reach such a happy state!

The higher primates, with whom we humans share a common ancestor, four to six million years ago, can also be observed to demonstrate not only close family bonding but also social and familial mutual support, often observed as food sharing and mutual grooming; both they and elephants appear to display behaviours which indicate both happiness or pleasure, as well as grief following the death or severe injury of one of their family group within the species. They thus demonstrate a sense of individual identity and awareness that other members of the species are like themselves and see the world similarly. These basic signs in several species as well as in man are the necessary building blocks of moral behaviour. Sharing of food, remarkable navigational powers and continual and systematic care of their young demonstrate that a basic morality has been maintained by elephants and some of the primates without their having had to be instructed by any supernatural being.

Members of the whale and dolphin family have been extensively studied both in captivity and in the wild and all show strong social bonding, not only with each other but also, in some cases, with humans. In this way they demonstrate empathy: a sense of self-awareness which supports the theory of mind, allowing them to recognise that each of them is like every other member of their species in terms of how they see their world. How they behave in it, structure their lives and rear their young shows a rudimentary moral sense like that shown by the other big-brained animals. Morality has its beginnings in such behaviours and cognate social awareness and bonding in humans is a prerequisite for us humans as well. All of these species have started down the path of fashioning a kind or morality for themselves hundreds of years before *Homo sapiens* even thought of appealing to any gods for guidance.

In earlier paragraphs, I have dwelt perhaps overmuch on verbal and discursive influences on humans which might determine how what we might call a popular morality might be generated. This, however, underestimates the role of modelling in family and other groups, something which can be readily observed in all the primates and man in particular. Cooperation, one of the basic requirements for the establishment of a morality (along with reciprocal altruism, mutually observed, within the group), can also be observed even in driver ants, groups of which will spontaneously form a bridge with their own bodies if the marching column comes to a stream or other watery obstruction. Some may perish in the process, but the majority survive. Such behaviours may be more the case of making sure the genes of the group survive than the result of planned decision-making guided by anything like a moral sense; still, the two processes are both ways in which socially appropriate and 'moral' behaviours might be initially developed and later sustained as behaviours whose perpetuation would be, in evolutionary terms, in the best interests of the species.

A number of leading contemporary biologists, zoologists and psychologists such as Barbara King (1994), Frans de Waal (2013) and Michael Shermer (2011) take the view that there are a number of characteristics or traits shared by humans and the groups of social animals remarked on above which are necessary for the formation of a morality substructure in all these species. Experiment and observation have shown that a number of 'pre-moral sentiments' have evolved in early human and animal groups: these have constituted the basis for an evolving set of pro-social or moral codes. Especially in the case of humans, such sentiments have gradually developed into quite complex and wide-ranging moral, ethical and legal codes. Again, no gods need interfere. The characteristics which have been carefully observed to exist in some higher animals include learning the benefits of attachments and bonding, cooperation, mutual aid, empathy, sympathy, reciprocity and altruism, detecting and using deception and even learning techniques of conflict resolution and the awareness of the rules of the group. These pre-moral characteristics are well researched in the bigger-brained animals contemporaneous with early and present man and are likely to have emerged and developed in parallel. The similarity in the size of social groups from five to ten millennia ago would have been comparable—say, between 20 and 50 individuals.

Even vampire bats will share regurgitated blood with another friendly vampire bat which has not been successful in the hunt or who has shared blood in the past with the successful hunter. It is not too hard to see how progressive refinements of these characteristics in man could form the basis of reciprocity in a rudimentary morality—all underpinned by the fact that such characteristics clearly have evolutionary benefits for survival of the species. It is the view of several modern social psychologists that very primitive emotions such as fear and disgust are also likely to have underpinned several elements contributing to the emergence of pro-social rules of behaviour in humans. Humanists are bound to be impressed by such evidence as these early origins of morality, later elaborated by the ancient Greek philosophers four centuries or so before the Christian era and before any of the traditional 'good books' of the Christians and Muslims were written.

Both man and the animals observed to demonstrate these traits and eventually social habits lived, as noted above, in relatively small groups, probably of between 20 and 50 individuals (as bonobos, chimpanzees and gorillas still do). However, as the earth became more populated, the size of groups, of humans in particular, grew into clans, tribes and nations. In his recent book *Moral Tribes*, Joshua Greene (2014) opens with a helpful parable describing how the growth of progressively larger organised groups of humans—with their propensity to clash or cooperate with other groups, to grow both larger and more diverse and to move to fresh pastures in search of food and power—sets up the conditions which would propagate, in the interests of the continuity of the species, a primitive morality in the form of simple rules favouring co-existence and cooperation, mutual trust and sharing. Even if I have made a connection between the development of parallel, if simple, 'moral' behaviours and attitudes in very early animal and human groups, the matter of fundamental importance is that both the animal groups and man, starting from perhaps up to 100,000 years ago, have, in adopting these cooperative and mutually supportive habits, all survived to the present day. The evolutionary value of these attitudes and behaviours have obviously served all well in evolutionary terms. Equally clearly, while humans have had to increase and complicate their moral practices, ideas and styles, in an increasingly complicated and more heavily populated world, the codes of behaviour have apparently continued more or less unchanged within the animal kingdom. Among the great apes, the mutual grooming continues as a bonding technique; the African hunting dogs continue their long-established hunting and sharing practices; the vampire bats continue sharing and repaying favours in the same way; and so on. Their worlds have changed relatively little compared to the massive changes in numbers, social organisation and competing behavioural demands imposed on *Homo sapiens* over the same period.

For example, the business of having to cope with sex and property has from the earliest days of our species demanded the emergence of 'rules of engagement' with other individuals and competing groups, usually of initially limited population size, from which could emerge moral codes and social regulation. Nevertheless, religious faiths, including Christianity, have seen fit to ignore the evidence that early pre-Christian man and several other animal groups had already devised and operated simple and beneficial moral behaviours, mutual trust and support, and reciprocated altruism. Instead, these faiths repeatedly claim that one of the most important functions of a god or gods is to provide a set of moral templates for followers to model, rather than allowing humans rationally and continuously to work out for themselves a set of moral principles which could work in practice and be acceptable to most. Many of these principles would, in modern times, be relatively inviolate, but others would be modifiable in order to adapt to new situations and knowledge applicable to the living conditions and cultural needs of the tribes/clans/peoples concerned. The unnecessary intrusion of new moral commandments by a god or gods is both gratuitous and redundant.

It is, of course, naïve to imagine that early man sat calmly around the camp or cave fires and, in the manner of Rousseau's *sauvages nobles*, calmly debated current ethical issues. It is much more likely that sudden disputes about food, power, wives, property and protection flared up and were resolved initially not necessarily by the wisest but rather by the strongest of men in the group. Misgivings and mistakes would be seen later and gradually corrected— 'emotion recollected in tranquillity', as the poet Wordsworth might have said.

The modern equivalent of many other ethical issues still follows such a pattern. Issues and their solutions to this day will, from time to time, flare up within a community. Many will be quickly forgotten, but others may be ruminated upon until the last juices of rationality have been pressed into a clearer jelly of a lasting ethic that can be wholly assimilated into that culture. Historical sources indicate that healthy debate about how to live a moral life has been practised down the ages, even if the outcome was not always effective. Some of the conclusions of these debates have been relevant for thousands of years. Others are new and not necessarily part of the canon. "Thou shall not kill a fellow human being" would appear to fall into the first category, but a similar precept like "Thou shall not edit any human gene" would clearly fall into the latter. A genetic manipulation which would eliminate the possibility of certain people suffering from chronic and/or incurable disease would likely be morally acceptable, whereas a genetic manipulation to produce unpredictable changes in the nature of one or all human beings would probably not be.

In earlier, often oriental cultures, some sense of how to live a good life was imbued in the (male) young by their hero-worship of contemporary masters or gurus—often 'masters' of martial arts, victorious generals like Alexander the Great and occasionally significant philosophers. The stress then was, however, on the moral and physical development of the individual rather than the group or culture more generally. Just in the past century, the wise (men, often) and leaders of several cultures have already had to wrestle with many broader issues: for example, deciding whether imprisonment has rehabilitation rather than punishment as its main aim. Other unresolved issues lead to debates about whether legalising so called soft drugs does less damage to users than is sometimes claimed. Legislative decisions allowing use by all of more dangerous, often illicitly traded and often ill-manufactured, and unresearched substances already pose difficult practical and morally conflicting problems to many legislators in many cultures. Such problems require specialist knowledge of several scientific and medical disciplines rather than the prayers and rituals of religions.

The understanding of and solutions for similar and other problems in earlier civilisations was that their jigsaw of knowledge about the world, its occupants and the universe was so rudimentary that only a few vital pieces could be put in place. The empty space (ignorance) beyond the last piece fitted was, and still is, immense and awe-inspiring. The modern world is not so easily awe-stricken, but in the simpler societies of early man, gods would have been created as a way of limiting the sense of being oppressed by the society's ignorance. Such gods could be blamed for disasters or praised for favourable events not otherwise explicable in terms that people could understand then. Gods were such that they could safely be appealed to for help, if the people offered them prayers, made sacrifices and did sufficient obeisance. Having created them, people then not only attributed everything they could not manage or understand (and there was a lot of that too!) to the actions and wishes of these gods. The result was that the gods were attributed powers beyond their creators' comprehension and thus the gods had to be feared, worshiped and propitiated. The gods were attributed powers and virtues in keeping with the pressing needs and aspirations of the tribes, peoples and cultures which sustained them. Although Christianity has it the other way around, history points to man having made gods in his image and with many of man's qualities, both good and bad.

Accordingly, the Nordic gods such as Woden and Thor were powerful warriors, manipulators of natural forces, good navigators who could exert massive forces in the interests of their worshipers. Rainmaking gods found a place in the religions of desert dwellers; sophisticates such as the philosophically aspiring ancient Greeks were impressed by the power of their top god Zeus and of Athene, their (interestingly female) goddess of wisdom; this deity, from which they believe they derived their knowledge of strategy, skills, judgment and almost every other known virtue, had a Roman equivalent in Minerva. Before that, the Egyptians regarded their kings such as Amun Ra as gods; even in recent times in Europe, kings and queens were thought to reign by 'divine right' i.e. their rule was sanctioned by a god or gods.

As Wikipedia has it, "Throughout history, humans have ascribed various powers to supernatural beings. Such creatures include the immortal gods and goddesses. Some are given credit for the creation of the world and mankind, or food, warfare, love, and all the other good and bad elements of life. The gods and goddesses may be worshiped with altars, elaborate or gigantic statues, mosques, cathedrals or sacrifices. Poets and other writers may tell stories featuring the traditional myths about the deities' involvement in human life. One can see great differences in styles of worship from one society to the next or from century to century within one society."

Daniel Dennett (2006), (2013) has described how the earliest religions (and the term 'religions' necessarily implies a god or gods to be worshipped) moved from primitive animism to a sort of folk religion for smaller groups; these then multiplied or merged to become progressively more institutionalised religions with national and even world-wide influences. As that elaboration progressed, the trappings such as music, ritual and liturgy tended to establish those major religions as powerful social/political organisations which in due course held their adherents in thrall. Other philosophers than Dennett, as well as psychologists, social scientists and biologists who have examined this process tend to agree with Dennett that the major religions such as Christianity, Islam, Judaism and Hinduism will resist the inroads of the scientific analysis of their origins, function, structure and beliefs for a century or two longer. Perhaps humanists should consider some of these social trappings to establish more active social interaction among themselves at a local level. I shall return briefly to this topic in Chapter 12.

Among the most persistent of gods were those mentioned in the previous paragraph, all of whom acknowledge one god. In an attempt to personalise their god, they graced their God, or Allah, with an initial capital. Hindus have Vishnu and Shiva but there may be other lesser gods among lesser religions elsewhere in the world. It is noteworthy that as the world's knowledge and understanding increased at ever faster rates, the need to invent and worship new gods, or even existing Gods, has diminished significantly. Around the world, new gods are being invented/discovered much less frequently, possibly because the current God tends to compel us to look down our noses at 'false gods' and makes edicts to forbid the worship of such creatures.

At various points in this book I shall refer to the work and thinking of neuroscientist, psychologist and historian of science, Michael Shermer, and one of his books, notably *The Believing Brain* (2011). In this, he describes how, like this author, he struggled to throw off the limiting shackles of a religious early life until his scientific studies and researches compelled him (as they did this author) to adopt a completely different and humanistic frame of reference.

Shermer exposes his early Christian upbringing, early university career and other influences as a background to his eventual and lasting scepticism about gods and religion. He is very frank about this but as founder and editor in chief of *Sceptic Magazine* and several books on science, philosophy and the religions, he is wholly committed now to a humanist position.   In the course of some paragraphs Shermer concentrates on the alleged characteristics of the Christian god in particular. He wonders why God should care whether he (Shermer) believes in Him, heaven and hell, or not. Shermer is much exercised by God's statement that He is a jealous, punitive and prescriptive God, visiting the iniquities of the fathers on the children – and down through several generations. This makes that God a very grim, relentless and unloving creation who simply does not recognise justice – a very different picture from that of the benevolent, all-knowing and ubiquitous being he is described as in the New Testament of the Bible. Shermer wonders, if God is omniscient, why should it matter whether Shermer's belief matters? Shermer sees God as being more like the ancient Greek and Roman gods who are portrayed as demonstrating ordinary human experiences and feelings such as jealousy, which humans, with effort, can get over, rather than cosset it, nursing His wrath to keep it warm, and working out harsh penalties on all and sundry. As I indicated above, Shermer draws attention to the Old Testament God, Jaweh, who in the first three of the Ten Commandments (Exodus 20 – 2-17) (King James version of the Bible) declares, "I am the Lord, thy God. Thou shalt have no other Gods before me. Thou shalt not make unto thee any graven image or any likeness of anything that is in heaven above or that is in the earth beneath or that is in the water underneath the earth. Thou shalt not bow down thyself toward them nor serve them for I, thy God, am a jealous God visiting the iniquity of the fathers upon the children and to the third and fourth generation of them that hate Me!" In the light of such diktats, I am not surprised at that hatred. It is perhaps worth noting how some Islamic principles have also been derived from these Commandments.

If God made man in his image, then he must have given him reason and critical faculties to exercise – even on God's claims and to query his very existence. Shermer declares, perhaps because of his early Christian background, that he has worked out moral principles for himself and done his best to live by them. This is exactly what humanists do as well. Shermer has despaired of following religions and gods at all, finally telling them in exasperation, to do with him as they wish.

Shermer here seems to be shuttling in and out of very different frames of reference. One moment the 'god' concept seems to be comfortably endorsed as real and relevant. In the next, it is discarded fairly peremptorily. If Shermer was confused by acts of God and the like, I can also draw attention to the confusion of frames of reference used by USA lawyers and the idea of "acts of God" and note something of the same lack of precision and determination which seems again to apply.

There have been, in the late 20th century, several cases in the USA of individuals whose insurers had refused them compensation for what were described in their policies as 'Acts of God'. The phrase, 'Act of God' or *vis major*, has been the subject of considerable litigation because a defendant who otherwise would be liable for the safety of another's person or property may be absolved of such liability when there fortuitously occurs an act of God. The defendant's main difficulties are in establishing that: (1) the particular occurrence was an act of God in the legal sense; and (2) the damage or injury incurred was proximately caused by the act of God and not by the negligence of the defendant. In the recent District of Columbia case of Garner v. Ritzenberg, a torrent of rain water entered the window of the plaintiff's basement apartment destroying all his personal property. The rain was of such intensity that parked cars were moved about in the street. The plaintiff alleged that the defendant-landlord was negligent in levelling the ground outside his apartment and that such negligence caused the damage. On the other hand, the defendant contended the rain was so intense that an unforeseeable 'flash flood' occurred. This, the defendant urged, constituted an act of God which was the proximate cause of the plaintiff's damage. The trial court found, as a matter of law, that the defendant was absolved, inter alia A.2d 353 (D.C. Munic. Ct. App. 1961). The United States Weather Bureau substantiates the court's holding, in that no extraordinary rainfall was recorded in Washington on the day when the damage occurred. However, the weather bureau has only two recording stations in the city and it is possible that this rain was localised and escaped recordation. Letter from Chief, U.S. Weather Bureau, William E. Hiatt to

J. L. Howe, III, Mar. lo, s96i. "The real issue was whether defendants were negligent in the construction or maintenance of premises likely to be inundated during heavy but foreseeable rainfalls."

What, then, is an act of God? Although the question is asked repeatedly, answers given in the cases are in conflict. In its broadest sense, an act of God can be defined as "every occurrence that takes place on earth". For legal purposes, this definition must be restricted. A comprehensive legal definition would be inaccurate without embodying the following elements: (i) unforeseeability by reasonable human intelligence; and, (ii) the absence of human agency causing the alleged damage. Generally, the controlling test of unforeseeability is that the occurrence be unprecedented in the particular area. Some courts construe the word 'unprecedented' quite literally; if the occurrence has happened any time prior to this particular occurrence, then it is foreseeable and will not absolve the defendant of liability. This construction is qualified only by the 'memory of man' which in its literal construction means recorded history.

"An 'act of God' as known in the law is an irresistible superhuman cause such as no ordinary or reasonable human foresight, prudence, diligence, and care could have anticipated and prevented." This requirement runs through all the reported cases on the subject. "The expression 'act of God' excludes the idea of human agency, and if it appears that a given loss has happened in any way through the intervention of man, it cannot be held to have been the act of God but must be regarded as the act of man."

In another case, in Ohio in 1961, a man initially won his case that an Act of God had caused damages which the court deemed due to him. Subsequently, papers suing God were presented to the court but the judge ruled that the recipient, (God), in spite of alleged omnipresence, had no fixed address and therefore the court papers could not be presented to him. An appeal to a higher court was sustained when the appellant pointed out that the intended recipient was said to be both omniscient and ubiquitous and therefore should have known the content of his summons as soon as the papers were typed! I suspect that the final outcome would have been unsatisfactory to the appellant on the grounds that the individual sued would have had no financial assets accessible by the courts.

This illustrates perfectly the logical chaos of mixing ordinary natural human realities with the supernatural. For obvious reasons, they don't mix! Many of these American court reports make fascinating, even sometimes amusing reading. They demonstrate the bizarre consequences of mixing logical debate about the boringly accurate but legalistic discussion of lawyers with notions of supernatural entities about which there can never be any broad-based agreement or definition. Acts of God appear to be repetitively malevolent and just plain nasty and on the part of a God whose adherents claim is benevolent. Positive events, like unexpected rescues from natural disasters such as volcanic eruptions, survivals of high altitude falls from aircraft or large lottery wins, never seem to qualify as Acts of God even though they are unforeseeable and unprecedented. This God of the lawyers seems to be a pretty unpleasant piece of work—shifty, elusive and far from dependable!

After this little legal diversion, we return to the earlier quotation from Shermer, the uncertainty of whose last sentence, seems to put him at a disadvantage. Writing in the terms he now does would probably have been harder for Shermer as an academic in USA than it is for myself and other humanists in western Europe. Britain used to be described as a 'Christian country' but the 2010 national census returns show that this is only narrowly the case. Just over half (59.5%) of the population declare themselves as Christians and a further 32.8% either say they have no religion or do not state any religion when asked which religion they are affiliated to.

Originally the Christian and Islamic gods were competitive in their powers and influence—and to some extent they still are. They were all punted regularly from their invention by their chief exponents (disciples) as far better than their predecessor gods like Zeus, Wotan, Vishnu, Shiva and the rest. The highways and byways of history are littered with the relics of past gods, false gods and mini gods of various potencies in their times. Some of the more obsessional historians have traced the names and some of the characteristics of nearly 36,000 gods or goddesses now 'demobilised', discarded and forgotten, no matter what wonderful powers had been attributed to them in their heydays, just as present ones will in the next few millennia be similarly discarded. After all, every religious devotee of one of these gods is an atheist so far as all these other gods are concerned.

A new god has not appeared for some time now. No doubt, however, in the next couple of millennia some new god will appear in Haiti, Tibet, Texas, Chipping Sodbury, Macduff, Ouagadougou or somewhere else in the world. There is an English saying, 'Every dog will have its day!' Perhaps that was first written by a dyslexic who wrote 'dog' instead of 'god'. The emotional need for the security and succour of religion is too strong for the huge numbers of the already indoctrinated, the poor, the frightened, the deprived, the uneducated and the intellectually lazy social conformists among the more economically advanced groups, to ignore.

The prophets and disciples can be seen as the public relations specialists of the gods just as the 'messenger god' Mercury was, to the ancient Romans. These disciples were the 'spin doctors' of their time, and in retrospect, just about as trustworthy as our contemporary equivalents. Looking at the history of gods over, say, the past three or four thousand years, it is clear that there is a strong negative correlation between the number of gods with the powers attributed to them and the progressive growth of technological and scientific knowledge. As more and more of the natural world is known and understood, so the need for various kinds of supernatural 'heavenly support and interventions' and aid in agriculture, warfare and coming to terms with the fact of death progressively diminishes. Whereas the hypotheico-deductive method and internationally cooperative style of scientists has hugely and obviously improved the lot of mankind, the dogmatism, certainty of philosophic rectitude and mutual intolerance of many religions over the same period have been damaging to and restrictive of human progress, wellbeing and happiness. Several of the most destructive wars on our planet have been not only triggered or instigated by mutually antagonistic religious groups but underpinned and maintained by the intransigence of religious bigots, dangerously aware of their own certainty. As has been already indicated, from the Crusades to the Spanish Inquisition to the 'Troubles' in Northern Ireland, Palestine, the ethnic cleansing of Muslim Rohingya by the military government of Myanmar and the running sore of Israel and Palestine—to say nothing of the present (2018) awfulness of Afghanistan, Syria and Northern Nigeria—the failure amicably and rationally to reconcile different religious beliefs is all too manifest. In their own eyes, each of them is right. By contrast, no wars or uprisings, no murders or riots, no sedition or bombings can be laid at the door of humanists. (It should, in passing, be noted that neither Hitler, Stalin nor Hirohito were humanists as has sometimes been alleged.)

Daniel Dennett, to whom I have already referred, while expressing in his own way the content of much of what I have written above, takes the view that formal religions and all their trappings and practices (like, for example, belief in the value of prayer) will remain, for many years, even centuries, in spite of the march of science, simply because centuries have seen many religions institutionalised and woven into the fabric of people's lives. A notable example of that resides in the British people continuing to reserve a number of places in the House of Lords for bishops of the Church of England. British monarchs have been for long described on coins in circulation as 'Defender of the Faith'. That may well have signified an important role in stabilising society from the questions raised by the Enlightenment two or three centuries ago. Surely, by now, that role should be quietly dropped in favour of linking our monarch to, for example, supreme patronage of The Royal Society and several other organisations known to be committed to reason and the scientific method, the extension of knowledge and its recurrent re-validation by observation and experiment. Government, too, should try to advocate rationality rather than faith or unreason. In particular, it should foster an educational system which constantly monitors the curricula of so-called 'faith schools', lest they move from a broad general education designed to increase independent critical thought and analysis in the standard school subjects—for example, the teaching of science and evolution—towards religious indoctrination.

These faith schools are seen by many as a form of social engineering which accentuates rather than minimises differences between groups of pupils and individual pupils from different religious groups. Surely the really well educated cannot ignore the vast swathes of our national history—and of world history—which have exemplified the destructiveness instigated by apparently irreconcilable religious differences, even bigotry and inflexibility. While I strongly advocate that all faith schools be done away with in favour of schools which accommodate all pupils, and teach a general curriculum, leaving matters of faith to be attended to in the home or other institutions, I also feel that universities should make compulsory for all students at least a year's course in a science such as biology, geology, physics or psychology as well as one year's study of a language other than the student's own. This is not so far-fetched an idea as it may seem. As early as the 19th century, and up to the mid-20th century, several of the ancient Scottish universities, including my own, imposed similar conditions on their students, except that Latin was the other language.

High-level scientific education will take a long time to spread its counteractive influence on the less educated masses. There is also the solace and reassurance about the nature of things like life and death which religion tries hard to provide. This will be a strong psychological reinforcer of people's religious behaviour and beliefs. The content of these beliefs is also easier to teach and learn than higher mathematics, molecular biochemistry and quantum mechanics. Daniel Dennett (2006), Sam Harris (2004) and A C Grayling (2013) have all pointed out that the formal organisation of religious sects and the content of education in many countries have all contributed to the fact that longstanding habit, tradition and even deep-seated prejudices and intellectual laziness, will make it hard to reject the comforts that religions offer. All of that, however, does not make religious belief rational or compatible with the scientific outlook. New pieces of the jigsaw of knowledge will slowly extend over the great blank area of human ignorance as the picture emerges of how our brains and the universe work and progressively interact.

What all gods and goddesses were thought to have in common was that they were considered to be 'supernatural'. This is both a curiously useful concept for magicians, fortune tellers, fiction writers, theologians and spiritualist mediums and at the same time, a useless one for scientists, economists, detectives, engineers and financiers. The supernatural is usually considered to be all that is not accessible to study or not governed by the so-called laws of nature. In one sense, that can mean that it includes everything that has not yet been discovered and is therefore 'not known' and indeed may not exist in any way at all. As soon as unknown forces, objects or events become apparent to any observer in the universe, then of course these events, objects or forces become subject to scientific scrutiny, description and measurement. They are then immediately part of the natural world and not in any way supernatural.

To attribute phenomena to the supernatural was useful at a time when little was known about the observable world and it gave great scope for imagination and the creation in fantasy of all sorts of mystical beings, events and ideas. Philosophers and theologians loved the concept of the supernatural (similar terms are 'transcendental' in philosophy and 'ineffable' in theology) because, by their very nature and definition, they were defined as not open to observation, description, measurement, experimental verification and testing. Indeed, they were beyond human understanding. If that is so, however, why use such words at all? They can have no meaning. Angels and gods as well as dead humans could populate the supernatural world untrammelled by scientific interference, exploration and experiment. If there is nothing in the 'supernatural world' that can be perceived, measured, examined under controlled conditions and clearly defined in terms of its nature and function, and nothing from that supernatural world appears to interfere with the way in which scientists, and indeed ordinary people, experience and understand phenomena, then it is sensible and intellectually economical to discard the concept as worthless, meaningless and irrelevant to rational discourse, our understanding and control of ourselves and our known environment. I never cease to be surprised at how apparently easily various religious people and theologians seem to be able to 'eff' the ineffable when, by definition, no-one can! Of course, in several decades of my professional work in psychiatric and other hospitals, I met many 'gods', 'spiritual healers', 'wizards' and 'devils' whose delusions and self-concepts were determined by paranoid schizophrenia (and occasionally by the drugs used to treat it), other psychoses anoxia and occasionally, brain tumours, as well as other brain dysfunctions such as temporal lobe epilepsy treated by neurosurgery or chemotherapy. Mostly, these examples were male. I never came across any 'goddesses' though I remember one female 'angel' who, unfortunately, failed miserably to live up to her job description. Psychotropic drugs and psychotherapy usually, but not always, retrieved them from the supernatural world they had temporarily inhabited.

In the absence of any clear definition or description of characteristics and function, gods remain elusive and don't seem to interfere with our normal understanding of the world and its ways. As for the Christian God who maintained that "I am the Word!", He seems to have been sparing in His use of words and to have been remarkably uncommunicative over the past couple of millennia. It is not easy in this 21st century to see what a God is or what gods are for. (You will have remembered my earlier question to the four hospitable Jesuit priests.) How do gods operate? What is their function, and would we notice if a god went on strike or just got tired of doing all the things she, he or it once did? How would we recognise one in the street–or anywhere? In spite of their declared omniscience, omnipotence and ubiquity, they remain elusive and don't seem to interfere in the work of scientists, politicians, bankers, bakers, butchers or candlestick-makers. Lawyers may, as we have seen, from time to time, debate whether certain events were acts of men or otherwise.

'Acts of God' seem to be relegated to the small print of insurance policies and terms and conditions, at least for the time being. Because legally certified acts of god are so infrequent, gods appear to be relatively unemployed, even unemployable—at least in our corner of the universe! What a waste of talent if all that overweening benevolence, omnipotence and omniscience were to remain unused. Personally, I have never in my quite long life experienced anything that might have led me to form a hypothesis that the existence of a god or gods determined its happening. Always there has been a rational, even banal, scientific explanation for my experience. Maybe that's why I'm so boring! Nor do I put it down to a gene for irreligiosity. My guess would be that that characteristic is both polygenetically and environmentally determined.

Nor have I ever seen a ghost, holy or otherwise. In a determined effort to do so when I was in my early teens, I won a bet for ten shillings by spending part of a dark night, near midnight, alone in Banff cemetery, on the very edge of the town. My two baby sisters, one tragically stillborn and the other stricken by pneumonia when only months old, lay buried in a quiet corner so I was familiar with the place. My spell among the gravestones was uneventful until my pals, who I suspected had been making supposedly ghostly noises from the adjacent woods, turned up to be absolutely sure I had met the conditions of the bet. This was during the latter part of WW2 when there were no lights anywhere and there were graves of both British airmen and German prisoners of war killed by their own airmen on a strike on Duff House (then a prisoner of war camp) in 1940. I spent most of my required hour nearer the British graves rather than the German ones—just in case. But I won the bet!

A C Grayling, a contemporary academic philosopher and journalist, writes in *The God Argument* (2013) that "Religious ethics is based on the putative wishes—more accurately, commands—of a supernatural being. For the humanist, the source of moral imperatives lies in human sympathy and a balanced perception of current human affairs." Grayling continues, "If I see two men do good, one because he takes himself to be commanded to it by a supernatural agency and the other solely because he cares about his fellow man, I honour the latter infinitely more." As do I.

I have quoted that little preamble simply to outline a significant way in which the humanist position differs from many religious ones. The humanist envisages a morality founded on human sympathy, empathy and kindness which can guide one's judgment in many different kinds of human situation and which can be seen rationally by the agent and those around him as a worthwhile action leading to the betterment of the human condition.

I have already looked at the need for a god or gods to be 'first causes' and have disposed of that by pointing out that space/time is curvilinear, even though many non-physicists still think it is linear, that a timeline has a beginning and an end. The timeline of the universe is, however, curvilinear, like a line drawn as a circle with no beginning and no end. The proposition is that the universe, and perhaps other universes, simply run on and on even as parts of it/them are constantly dying and are replaced in a constant state of endless renewal. There has, therefore never been 'nothing' from which the universe sprang. To look for a beginning is simply the habit of some human thinkers to require a start of things from 'nothing'—a very difficult notion to define and get to grips with, in any case! Because each of us, and our brains, had a beginning when an ovum was fertilised, and will have an end when we die, and because, as a result, our brains tend to receive and to organise sequenced sensory and associative events as they occur historically, we are biologically predisposed to think of everything as having a beginning, a middle and an end. We may conclude therefore that there need be no 'first cause' (of the creation of everything) such as a god, but that order, a very human concept, is constantly emerging from entropy and vice versa, in all existing formed matter and energy. Thus the concept of a creator/god is unnecessary.

A second argument proposing a need for gods or a God is often based on the need for us to be guided toward a sound morality or knowledge of what is good. This topic has already been touched on and will be again. Christians, for example, set great store by some contents of the Bible such as the commandments of Moses or the beatitudes of Christ. The Koran sets similar standards but becomes less appealing to the dispassionate reader when it encourages the killing of infidels (non-believers) and apostates, even in retribution for a previously committed wrong—hardly the essence of tolerance! Many laws of many lands have been derived from the dictates of holy books written by those who believed they were privileged by a god to be his/her/its messenger and interpreter. As I remarked earlier, kings also assumed this mantle and variously wrote their own legal scripts to suit their own personal and political ends. Luckily, there were some good disciples and some good kings, so we have generally benefited as a species by having a codified morality which has been successively shaped by experience and other good men, religious or otherwise, into sensible laws as well as sound ethical guidelines.

However, tradition and the written word are not the only way in which a morality can be formulated. The law, of course, deals only with a tiny aspect of wider moral behaviour. There is no law (as distinct from the exhortations of, for example, the Bible, Talmud, Torah or Koran) which compels you to be kind, generous and loving. It is patently wise and civilised for men to be so. Our reasoning about how mankind can best be preserved and progress sees such precepts to be good starting points against which few would rail. Certainly, no humanist has any quarrel with kindness, generosity and love. On the contrary, laws can be fiercely harsh, rigorous and sometimes cruel beyond belief—for instance, the Talic law of 'an eye for an eye and a tooth for a tooth', or the burning of witches and apostates, or the stoning to death of fornicators and adulterers. That there have been refinements in the exercise of judging the moral from the immoral is especially clear in the so-called developed nations. What is equally clear is that there remain considerable variations in how behaviours are judged as moral/immoral or legal/illegal in many other parts of our world and in different cultures. In the Mormon headquarters of Salt Lake City, premarital sex is considered as immoral whereas in some Polynesian islands, it is not only moral but also desirable. The stoning to death of women caught in adultery is still deemed appropriate in some Muslim cultures whereas it is considered barbaric and immoral by other cultures. Absolute rules of morality clearly do not exist except in the mind of the 'infallible' Pope of the Roman Catholic church or in verses of the Mohammedan Koran. What is good or bad appears to be determined in practice by the culture in which such decisions are made, and particularly by what has been written in the 'holy books' venerated by that culture.

No Inuit out seal-hunting on the Greenland ice cap or tribesman of the central Brazilian rainforest is going to worry about the morality of animal or human cloning. The former will, however, trust that his brother or friend will help to drag home the seals he kills just as the indigenous Brazilian will consider whether or not to tell others in his village of the wild bees' nest full of delicious honey that he has found. Following how evolution has determined the end state of many animal and human behaviour patterns, we might reasonably suspect that the behaviours most appropriate to the survival and success of our species in different local physical and social environments will eventually prevail as 'the good' or the morally correct. Continuing segregation of cultures will slow down this process because then the differing ways of living in different cultures will not be made apparent in ways which compel individual humans to weigh and consider which lifestyles contribute more to the sum of human happiness for both men and women.

Because we see significant differences in what is judged as moral behaviour at any one point in time within a culture, or between cultures, it is not easy to assess how far evolution will modify what rules survive down the centuries. It is reasonable to take the view that social groups which propagate behaviour which is consonant with long-term species survival will be more likely to sustain themselves than those which habitually encourage aggressive, dishonest and/or wholly selfish behaviours. In several advanced cultures moral codes have been written down and can be modified as required by changes occurring in the wider world. The Human Rights Bill is an attempt to move from moral codes to legal requirements. One of the most potent mediators of change in moral perceptions and behaviour is the relatively recent expansion of numbers of people from any corner of our earth to any other facilitated by long-range air travel, and various representations of widely different cultures by television and cinematic programmes, and the content of the internet. The effects of social media such as Facebook and Twitter probably initiate and sustain the constant interchange of moral and other ideas (of sometimes distressingly variable quality!) than does any commitment of religious fathers, priests or professors to passing on the guidance of their gods.

Most medical and scientific researchers, including myself, have had or have to submit the nature, planning and executive content of their proposed research to an appropriate ethical committee before permission is granted to go ahead. Western democratic governments in particular are increasingly finding that new issues in science and political thinking require the peoples' representatives to formulate new legislation which will guide the governed when they face new ethical/legal dilemmas with which they have never before been faced. Examples of such issues might include, in the USA, citizens' rights to hold personal firearms, or, in Britain, the use by doctors of stem cells (and their foetal source) in therapy and research. There are several live moral issues, including an individual's right to end his or her own life when suffering a terminal illness; the right of a woman to have her child aborted (in a variety of reported circumstances) and, of course, the right to express in speech or print views which may not be those of a government or some other political/religious majority. All of these examples are commonly debated and discussed in small social groups, university classes and common rooms, newspapers and magazines, and the publications of opposing or sympathetic groups. As I have noted above, Twitter and Facebook on the internet now also comprise another very active forum which itself is proving to be a new moral minefield because of its capacity to propagate 'fake news'—an example of our brains being too clever for their own good. One has to ask, as an evolutionist, whether ways of safely detecting 'the truth' will be found, or whether 'the fittest' will be either those who most skilfully either do so or those who bend the majority to their will, regardless of content. I am cautiously optimistic that the appropriate correctives will gradually emerge.

Socrates, Plato and other ancient writers have, in their time, fulfilled something of a monitoring function over moral and social change on behalf of a wider society. Philosophers from Hume to Voltaire, Descartes, Kant, Bertrand Russell to Gilbert Ryle and A J Ayer have, in the past, carried on this noble tradition. For most people who care about how our society maintains its moral course, however, they will depend more on doorstep and pub discussions, what can be heard and seen on the media, and sometimes personal discussion with priests, pastors, pals and psychotherapists. Even the sporadic reading of history books, magazine articles or even selected snatches of the Bible or Koran may increase the engagement of many with contemporary moral issues. There are currently some excellent television programmes such as 'The Big Questions' and, on radio, 'The Moral Maze' which engage with and present a variety of people of all abilities and interests in current ethical dilemmas. In this way, moralities and the definition of the good life may also emerge and evolve. Being international, the internet expands, though not necessarily improves, the range and quality of discussion of contemporary moral and ethical issues. So far, the extent to which its involvement might resolve these issues is, for many, an open question.

In earlier paragraphs, I have dwelt perhaps overmuch on verbal and discursive influences on humans which might determine how what we might call a popular morality might be generated. This, however, underestimates the role of modelling in family and other groups, something which can be readily observed in all the primates and man in particular. Cooperation, one of the basic requirements for the establishment of a mutually practised morality within a group, is certainly evident amongst humans, as well as primates and cetaceans. Even driver ants will spontaneously form a bridge with their own bodies if the marching column comes to a stream or other watery obstruction. Some may perish in the process, but the majority survive. Such behaviours may be more the case of making sure the genes of the group survive than the result of planned decision-making guided by anything like a moral sense, but the two processes are both ways in which socially appropriate and 'moral' behaviours might be initially developed and later sustained as behaviours the perpetuation of which would be, in evolutionary terms, in the best interests of the species.

Primitive man had few possessions, simple tools, dependants and modest food stores which had to be constantly supplemented and defended. With property ownership, of course, came envy and greed. The simple rules already tacitly adopted became progressively more complex, disputed and numerous. As the earth became more populated and group sizes also grew into hundreds, then thousands, then tens of thousands, the demand for land and foodstuffs increased likewise. Tool (and weapon) makers became more skilled and sophisticated and ways of organising tribes, clans and then nations made progressively greater demands on a hunter/gatherer population to live peaceably together and to attempt reconciliations when eventually quarrels and fights got out of control. In the course of what some historians describe as the Agricultural Revolution, the marking off of private land as agricultural took the place of hunting and gathering. It also compelled man to establish more wide-ranging codes of moral behaviour. More detailed elaboration of these rules formed, in due course, the basis of property and civil law. At the same time as *Homo sapiens* were struggling to become a rule-observing society or societies, subgroups were moving out into new territories seeking *Lebensraum*, establishing group identities not necessarily wholly compatible with the needs or wishes of other clans or nations around them. Contemporary replication of such problems with immigration remain to this day. Even the cleverest among those found out that there was so much more of the world, with other animals and humans yet to be discovered, that recurrent modification of the rules would be inevitable. Painfully aware of their own ignorance, the opinion-formers of the time sensed that the only immediate solution was to attribute to spirits or gods the powers that seemed to be important but which had so far eluded their reach or understanding. It was at this stage, about two millennia ago, that there were so very few of the pieces of my jigsaw of knowledge placed on the vast field of ignorance that there seemed no quicker way of acquiring the knowledge needed to fill in the unknowable blank area other than legends, the *obiter dicta* of 'prophets' and ideas from seers and scribes, holy or otherwise.

Thunder and lightning, tsunamis, earthquakes, volcanoes, blights and diseases that killed their babies, floods that swept away their houses and strange kinds of madness in some of their fellow creatures were all seen as various expressions (usually of the displeasure) of the gods. It became imperative then to worship and propitiate these gods, sometimes by prayer, sometimes by sacrifice or gifts. Abraham was even expected by his God to sacrifice his son! The smartest of men then quickly found they could achieve more control of their fellows and effect other clandestine results in their own interests by becoming the only ones (priests and disciples) who could truly interpret the wishes of the gods and instruct their weaker brethren in the obedience to the gods that was required for them, their families and their then moralities to survive. That sort of misguided, unthinking obedience was seen in the Nuremberg rallies in the 1930s and 1940s, when Nazi supporters submitted wholly to Hitler; it is still to be seen when Muslim Jihadis and their like strap bombs to their waists under their cloaks and blow up themselves and many innocents, for the greater glory of their god(s).

In the middle ages, in England, those of a religious persuasion, mainly Christian, were wont to define strange or disturbed old ladies as witches and to insist that they be ducked, and often, as a result, drowned in the village pond for no more reason than that they were somewhat out of the ordinary in behaviour or personal characteristics. Similarly, the high priests of the Roman Catholic church formed the Spanish Inquisition and assumed the right to question anyone found not to be fully indoctrinated and their behaviour to vary from that specified by their holy writings and interpretations. Agnosticism, or the demands of rationality, were not permitted. Both reflected a form of independent thought which would have been dangerous. Thousands of innocents were tortured and many more were burned at the stake if they failed these doctrinal (though often quite cursory) examinations—and all that in the name of a loving Christian God.

It is no wonder, therefore, that the rules of morality have had to become more sophisticated and complex when one huge group of religious people take 'Thou shalt not kill' as a commandment from God and another huge group of a different religious faith urge its members to 'Kill the infidel'. Many civilisations in the course of the last three thousand years have discovered that many of the features of living a moral life had to be made explicit rather than tacitly observed and sustained. With the development of writing and the use of symbols, hieroglyphs and eventually alphabets, rules of behaviour for individuals and groups were slowly codified and became law. The law then enabled sanctions to be imposed to ensure that good moral and legally-enforceable rules were observed by all individuals and groups for whom the laws were written. Tribes or nations sufficiently civilised to have thought through and constructed appropriate rules became more stable and successful—until new problems presented themselves to challenge the ingenuity and wisdom of the leaders. Several modern organisations such as the United Nations and International Courts of Justice, of which great things were expected, have proved a disappointment to many: slow in action and cumbersome internationally because of veto systems built into their operation. The disappointed then look inward to their own diverse, national and even idiosyncratic approaches to making ethical decisions which, in turn, may or may not progress from a local value system into legislation.

Ancient Greek, Roman and oriental civilisations were early codifiers of moral and legal behaviour which in turn led to rules about ownership of such assets as wives, property, land and other goods. The ideas underlying and reinforcing moral behaviour did not necessitate the existence of gods. Aristotle, Socrates and the Stoics debated such matters without necessary reference to Zeus or any other god of their time. The four Jesuit priests of Chapter 2 seemed to have forgotten that. The ancient Greeks held that morality was a principle that man on his own should struggle to define and develop. Humanists still do. The guiding principles emerged often enough from the simple transactional behaviours of human individuals and groups in ordinary human situations. This is still beautifully illustrated in school playgrounds as one observes how early and firmly notions of 'fairness' and 'unfairness' are declaimed, developed and upheld by quite young primary school children. A dozen years on, these early, almost intuitive, ideas of justice will be seen as requiring qualification and refinement.

Adults seeking to live a good life will become familiar with the need to grapple with and live through increasingly complex ethical problems. As the early Freudian psychoanalysts pointed out, we all learned from parents, teachers, priests and other authority figures to develop an internalised conscience about what was right and wrong behaviour in the eyes of our 'elders and betters'. We also developed an even stricter 'unconscious conscience', the superego, which could create a legacy of guilt which often feels more compelling than rational in ethical decision-making. This rudimentary process is what laid the foundations on which many, as a result of normal behavioural and discursive interactions with adults later, would build a knowledge (however incomplete) of 'right' and 'wrong'. A schoolboy who sees a bully strike a harmless child without apparent provocation would probably react by treating the bully to some retributive justice there and then. Later in life, however, such decisions become more complicated, often because others are involved. The bully might, after all, have been the headmaster's son, and alternative outcomes present themselves. Most modern ethical decisions involve more than the agent and the respondent. Many have encountered the much-quoted theoretical ethical problem involving a man on a runaway railway trolley who is in the position of having to decide whether to kill several workers on the line who cannot get out of the way, or to throw a points lever which would direct him and the trolley away from the group of men, but down an alternate line and into a brick building which might or might not be empty or packed with tons of dynamite. Theoreticians of risk-taking love to present increasingly complicated outcomes in such a situation. For example, the men on the track are all convicted murderers from a nearby prison but in an office in the brick building is an eminent scientist working on a new 'miracle drug'. Yes, yes. These are manufactured situations designed to prompt ethical discussion, but there are many similar 'real life' dilemmas in science and medicine alone, which have to be solved in daily practice, sometimes in courts of law. Only by keeping abreast of such matters can the humanist, or any citizen seeking the good life, begin to adjust attitudes and moral decisions.

An organ transplant surgeon holds a single donated kidney but has six waiting patients only one of whom he can help. Can he and does he alone decide, and what criteria should determine the choice of recipient and outcome? Should it be the youngest, with most of her/his life to come, or the clever researcher whose work is on the point of saving thousands of lives, or one of his surgical colleagues who has been in the queue for two years? Ethical decisions of that sort extend the parameters involved and go well beyond the childhood learning of most individuals. They force refinement of the nuances of decision-making in the modern moral context.

Inevitably, because of the low levels of human knowledge about the universe, the world and human nature, those members of the human race seeking power and the control of others became involved, sometimes disastrously, in re-formulating many of the spontaneously generated rules to further their own ends. A few years ago, penniless Indians were persuaded by ruthless entrepreneurs to sell one of their kidneys—which were later sold on, at extortionate profit, to hospitals and surgeons. To this day, it is easy to see examples of such self-seeking amendments to the bases of moral and legal judgments within groups of all sizes and complexity up to nations and even international organisations. For contemporary examples of the latter, just see the content of various countries' laws on immigration, the attitudes of different religious faith groups to contraception, female genital surgery, organ donation or the pay arrangements of international bankers!

The general thrust of the argument in the foregoing paragraphs has been that morality is an evolving social process, sustained by the fact that some 'moral behaviours' such as cooperation and mutual support will be more likely to lead, in the long term through the survival of the current participants, to the survival of the species, whereas others will either be discarded as unhelpful or will lead to some kind of a deterioration of or even the extinction of the species. This is all about the persistence of memes rather than genes. I incline to the view, however, that those very memes are sustained down generations by individuals whose gene patterns make it easier for them to continue demonstrating the behaviours in question. As I have already remarked, the qualities and characteristics necessary for the beginnings of morality have existed in some animals and in man for long before thinkers and the writers of holy books and catechisms even in early pre-Christian centuries ever sought to propose that it required gods or their messengers to declare to humankind what the 'true' codes of morality were. Mankind is now committed to re-establishing moral codes and ethical judgments which take account of circumstances and events which were unknown to any of the writers or interpreters of holy books. Moses could come on strong about not killing, not coveting neighbours' wives and honouring fathers and mothers, but he never uttered a squeak about the advisability of cloning animals or humans, modifying the genes of grain or spreading damaging rumours about people to all and sundry around our world on the internet.

As scientific knowledge expands, it will present ever more complex moral and ethical issues. Just consider the recent problems created by the dissemination of 'fake news'. Different religious and other subcultures will formulate different ethical solutions to the same problems. This means, as I have stressed several times, that the notion of moral absolutes becomes more and more tenuous. At the same time, however, it leads to variation in human responses in human situations—a necessary requirement for natural selection and evolutionary effects to take place. If moral notions have evolved, then so must they continue. Having a strict, never changing, absolute moral code written several thousand years ago, in holy books or elsewhere, means that adaptation to a changing world with changing problems is slow or negligible and does not allow for the variations in coping styles necessary for evolutionary effects to happen.

As previously mentioned, almost all well-trained and responsible scientists, and even students preparing research dissertations, have to submit their proposed work to various ethical committees for prior approval before proceeding. Among Western populations at least, however, it is expected that the ethics of the work will be discussed on the basis of evidence and rational analysis of the issues arising from the work or research proposed. Some distortion or misrepresentation of the facts reported may, however, derive from the 'spin' placed on them by the media anxious for 'a story'. It is not uncommon for what are basically preliminary research findings to be seized upon by enterprising press columnists who may tend to exaggerate the nature or the effects of the research beyond what the science has reported. As happens in science itself, there will, of course, be a gradual moderation and refining process whereby information is agreed and disseminated more widely throughout the world. Moral philosophers, to say nothing of the common man, need to be aware of and incorporate into their thinking as much new knowledge as possible if their moral and ethical judgment is not to be corrupted by ignorance of matters of material fact.

The humanist position on morality is that sound ethical behaviour can be seen to substantially encapsulate two main principles. The first, "Do not knowingly harm any man or animal" and the second, "Do unto others as you would wish them to do unto yourself". This is, of course, The Aristotelian Golden Rule: an oversimplification perhaps, but not a bad starting point. Beyond that, however, humanists, like the ethical committees referred to above, have to look for other general principles which are based on reason and a balanced analysis of the facts. Such an analysis needs to take account not only of developing issues that arise from changing events, social structures, the political environment and an expanding knowledge base, but also the political and cultural history of the population which will have to attune itself to any consequent change in moral attitudes and the altered laws that may follow. How power is gained and exercised is beyond the scope of this book; however, it is a topic which one can only hope will be thoughtfully discussed by many—especially those who currently wield that power.

Humanists concentrate too on the individual differences in the individuals at the centre of all ethical problems, their backgrounds, prejudices and personal characteristics. Humanists will consider the need for personal and social fairness and justice, tempered by tolerance, empathy and other rationally based rules fostering and expressing gentleness, understanding, kindness, the principle of reciprocity and recognition of the deeper emotional and physical needs of others. Tolerance is, at heart, a principle which appears to be laudable and safe. Unfortunately, it depends on reciprocity, on all others recognising that there may be heavy emotional loadings involved but nevertheless taking a rational approach to conflict resolution and mutual understanding—something which is almost utopian and certainly not widespread even in allegedly advanced societies. In our present world as a whole, there are now too many situations where that general principle cannot apply, simply because there are religious, political and other groups who do not in principle tolerate those who disagree with them. The 'Holy Grail' of reciprocated tolerance and understanding has already been passed around the international scientific community. Equal draughts from the magic goblet may not yet be evenly shared because national or even international 'security' may be put at risk.

A similar principle of reciprocal tolerance and understanding, however, away from the fields of science and humanism, leaves the world wondering when the leaders of the great religions may at long last come together to sup from that same goblet of tolerance and mutual understanding.

Chapter 8
Values

Politicians, plutocrats, priests, Popes, potentates and proselytisers in our allegedly civilised world never tire of adjuring the rest of us to 'get back to' good old family/Conservative/Labour/Christian/Islamic/New Testament /Old Testament/ educational or even business and banking values. How these power brokers have assessed in detail what these values are that they have referred to is often left unspoken. The values most ordinary people are already holding onto are never revealed, or even considered to exist. Very seldom too do any of those who shout loudest about values either adopt them themselves or clearly articulate them to whichever general public they are addressing or representing. There must, however, be some way whereby groups of people, tribes, nations or organisations come to be of the same mind, at least within their own groups, about which rules or values are for them and which they would hate to be without. This is simply because, as I have already indicated, people living in different cultures, in widely different geographical locations and climates, with different histories and faced with different social and personal moral problems, have to settle for different ideas to guide their moral and ethical decision-making.

For too long it has been left to religious leaders either to impose, or at least to articulate their values—a very mixed bag of archaic nonsenses and reasonably appropriate values which are still acceptable to many, including non-religious people.

History and knowledge offer an overview of those moral principles and values which have led to good governance and a measure of good will, political stability, personal satisfaction and happiness. Level of education available to societies will determine the capacity of members to review how far certain principles of thought and behaviour have led to goals with which most can concur, as against those principles which have historically caused more trouble than they are or were worth. Even so, in almost any European small town of today there is likely to be found a mix of more general social values and of personal values, some or all of which may be wholly consistent with the general social values, while others may be drastically opposed to them. For example, while a given group of adults may publicly support the view that children's education should be as encouraging, stress-free and interesting as possible, this group may also include members of the "Spare the rod and spoil the child!" school of thought who privately favour physical punishment and 'strict discipline', often a euphemism for harsh educational regimes. It is this sort of mix in which individual members of a community may covertly hold to a personal value system while apparently concurring under social pressure with the wider community view. Another, starker example is of the values widely held and endorsed by Hitler's National Socialists and thought to be the values of Germans as a whole. In that setting there were still, in the 1930s and '40s, a significant number of Germans, both Jews and Gentiles, whose more liberal personal values conflicted with the state system. Situations like these are the pollsters' nightmare. Later I shall say something about purely personal values but will first consider group/social/community values. These are the ones that seem to preoccupy the minds of governments, the media, other policy makers and, less so, religious leaders.

In the previous chapter consideration was given to the interactions of gods, morality and religions. In ethics, a sort of subsection of morality which looks more at personal interactions and decision-making, the term 'value' denotes the degree of importance of some object or behaviours, with the aim of determining those actions or behaviours which are consonant with living the best kind of life possible for oneself and for all others in the culture one lives in. In its plural form, 'values', the same term may describe the significance of different actions moderating conduct and living a good life, in the sense that a highly valuable action (relatively speaking, at least) may be regarded as ethically 'good' and that an action of (relatively) low value may be regarded as 'bad'. Values are therefore clearly related to and emerge from principles of morality in a given culture and at a given time. Another definition may see them defined as broad preferences concerning appropriate courses of actions or outcomes. As such, 'values' reflect a person's sense of right and wrong or what 'ought' to be. As this chapter progresses it will be seen that "Equal rights for all", "Excellence deserves admiration", and "All people should be treated with respect and dignity" are representatives of values. Our values can be expected to influence attitudes and behaviour and to some extent be modified by circumstances and experience.

Pre-Christian values tended to be dictated—often literally—by the most powerful. The power might have been intellectual, as in the case of the ancient Greek philosophers; military, as in the case of the ancient Romans or Persians; or wealth-based, as in the case of the Minoans in Crete or Maharajahs of India or the huge global business consortia of the 21st century. The more modern examples of these can easily be found in the history of the past couple of centuries. In communities dominated by two of these principles, power and wealth, there would have been less participation in discussion of social or political values amongst the general population—even though, as now, ordinary people would hardly have been devoid of ideas about what they value in the moral glue that held their society together.

In spite of the considerable differences in values adopted in other cultures, there is one set of values which has trickled down, furthering the evolutionary process, over tens of thousands of years and which appears to be well established and to the benefit of our civilisation. It is the relatively protracted protective care of the young in families. Earlier I indicated how several species other than man have demonstrated how protection from predators, adequate feeding and training of the young in important survival skills by parents have all underlined the value of the **family**. This has been most apparent of course in ourselves, the higher animals like the great apes, elephants, cetaceans and—one of my favourite examples—African hunting dogs.

Now, the latter set great store, and rightly so, by the value of the integrity of the pack, the extended family as a unit which has been sustained and developed by more than just the basic needs mentioned here. Its value now additionally incorporates not just a home, food supply and protection, but also bonding and behaviour modelling in both man and animals. From these early habits grow, in man, mutual love and respect between parents, between parents and children and between siblings and even wider relationships, with, for example, grandparents and grandchildren, uncles and aunts and so on. The wish to keep the supportive integrity of the family is probably the most fundamental value recognised and sustained by humans across cultures, locations, religions and political systems. Keeping the family (in any of its several forms) as an institution is therefore the basic value we probably share most with our kind. Within that, there are bound to be a variety of structures and practices deriving from different family styles in many cultures which determine sub-values which change with time. For example, structures such as matriarchy versus patriarchy, nomadic versus fixed home-based lifestyles, the distribution of labour among hunters versus gatherers, adults versus children, males versus females and so on all generate differing sub-values. In more modern times family styles show even more variation. For example, there are families run by two same-sex parents; very large extended matriarchal families where this is necessary for food production or mutual care; and of course, single parent families (well known in some other species in the wild such as elephants and the big cats) where care burdens fall on only one, usually the mother.

Related to the need, in early civilisation, to keep families together, there came pressure to value highly **security and protection from harm**. It is not surprising, therefore, that we still value protection from harm to our persons or to our offspring or to our possessions. This remains as the value which reinforces the rule of law and strong but sensitive policing by consent in well-developed societies. In this context, **justice** is a key value.

As every school teacher knows, the notions of justice and fairness are formed early in young minds, so it is little wonder we grow up to value the security of a justice system which is free of corruption and false representations. In the UK, it is still generally the case that we can walk about safely and securely in our towns, cities and the countryside (with a relatively small number of exceptions) whereas I have lived, much more uneasily, in several countries where the rule of law could not be taken for granted and where more murders are committed in one city in a week than we experience in the whole of the UK in a year and where civilians carrying loaded guns is considered not only as a right but as a necessity. Even in the developed world, then, it is easy to see differences in the weight given to several civic values by the populace at different stages in their civic development. However, it bears repeating that variance is the prerequisite of evolutionary change.

Looking at the current scene, there is a sense in which we are all the arbiters of what we take to be 'the good'. We read and write letters to the media (which in former times would have exclusively meant newspapers and magazines), we tweet and blog on the internet, we discuss all sorts of things with our friends and workmates, in the street, in the pub or in our homes, schools and universities. We watch programmes on television and listen to radio discussions from anywhere in the world. We consult close friends or advisors, clinical, legal or spiritual, the better to make our own judgments about human dilemmas and ambiguous situations. Modern communications media now enable us to scrutinise other values adopted by populations throughout the world and to consider the differences and their effects and make comparisons with our own which might allow us to better understand how value systems arise and develop. This, however, is still a preferable method for people to work out for themselves, in the context of their own cultures, what should be the values they keep, rather than having these thrust upon them in the form of *ex cathedra* statements from a miscellany of clerics and theologians, or even military dictators or political agitators. The stability of such value systems was originally sustainable until much of the developed world began to feel the pressures of recent mass migrations by refugees and others across cultures and national boundaries. This in itself has created new moral issues and problems. More recently, the fabrication on the internet of 'fake news' by individuals, hostile nations and other agencies is undermining the ability of even the best organised companies and governments to establish the truth of all kinds of political and other situations.

From simple observation we can see that such activities and the thinking that accompanies them and is most likely to resolve them, is most likely to flourish in the political organisation we call **democracy**—one person, one vote, for all adult citizens, male and female, have a vote. A by-product of this is that we have come to value what we call '**freedom of speech and expression**'. This, I suspect, would come very high in the value system of the most developed Western societies/nations today. In *Areopagitica*, John Milton (1664) took a break from writing his elegant poetry to pen a strong defence of freedom of expression in equally elegant prose. He vigorously defended the right to publish books uncensored by any government or other self-styled authority. A brief quotation will afford the reader a taste of Milton's 17th century style: *"For books are not absolutely dead things, but doe contain a potencie of life in them to be as active as that soule was whose progeny they are; nay they do preserve as in a violl the purest efficacie and extraction of that living intellect that bred them."*

Freedom of expression is, of course, not unqualified. Philosophers can happily while away an hour or two recapitulating instances where freedom of expression has had to be curtailed. Sedition, lying, libel, slander, inciting to hatred and, until relatively recently, blasphemy, are but examples where freedom of expression may be or has been limited. But even these examples are being eroded year by year in the Western world. How, for example, in the case of blasphemy, can one take in vain the name of a god the sheer existence of which is unsupported by any scientific, empirical evidence that would stand up in any laboratory—or court?

There are, too, occasions when, unfettered freedom of expression might generate significant difficulties when matters are discussed which reveal very great differences of principle between, for example, people of different faiths or between people such as Adolf Hitler and Winston Churchill who determinedly held on to very different political principles. Because the former will often have suffered a lifetime of indoctrination in churches, temples, synagogues and mosques, town squares, meeting halls, schools and even in their own homes, they will often brook no discussion of matters of dogma according to their prophets, gods or political champions. Indeed, they may take offence even at an attempt to provoke open discussion about the nature of faith itself—to say nothing of the many details of belief which to them are unchallengeable. This is what led to a death fatwa against Salman Rushdie in the late 1980s. Similar pressures are currently causing great distress to two or three sects of Muslims both in the Middle East and in the East Midlands of the UK. Roman Catholics and Protestants are not immune from such disputes as the strife in Northern Ireland has demonstrated. One of the key characteristics of humanism is the willingness and openness its adherents demonstrate to discuss freely, respectfully and without being embarrassed or causing embarrassment or distress, any matter of interest at all, whether it be philosophical, political, religious or scientific. One of humanism's commitments is to propagate similar openness and freedom amongst all of humanity. It will not be easy to implement.

Many people of this 21st century form a view of Islam which is based on only the current Muslim religious philosophy of either Shia or Sunni varieties. They fail to realise that mediaeval Islamic philosophers were much more open in many aspects of their thought. Their thinkers pursued what we would now describe as humanistic, rational and scientific discussion in their search for knowledge, meaning and an understanding of values. A wide range of Islamic writings on love, poetry, history and some philosophy demonstrate that mediaeval Islamic interest in such topics as individualism, scepticism, even secularism and liberalism were so far from being a closed book to their thinkers.

Unexpectedly, but according to Imad-ad-Dean Ahmad, another reason the Islamic world flourished during the 12th to 16th centuries was, of all things, an early emphasis on freedom of speech as summarised by al-Hashimi (a cousin of Caliph al-Ma'mun) in the following letter to one of the religious opponents he was attempting to convert through reason. "Bring forward all the arguments you wish and say whatever you please and speak your mind freely. Now that you are safe and free to say whatever you please, appoint some arbitrator who will impartially judge between us and lean only towards the truth and be free from the empery of passion, and that arbitrator shall be Reason, whereby God makes us responsible for our own rewards and punishments. Herein I have dealt justly with you and have given you full security and am ready to accept whatever decision Reason may give for me or against me. For there is no compulsion in religion (Qur'an 2:256) and I have only invited you to accept our faith willingly and of your own accord and have pointed out the hideousness of your present belief. Peace be with you and the blessings of God!" Now, apart from the little dig about the 'hideousness of your present belief' this is a remarkably liberal defence of a freedom of speech and expression which is rarely expressed by the current imams in the UK, if at all. To a modern mind also, there is a curious juxtaposition of the conflicting ideas of 'God' and 'faith' on the one hand and 'Reason' on the other. Nevertheless, to have read such an acknowledgment of the value of freedom of expression from a Muslim, even if a mediaeval one, is encouraging. It would be enlightening to have the comments of a contemporary imam on these passages.

The humanist would never prohibit the freedom of speech which allows all of these religious groups to proclaim their beliefs, but he or she would most strongly oppose the view that any belief system or other branch of knowledge should not be open to frank and free discussion and argument. Humanists favour the view that only by more open, rational and balanced discussion of any and every topic which may cause conflict can mutual tolerance and friendly understanding be facilitated between individuals and groups who find reconciliation of their views difficult or undesirable.

Support for the value of freedom of expression necessarily implies that many differences of opinion will be expressed whether supported by valid evidence or not. Differences among scientists on scientific matters can be resolved by further observation, the accumulation of evidence and experiment. Differences among lay people and scientists alike on non-scientific issues will not yield to any comparable discipline. The chances are that many people will not or cannot accept any rules of debate and substantial differences in background knowledge would inevitably lead to misunderstandings and even conflict. That is when tolerance becomes relevant—even imperative. Most of us would probably consider ourselves to be tolerant, but can we be sure that those on the other side of the argument will share that ideal? Only a short time ago I heard the then UK Prime Minister David Cameron declare, "I will not tolerate intolerance!" He appeared not to notice the paradox. If tolerance is diminished, then conflict is likely, perhaps even inevitable. Tolerance does not, of course, entail agreement. But sustained disagreement should certainly never lead to harm coming to any of those with whom the disagreement is expressed. If we are to value tolerance then, it is crucial that it should be a reciprocal principle. It is sad to note that the greatest lack of mutual tolerance for each other's point of view is often observed between exponents of the great religions of this world. They all depend om dogma so much that the notion of tolerance tends to leak away. Their problem is that their authorities are derived from the 'given word' of their prophets or gods rather than from well observed social, historical and scientific evidence or the deeper understanding of the natural world and human characteristics. Humanists notice that there is a tendency for religious leaders to venerate ancient texts and stories rather than to review their applicability to present conditions of the wider world and base their moral teachings on these new findings. There are helpful methods of trying to resolve conflicts. Contemporary psychologists can give useful guidance on principles and practices of arbitration and conflict resolution, but it is seldom sought except by well-informed, modern politicians, lawyers and businessmen.

The jigsaw of accumulated knowledge that I animadverted on earlier was tiny two or three thousand years ago compared to what it is now. Theological historians and various other sages have to struggle to find any useful relationship between what gave the scribes and Pharisees writer's cramp and what really relates usefully to the values and moral and ethical issues of the 21st century. The conditions in which we now live on our planet have changed and developed as much in the past hundred years as they had done during the previous two thousand years—and even faster change is to come! The great jigsaw, in the form of technological and many other fields of knowledge, is likely to change and develop in the next twenty years by as much as it has done in the past hundred. What values people will wish to endorse as they observe the changes in the moral climate, to say nothing of the actual climate, of their corner of the world has to remain an open question. So many thousands of people travel across the length and breadth of the globe each week, watching, reading and often discussing differences in values, living conditions and lifestyle that many gradual convergences in ethical and moral attitudes will spread across cultures. One can only hope that those convergences will occur between the more intelligent and best informed from among the travellers.

It may surprise some that no mention has been made so far of the value of **freedom**—except in the context of freedom of speech and expression. All over the world there are self-declared 'freedom fighters' whose concept of freedom is wholly dependent on the lack of value they have placed on their former governing regime or from the effects of some of its enactments. It is all very well to value law and order but that brings with it detailed prescriptions and enforcements which can produce unforeseen anomalies and irritations. The **democratic process,** mentioned earlier, should usually allow the overweening value attributed to an object, action or point of view, to overcome any possibly idiosyncratic, personal views or proposals. Quite close to home, I have seen objections from government (local or national) raised to the building of inappropriate housing within a National Park proposed by individuals whose personal values clash with those of the wider population. Establishing the moral boundaries of differing kinds of freedom is often the stimulus to refining what the word 'freedom' means. Parliamentary democracy is possibly the condition in which such refinements can be made, and those fortunate enough to enjoy the latter will require to keep a watchful eye on other national groups whose understanding of democracy may not nearly match theirs.

Personal values are very much the product of some sense of individual responsibility in persons to interact comfortably and consistently with others amongst whom they live. Many religions, driven by what are thought to be the injunctions of their gods or prophets, lay down, sometimes in great detail, what their values must be, and the various sanctions, i.e. rewards and punishments, which will follow in the wake of behaviours which comply or transgress these values. Humanism, by contrast, requires its adherents to acquire and develop their own guiding values. They exercise their own responsibility for sensible scrutiny of what is best and worst in the world and use careful observation and judgment to create for themselves a rational basis and as wide a knowledge base as possible, a system of values which will allow them consistently to pursue the values that all humanists, and indeed everyone else seeking to live a 'good life', can recognise as contributing to the greater good and general welfare of all concerned.

Privacy is a valued condition that spans the border between personal and more general values. In both areas recently there have been challenges to that value. Private assumptions that anyone might enjoy total privacy within the security of one's back garden have been ruined by curious and intrusive others who are prepared to fly camera bearing drones gratuitously to disturb such privacy. The owner of Facebook, a supposedly innocuous internet social medium, has just been interrogated by USA Congress about the sale of huge amounts of data culled from personal entries some of which might have been used to influence national elections or foreign affairs. From this it is becoming clearer that new definitions of privacy must be formulated, and as promptly as possible.

Changes of values with the passage of time can also mislead. In recent weeks there has been active debate in the UK about the validity of commemorating the life and work of Cecil Rhodes. Was he a colonial supremacist or a patron of education and development in the part of Africa to which he gave his name? The debate about how he should be commemorated continues. More than half a century ago, over the main gates of the Nazi concentration camp at Auschwitz was (and remains as a solemn reminder) a wrought iron expression of value—'Arbeit macht Frei' ('Work liberates you')—except that it presaged misery and death for many of those who, prior to 1945, entered beneath it.

Our contemporary democracy should incorporate most if not all of our agreed values, but in the politics of advanced societies sub-sets of a population can quickly associate themselves with significantly varying sets of values which they think should determine political and social outcomes. It is therefore necessary to take a very long view of history if one is to settle for an agreed value system which might be both widely applicable, widely accepted and widely defended.

It is equally clear that general agreement about a system of values depends on the size and influence of the group seeking to establish them. In the years when a far higher proportion of the UK population than the present 58% declaring themselves in the most recent census as Christian, many towns and cities put up war memorials to men who died in wartime 'for the Glory of God'. Over a main entrance to my own ancient university there still remains an inscription in Latin which reads, "*Initium sapientiae timor Domini*" ("Fear of the Lord is the beginning of wisdom"). My personal interpretation, taking account both of my atheism and knowledge of Latin is: "Respect for the master is the beginning of wisdom." The inference to be drawn from these inscriptions is that high value was attached to the notions of the greater good being fostered by a willingness to die 'for the glory of God' and that honouring that God was a necessary precondition to becoming knowledgeable and wise. The values that a country still endorses for its armed forces probably continue to include the basic ideas of being prepared to die if necessary and of exercising learned skills and good judgment in the pursuit of military duties. The religious underpinning of such values, however, has now diminished in favour of more recent, democratic and socially relevant evaluations of the kind of country most Europeans would wish to live in and sustain.

But where in a given population educational level is low and experience of all kinds limited, then there is bound to be less independent evaluation of moral issues and a greater need for 'ready-made' solutions to moral problems such as religions, and some political organisations provide. The difficulty with these solutions is that they too, are often, as I have already remarked, based on 'the given word' of some 'supernatural being' or cult leader who claims god-like powers. L Ron Hubbard of the Scientologists and Kim Il-sung, the 'great leader' of the North Koreans (grandfather of the current leader Kim Jong-un), are notable examples. Many of the precepts of earlier 'authorities' such as these have been handed down for centuries from a time when the world was, in geographical and human terms, larger and simpler. Modern travel and communication media such as the internet have shrunk it for many. The origins of moral ideas and values were in times when people were more ignorant of natural processes and were unable to construe human problems in the light of modern knowledge, especially in psychology, physics, medicine, biology, engineering and neuroscience. The humanist is therefore very wary of that sort of dated ideology because it often allows irrational and special interest groups of the aforementioned politicians, priests, plutocrats and other plunderers to cash in and supply their own 'infallible' answers.

Humanists, in the light of history, expect the quality and quantity of knowledge to increase with the years. They also see that the definitions of moral behaviour tend to lag quite significantly behind scientific developments. People and politicians alike need time to understand not only the nature and extent of new scientific developments, but also to pursue the implications for human behaviour that they carry. For example, genetic engineers can isolate and, in some cases, remove, a particular gene from DNA, but lay people might well have views about which or whether particular genes should be manipulated at all no matter whether the gene is in a human or a grain crop. Sometimes in such contexts, scientists will be accused of 'playing God' in spite of the fact that most scientists, 93% according to Stenger (2009) and a growing number of non-scientists, will not have the slightest notion of what that means. The scientists see themselves as simply building up new knowledge on the basis of what is already known. That is what scientists have always done, and there is no sign of any god, unlike the one figuring in the insurance markets, having interfered with that process so far. Scientists are simply trying to design more intelligently and more effectively. Harari (2016) in his book *Homo*

Deus has suggested that intelligent design is rather a good idea—but only if we remove it from the Designer of the religious, God, and pass on the task as soon as possible to Man, who will do it much better. Omniscience is now better and more evenly distributed.

This may well be the point at which it is worth reiterating how important it is for our species that we should endorse the value of **education for all**. The more people understand about the world we live in, and about each other, the better will we be able to make informed judgments about all the other values we should embrace and foster. We will also be the better able to keep up with and put to good use the perpetual growth of the great jigsaw of knowledge. Most of all, as wide-ranging an education as possible would enable us to develop our critical faculties, to look beyond the obvious and to empower us to recognise the possibly specious arguments of those who would manipulate our freedoms, our ideas and our open and democratic lives. Only a good education which trains us to discriminate the different kinds of rational and irrational methods of persuasion attempted by newspapers and other media can inoculate us from the hidden persuaders. Television in particular can be used by governments, multinational and even more local agencies to manipulate 'public opinion' or certain segments of the public by creating tastes for programmes which cater for uncritical, uncomplicated and often pleasurable, but passive, viewing which is simply a process of 'dumbing down' and massaging away the critical faculties of those who might otherwise rebel or, at least, disagree. George A Scott, my much-admired English and History master at Banff Academy through my teenage years, and later, Rex Knight, Professor of Psychology at Aberdeen University, both saw education of the sort they both imparted to us as a means to sharpen our critical faculties and as a lifetime intellectual safeguard. It would be a safeguard against the hidden and subtle assaults to which we, as reasonable people (in our roles as consumers, subjects or constituents), might, all our lives, be subjected by all those politicians, salesmen, prophets, propagandists and charlatans who would serve their own vested interests. Since Rex had served, alongside the novelist Nigel Balchin in the Department of Psychological Warfare throughout World War 2, we paid particular attention to what he had to say on such topics.

The advanced civilisations have always favoured the freedoms which allow people the opportunity to observe how the moral climate of the society they live in may change. More importantly, the right to discuss and openly criticise what may be seen as misguided moral decisions is highly valued and sometimes enshrined in law or even fought over in battles. This fundamental freedom of speech and thought, if sustained, breeds mutual tolerance and respect for the soundly based arguments of others, thus allowing compromise and flexibility to guide, without prejudice, the outcomes of debate and the rationalisation of differences. For the generality of people to have the freedom to discuss and later to effect decisions, however, they need to live in a mature democracy. The word itself derives from ancient Greek, '*demos*' meaning 'the people' and the verb '*kratein*' meaning 'to rule'. Plato's democracy was rather more elitist and authoritarian than that of Aristotle, but guided by the latter, western European civilisation has, over the past two and a half millennia, struggled to make it work, in spite of the destructive efforts of numerous totalitarian regimes in the interim. Currently there are parts of the world where it is simply unacceptable to attempt to impose democracy as a principle because of major differences in cultural patterns and religious sanctions.

Patently, differences in the histories of different civilisations and cultures throughout the world mean that all are open to the scrutiny of all others. People can therefore see what effects on wellbeing, social harmony, economic prosperity and cultural development are reached in all of them. Often this scrutiny is tacit and may take years to be fully articulated and to demonstrate its effects, but that is how we come to establish those aspects of our lifestyles that we value. We, in a particular country, subgroup, culture or organisation, tend to believe that at any one point in time, not only are our values the best for us but also that they are unlikely to change too quickly and may also be the best for some others. Such complacency can be dangerous. One look at the history of the Tudors in England, the Victorians in the UK, the Moors or the Scandinavians in the 10th and 11th centuries shows how wrong that complacency can be in the moral stance our group happens to have adopted. All these groups I have just mentioned moulded some of our values even if few of theirs met the criterion of doing no harm to others—one of the most important of humanist principles. Just as our moral and ethical judgments have to keep pace with new knowledge and experience, so also do our value systems change with them.

A fairly recent fine book by Yuval Noah Harari (2011), *Sapiens, A Short History of Mankind*—to which I shall refer later in this book—lays out in fascinating range and detail how the great sweep of history can demonstrate the dynamic interaction of events, ideas, values and conflicts which have allowed evolutionary changes to occur almost imperceptibly. Some genes mutate, some genes survive and some die. That process changes how individuals and groups then behave and think, which in turn modifies social aspirations and valued behaviours.

Yet again, it is our political and religious leaders who are the reactionaries in this. They will be the first to resist any suggestions of change in our value system, to advocate 'family values', 'national standards', 'Christian values' and so forth. As I remarked in the first paragraph of this chapter, they do so generally without ever defining in any detail what these values are or what they entail. Worse still, many of them do not unfailingly uphold or live up to the very values they claim to be so vital. For example, what kinds of 'family' do they refer to when only one family in four in the UK currently (2018) consists of two differently sexed parents and, say, two children of their own? Do they mean a family of two unmarried partners both of whom have been previously married and who share four children from previous relationships? Do they mean the extended Hindu family of Indian or Pakistani immigrants comprising two parents, one or more grandparents, several children, an aunt and two cousins, all living in the same house? Do they mean a lesbian or homosexual couple, married or not, living together and applying to adopt a child? Indeed, can there even be a 'typical family' ever again when multiculturalism and mass population movements are the norm in the more developed countries? Finding common moral values among such diverse backgrounds is bound to be difficult psychologically, socially and politically. People who have already thought deeply about what values mean most to them will be very reluctant to change.

If empirical solutions to such diversity are to be found, then, as a psychologist, I would suggest that long-term, longitudinal research should be established now and continued over several decades. This would be designed to examine what parameters in the case of each type of family determine the success or otherwise of that type of family and of those individuals who comprise it. By success I mean what are the defining characteristics of the families which lead to the wellbeing, productivity and happiness of all its members, young and old, male and female, over the years, and indeed to the wellbeing of other families around them; how happy, stable and integrated are different sorts of family within the narrower societies in which they grew up and later in which they might move to. Do the next generations of different types of family demonstrate at least equal wellbeing, happiness and achievement to that achieved by their forebears? The findings of such a research (which ideally should be ongoing) should then guide the policies of government, educators and economists toward defining more particularly what values within family life determine a happy, integrated and achieving society. Factual evidence would then form the basis of governmental decisions at least in the fields of education, child care and family welfare and styles. The findings of such research might not suit everyone. Humanists, for example, might find that their child rearing and education practices produce more disturbed and unhappy children than do those of families with a strong religious faith. (I think that is an unlikely but still possible outcome.) Or it might be otherwise or indecisive. Or there might be no significant differences determined by faith differences at all. But at least the cries to return to certain values could then be founded on evidence rather than only on evidentially unsupported affirmations.

It is simply the case that sub-populations will tend to cleave to what they see as their own values even in the face of other pressures. Often these will be largely exerted by religious and political leaders (where there is no separation between the religion and the state, these will often be one and the same) and derived from the various 'good books' like the Bible and the Koran. These values need not necessarily be erroneous; many of them would not be and would be found to be a sound basis for living a good life.

However, the humanist position in this would be more rationally and securely founded on careful and graduated evaluation of how far the adoption of many of the Christian, Islamic and other value systems advocated by these past models have a sound rational basis and wide social and political acceptability. The humanist will be a careful observer of life's events so that his or her evaluation of these may be guided by good science, human sympathy, empathy, respect and the careful avoidance of doing harm to any person. In general, the humanist will favour the similarities between humans rather than the differences and the ready demonstration by all of kindness, consideration, gentleness, tolerance and cooperativeness—and all without the need to invoke the help, hindrance or interfering judgments of gods or any other supernatural phenomena.

Up till now, I have touched on what one might describe as institutionalised values. Most people who think about what they value in their way of life, however, tend to quote ordinary, everyday characteristics of individuals in the culture they habitually interact with. They tend to value the security of the impartial rule of law, their privacy, their freedom to make their own choices about such things as how they raise their children (within the law of the country they choose to live in,) and to attribute value to a number of smaller civic freedoms such as being able to plan and enjoy an annual holiday, being able to dress as they wish (though within the styles and local clothing habits of the country they choose to live in), or the freedom to redecorate their home as they wish.

In recent casual but deliberate conversations with a fairly wide range of others, mostly adults but with a sprinkling of children and young adults, I have elicited some of the features of the behaviour of other persons that they value. These valued characteristics include being fair to others, seeking justice for all, being honest, not telling lies, being generous, humble and tolerating differences, being brave, never cheating, being dependable, loyal and respecting others, keeping your integrity and self-control and, above all, treating others as you would wish to be treated yourself. These are not reported in any order of importance held by those who expressed their thoughts. Had I been doing a proper psychological analysis of the results, I would, among other things, have had all the respondents look at the list of all the injunctions suggested here and rank the items in order of importance for them. I might even have applied a Kelly Repertory Grid to see what clusters of constructs emerged. The lightly informal level at which I was then working, however, hardly justified that. The items I have quoted were not in response to specific questions on my part, nor did every conversation elicit all, or even more than four or five of the 'values' reported. I suspect that the Golden Rule, "Do as you would be done by", which precedes historically the major contemporary religions and their various commandments, would likely take precedence, with mutual tolerance and respect for human life coming close.

What people often talk about, as we can see from this example, are more often personal characteristics and behaviours rather than value systems themselves. It is, however, possible to see how, in any given culture, these desiderata could lead to incorporation into a more general, principled system of values. In other words, the kind of society in which my respondents would wish to live out their lives would be one in which such qualities would be generally adopted and encouraged.

Had I put all these questions to groups in China, Iraq, Polynesia, North Korea or Tibet, the responses would probably have been slightly, but not hugely, different in younger respondents but there would have been more variation among older respondents. Other ideas fundamental to the lives in these lands with different ecologies, climates, religious and political systems would have reflected different priorities for living together. Only the reduction of many of these differences by equalisation of the distribution of the world's wealth and knowledge among peoples, together with the effects of intense and prolonged education to the highest levels will reduce these variations in value systems, cultures and the divisive effects of religious and political systems in a way which allows growth and openness to be fostered. The humanist would wish to see these replaced by rational, evidence-based ways of solving conflict and seeking the security and wellbeing of all with a gradual convergence toward common values, upheld by sanctions supported by every citizen of every country. Perhaps this is a foolish Utopianism, a search for the holy grail of human harmony and value, but well worth striving for.

Chapter 9
Purpose in Life

One claimed justification of the 'God hypothesis' is that it can provide a 'purpose in life' or that it can give life 'meaning'. This, of course, assumes that there are such abstractions as 'purpose' or 'meaning' disconnected from the nature and behaviour of human beings. It is like asking what the purpose is of electricity or digestion. The answer in the case of the former is simply that electricity, as energy, cannot have any inherent purpose of its own. It simply exists—but can be purposively utilised by man if required. But the purpose is man's. In the same way, digestion is an abstraction encompassing many specific digestive processes, each of which might be seen as having as its purpose the triggering of the next event(s) in a chain of physiological events, all of which comprise the process of digestion to sustain life in man and animals.

People generate purpose for themselves. Life in the abstract has none. Individual humans create purpose and intentions for themselves. Humans may well consider that single-celled organisms have some sort of purpose within the general ecology of all living organisms—but it is humans who, for human reasons, see or create that purpose for microbes and the rest. Meaning, applied to life in the abstract, is, similarly, an exercise in futility. What is the meaning of clouds, tsunamis, volcanoes, lightning, tsetse flies, birth, death and illness? There is none that is intrinsic to them except any that we humans impose on them. They simply exist, come and go; they remain as meaningless as they were long before man ever appeared on earth. In due course, in the perpetual struggle to understand, some humans would try to attribute some meaning of their own to them—which matters not at all to how they are and what effects they might have on humans. Our ignorant ancestors of course attributed meaning to them as, for example, expressing the 'wrath of the gods', but that has no meaning for an oceanographer, volcanologist, entomologist or other scientifically trained persons. Calling such things 'the wrath of the gods' adds nothing to our understanding of the phenomena. Nor does it say much for the putative beneficence of the gods. Contemporary biologists and psychologists, for whom all life forms are simply organisms which have evolved after the earth had already existed without them for millions of years, will similarly declare that life forms, including man, just exist. Having survived and evolved in a very competitive earthly environment, they will all simply get on with living in a way which favours the protection and continuance of their genes and the potential lives of their descendants. If any purpose is needed, that could be it. Most living creatures pursue that purpose entirely unconsciously.

'Meaning', as I have ben referring to it, should be distinguished from 'significance'. For example, Koplick's spots—little red spots in the buccal membranes of a child's mouth—have no meaning in themselves, but do have, in the presence of other signs of measles, diagnostic significance for an examining doctor. In the same way, powder burns near a bullet entry wound in a body is, to a policeman or forensic analyst, significant of close-quarter shooting. It is the context in which the phenomena—the red spots or the burn marks—occur which gives meaning.

Most humans, however, tend to forget or to ignore the fact that, so far as they are concerned, any detected 'purpose' is always an inference from observed speech and/or behaviour. Behaviour which is reviewed after it has occurred and which seems to have had particular consequences related to it in the eye of the instigator or others is often described as 'having had a purpose' or as having fulfilled an intention. Where that has happened, as when a billiard player says, "I shall play in-off the red here," and does or does not, his behaviour is said to be purposive. But he has simply planned a chunk of his future behaviour, and, successfully or otherwise, enacted it. It is, therefore, entirely possible for people to plan their life on a larger scale in a similar way, directed by some similar fantasy or plan of what they wish to achieve or bring about. Such forward planning is of course just one other function of that superb organ, the human brain. In other words, we can construct for ourselves great or small purposes within our lives, from moment to moment or from year to year. We do so in the same way as we can construct 'in our heads' such things as a composite image comprising a lion's head on a horse's body with a forked tail and webbed feet. We can do this because we have previously seen each component of this bizarre creature. A civil engineer, before he even puts pen to paper to sketch his first working drawing of a new bridge, will have mentally 'constructed' it. Purposeful plans represent our intentions and in due course emerge as behaviour. These will vary in scope and duration depending on the motivation and pattern of specific reinforcements we may be subject to from time to time.

As a late adolescent, my main purpose in life was to achieve, first, a place in the first eleven in the school football team, and then a university education. For that to happen, I needed to fulfil other lesser purposes such as achieving the necessary prior qualifications. As these various purposes were fulfilled, adulthood saw me setting up other purposeful behaviours such as finding a wife and raising a family. Within that process were embedded many other smaller-scale purposive behaviours. The lives of most humans are filled with purposes of their own making which give their lives a shape, structure and significance or meaning—for themselves, at least. Our goals may well direct much of our behaviour, but our behaviour may also determine whether or how far these goals are achieved.

Take, for example, the case of a young executive driving to work. Her main purpose, intention or ambition, as a long-term goal, is to become CEO of her business. In the course of her drive, she stops at a delicatessen to buy a snack for lunch. The purpose, or short-term goal, of doing so is to save time by not having to leave the office and find a snack bar or restaurant. A third purpose in doing all this is that she can grab an opportunity to telephone her home in privacy to reassure herself that her home-based husband and baby are all well and happy. Purpose thus expressed is clearly of value as a guiding principle of behaviour, but it is wholly available to all without having to be either endorsed or instigated and structured by any god or other external agency. The business of intention and planning in humans is wholly a function of their own brains, together with autonomic and neuromuscular processes. Purpose in life is present in most of us all the time, sometimes at a very modest level, sometimes in a rather grandiose way.

When we see cattle heading toward a trough of water in the corner of a field, it is easy to think anthropomorphically and to impute purpose or intention to their behaviour, but whether it can be said that the beasts are demonstrating purposeful behaviour is only an inference we draw. If we observe humans doing things that seem to be non-random, then we can ask them "Why are you doing that?" They may tell us what is or was their intention but of course they may not know, or they might be lying. They might also tell us to mind our own business. Similarly, the details of their intentions may be quite different even if their observable behaviour at a certain point is the same.

For example, two wives say to their husbands, "What's your purpose in going out on a horrible morning like this?" Both husbands reply, "I have to get to the bank!" The stated intention is the same for both—but, unknown to the observers, one husband's briefcase contains his office papers, a sandwich and his bank card. The other's briefcase contains a balaclava, a face mask, a 9mm loaded pistol and a small crowbar. The stated purpose 'going to the bank' is truly reported but the men's more detailed intentions embedded in their first statements would have become much more accurately defined during subsequent police questioning.

Similarly, the 'purpose of life' means little and could be interpreted in thousands of ways depending on what lives one is talking about, in what context and circumstances. 'Purpose' or 'intention' are entirely human notions and apply to all manner of specific human activities whether these are enacted by groups or by individuals. All individuals, if challenged, may have a pretty good crack at saying what they think their 'purpose in life' might be, but most would answer in terms of what their present ambitions or intentions might be as short- or long-term goals. There is no necessity for any god to lay down what he/she/it states to be 'the purpose of life'. What we observe in ourselves and others are predictions of how far we and they are about to fulfil plans in our and their heads to achieve chosen ends. Most sensible people work many intentions out for themselves—and it will almost certainly vary in scope and goals as their lives progress. The suggestion that I should be told by others what should be my 'purpose in life' would generate in me a certain resentment. Christians and some other religious people may declare that man's purpose in life is 'to worship God'. If they need that belief, then let them have it. However, for those of us for whom such a phrase has no meaning, it is a pointless adjuration. It also demonstrates a failure to see that others can reasonably work out for themselves a way of life which is filled with a whole range of very productive and personally satisfying purposes. Purpose in life need not, after all, be applicable to our own species only. Other living things, even very simple organisms, have a purpose—to preserve and pass on their genes.

So far as I, as a humanist, have been concerned therefore, I have created my own purpose in life—knowingly to harm no other human, to achieve through my deeds, my relationships with all people and other living things and my progeny changes which will be of evolutionary value to the species, or, more modestly, which will give added value to the lives of others that my life might impinge upon. At a more personal level, my aims have been very close to those that the psychologist Abraham Maslow (1987) has considered to be important for what he calls 'self-actualisation' in humans. These are to have a sense of one's own worth; to be able to give and to receive love; to be able to work and to play with pleasure, satisfaction and creativity; to be able to interact freely with, possibly enhance and never harm my fellow humans and to be able to extend my understanding of the properties of this tiny planet that I have inhabited for this infinitely brief period of cosmic time.

It is a pleasure to acknowledge how far I have been helped in achieving such a sense of purpose by other people around me. Parents, wife, children, grandchildren, teachers, professors, colleagues, neighbours, friends, enemies, thugs, cheats, soldiers, poets, patients, artists, madmen, murderers, musicians and mountaineers, to name but a few, have all played their part in fostering my understanding and extending my experience. There will be others. All that one may usefully wish for is that one will have a continuing openness to experience and the capacity to rationalise it into a system of thought which might give 'added value' to the species. That is but one other important aspect of the humanist viewpoint.

Chapter 10
About Consciousness, Life and Death

When I penned the preface to this book, it was not my primary intention to devote all its content solely to a polemic against all gods. That element has, I hope, been sustained, but it was intended much more to be an 'apologia pro vita mea'—an attempt to present a systematic understanding for myself, and perhaps for others too, of how all the external events I have been subject to and all the internal experiences and thoughts of my life could be rationalised so as to afford me a comprehensive and rational understanding of my brief existence in space/time.

Religions tend to make much of the fact of death and to weave their fantasies of an afterlife and the contents and nature of that through their belief system and that of their followers. De-mystifying death and facing up to its reality can be liberating and rational, softening the blows to those individuals who have been bereaved and encouraging the humanist standpoint as a resource and source of strength.

Accordingly, what about the nature of consciousness—of life, for that matter—and what about what happens after life ends, after death? These are the kinds of question that many people find easier to rationalise in terms of religious beliefs. My own view stems from my understanding of how lifeforms appear to have evolved in finite time from some random variation in the apposition and fusion of certain molecules in the appropriate conditions of atmosphere, temperature, electrical charge, humidity and so on. From that first dramatic evolution of the organic from the inorganic, very primitive lifeforms, as small as a single cell, emerged, only to be eliminated if they did not further adapt to the conditions surrounding them or to survive if they varied sufficiently for some to have the properties appropriate to survival in their conditions and at their time. There is every likelihood that similar processes may be occurring either on our own planet or on other planets in other galaxies right now. Some astronomers and cosmologists think that, in our solar system alone, several of the necessary conditions for life may exist on, for example, Titan, one of the moons of Saturn, and elsewhere, to say nothing of on other planets as yet undiscovered amid the trillions of other galaxies. We need to remember that although I have proposed in this book that the universe/s is/are continually regenerated *in toto* as systems, individual planets such as earth may be naturally created and destroyed within the system as a whole.

In our own planet, of course, since humans have become the 'superior' organism, they will always tend to wish to control and sometimes—even often—destroy emergent lifeforms, especially those seen as offering some threat. The constant battle between ourselves and the world's viruses are a case in point. As higher lifeforms developed over the millennia, those with more complex nervous systems appear to have had higher survival potential—although other species, like microbes, bacteria or the insects, seem to have achieved the same result by the simpler expedient of arranging survival by sheer numbers and highly routinised or 'hard-wired' behaviour patterns. As things now stand, however, man appears to have gained a substantial ascendancy over other species by the skills of manipulation and tool-making, by the evolution of language and symbolic coding systems and, most of all, by the development of consciousness.

The communication of knowledge arising from this has the result that every human being is at least potentially able to gain vicarious experience (data collection and processing, as well as problem-solving skills) far beyond what could be derived from simply copying the actual activities and experiences of the moment from others. Our complex brains are also able to store and process, both serially and in parallel, many kinds of data originating outside as well as inside our own bodies.

Some writers take the view that consciousness rather than speech and its internalised form, thought, are crucial to our development as a species. I favour the latter view. Even if it is consciousness that enables us, as it were, to monitor in living through often complex personal and social lives, the awareness that we are thinking, planning, using abstract thought and drawing on memory, being able to develop and use all of that is very much part of being human. Speech, which is mostly associated with conscious states, allows us to communicate with others, and allows them to infer consciousness in the speaker. "It enables us to create uniquely human cultures. No other creatures on earth can do this." (Baggott, 2015) In spite of this achievement, the debate about the nature and operation of consciousness continues. Perusing even some of the literature, I am reminded that I once watched three seagulls pulling and tearing, fairly ineffectually, at quite a large fish left on the harbour quay. A nibble here, a tear and drag there, a short but vicious squabble between two of the birds, and a lot of angry noise, did no more than leaving the booty unconsumed and provided little satisfaction for any. The parallel between that little scene and the intellectual exercises of both erstwhile and contemporary philosophers, neuroscientists, biologists, psychologists and others, is striking.

The title of this chapter makes the distinction between 'life' and 'consciousness' for the simple reason that we are conscious only for about two-thirds of our lives, and that, even within this time, there will be periods of reduced levels of consciousness. Most, if not every, morning we experience the recurring miracle of awakening to greet a new day just as eight hours or so earlier we set our brains and bodies to 'tick-over' mode and fell asleep, unconscious. The EEG record during this sleep would show absence of faster alpha rhythms and a resurgence of slow, higher amplitude delta rhythms. Levels of consciousness vary within this period as we may dream, sleepwalk or talk nonsense. Freud, originally a neurologist, thought that dreams were 'the royal road to the unconscious' and many contemporary neuroscientists still consider that we may learn more about the brain and consciousness from traumatic or natural disturbances of it.

When the 17th-century French philosopher René Descartes pronounced *"Je pense, donc je suis,"* he was proposing the view that while mental processes such as consciousness and physical processes like brain events appear to be correlated, they are really two separate domains—different kinds of phenomena. Descartes thought that any interaction between these two domains was mediated by the pineal gland—a small midline organ deep in the centre line of the brain. This separation of mind and body became known as Dualism, only for the progression of neuroscience to reject it and settle for Monism—that all mental processes are the actions of brains and bodies. No brain—no mind!

When I was an undergraduate in the 1940s, I was influenced enough by the 19th-century biologist Thomas Huxley and 20th-century Rex Knight, my own professor of psychology at Aberdeen University, to engage with the idea of epiphenomenalism whereby consciousness was seen as a by-product of brain function rather as carbon dioxide is a by-product of breathing. But at the time it expressed a kind of monism which contrasted sufficiently, to my mind, with Cartesian dualism. Descartes was probably attracted to the idea of mind because that was indicative of the possibility of a soul. Contemporary neuroscience, however, favours the monist view of the sage who remarked, "No body—never mind!" In other words, consciousness is a function or product of the body and brain in particular. Once you have read a little further, it will not surprise you to know that the human brain alone uses over 20 percent of the body's energy.

Most lay people probably think of consciousness in practical terms. It affords them the awareness that the sensory impressions they get indicate that something exists independently outside themselves and makes an impression on them. There is also the consciousness of knowing facts and how to do things, motor memory. (A part of the deeper brain, the thalamus, is important for this.) Finally, involving almost all the cortical and subcortical areas of the brain, there is the reflective consciousness which has so burdened philosophers down the ages. That is the capacity and readiness to give considered attention to the nature of consciousness indicated by the first two kinds above, as well as two further aspects of consciousness, one the initial reception of sensory data and the other, the imposition of meaning and significance on these data

A prominent theoretical position elaborating this, proposed by Block (1997), argues for those two types of consciousness, one described as Phenomenal (P) consciousness, and the other as Access (A) consciousness. P-consciousness is simply the awareness of raw input data. It incorporates static or moving shapes, colours forms, sounds and sensations, and includes the tensions in our muscles' internal soft tissues and physical responses such as sweating, feelings of needs to defecate or urinate that are generated when our bodies prepare for a 'fight or flight' response. These tensions may appear in P-consciousness as nausea or exhilaration, say, before, possibly, being interpreted differently, as a false alarm response by A-consciousness. These experiences, considered independently of any impact on behaviour, have been called 'qualia, that is, discrete inputs from the senses before A-consciousness interprets them by linking them to the memory stores of Access consciousness. A-consciousness is the phenomenon whereby information already recorded in our brains is accessible to introspection, for verbal report, for reasoning, and the control of behaviour. So, when we perceive (as distinct from simply receive), information about what we perceive is access consciousness; similarly, when we introspect, information about our thoughts is access conscious; when we remember, information about the past is access conscious; and so on. At this point, the importance of already stored memories is apparent. Every single new sensory input is devoid of meaning until it can be set into the immense array of preceding inputs—even if that precedence is no more than a fraction of a millisecond. Memory is therefore a crucial component of our consciousness. It is crucial to giving the experience of continuity. Imagine waking in the morning to recognise that you are in your bedroom, but have no sense of what a door is, or where it is in this room. You decide to walk round the room to find it. Trillions of brain cells have been purring away all night and day to keep alive for further registration to them of each new element of experience entering the system, and, as it were, to file it away in the right place. They will, all being well, be able to set in train billions of neuron interconnections which will activate all motor neurons in the muscles which allow you to keep your balance and walk, as you did yesterday, and the day before, without your having again to learn to walk. Again, all these functions happen without your awareness of the enormous detailed nerve and muscle activity involved. In my clinical experience I have examined and treated many patients who have suffered strokes or other forms of brain damage which have resulted in a breakdown in the links between P consciousness and A-consciousness. One patient woke up after sleep to find she could recognise her clothes on the bedroom chair but had no idea what to do with them.

Although some philosophers, such as Dennett (1991), have disputed the validity of Block's distinction, others have broadly accepted it. Chalmers (1997) has argued that A-consciousness can in principle be understood in mechanistic terms, but that understanding P-consciousness is much more challenging. He calls this, with some justification, 'the hard problem' of consciousness. Indeed, Colin McGinn of the University of Miami has proclaimed that no matter how much neuroscientists and others study consciousness, the mind is fundamentally incapable of comprehending itself. "We're rather like Neanderthals trying to understand astronomy or Shakespeare. Human brains suffer from a 'cognitive gap' in understanding their own consciousness," he said. Several commentators, including myself, find this an unduly pessimistic assertion. While the Neanderthals evolved only as far as stone tool-making and other simple skills, early Homo Sapiens did so in a huge variety of ways which, among other skills, enabled us to understand Shakespeare and astronomy. By the same token, it is not unlikely that we shall eventually find that the human brain has evolved sufficiently to become, if not wholly capable, then at least a little more capable of self-scrutiny and analysis, and by doing so, will deepen our understanding of consciousness.

My own understanding of consciousness has been contributed to by all these more recent sources together with the fact that consciousness is a variable condition, from full awareness through partial awareness to total unconsciousness. The latter, of course, may be medically induced by anaesthesia, traumatically induced by accident, illness or injury, or self-induced by drugs such as alcohol or opiates, and even these conditions may vary in depth of unconsciousness. In a general anaesthetic there will be reduction in all sensory inputs (P-consciousness) though in lighter anaesthetic conditions most P-consciousness and some A-consciousness may be variably affected. In hypnosis and deep meditation there is some reduction in full awareness, while sleep, of course, reduces consciousness considerably. Both deep, natural sleep and rapid eye movement sleep (REM)—when we may become slightly more aware of our surroundings—are vitally important for the rest and recuperation of all those trillions of cells which sustain waking activity and consciousness. The variations in level of consciousness can be monitored to some degree by electroencephalography: Here, sleep or deep drowsiness will be represented, perhaps rather coarsely, on a cathode ray tube, or computer print-out by low frequency, high amplitude (Delta) wave forms of under 8cps, whereas Alpha and Beta wave forms show lower amplitude and higher frequency wave forms of 10 to 13cps indicating readiness and arousal to engage in directed mental activity. For a more detailed analysis of brain activity, however, functional nuclear magnetic resonance imaging (fNMRI) or computer aided tomographic (CAT) scanning are more likely to offer insights into more detailed locations of brain functioning which may be carefully related to specific aspects of the subject's consciousness.

The huge, even astronomic, number of neurons in the brain (10^{11}) and the even greater number of potential interconnections between them (10^{15}) can be studied as static photomicrographic images or, as I and others have done, by simple observation and dissection of a human brain in the laboratory. The sheer complexity and compression of fibrous interconnections of neurons is mind-boggling—if I may use that term in this context! Schematic drawings from photomicrographs can only hint at the potential computing power of this incredible organ.

Consciousness seems to me to result from the concomitant of non-stop processing of our sensory and autonomic neural inputs to the brain. Stimulated afferent neurons feed in the sensory, autonomic and other action potential data via the spinal cord and collateral neurons in a small bundle of neurons at the top of the spinal cord called the limbic system, which contains a segment known as the ascending reticular system. This small but important neural system both controls the general level of arousal, sometimes called activation, and acts as a filtering system to control overload from all peripheral inputs from the spinal cord. It has been thought by some neuroscientists to be the first stage whereby the brain as a whole recognises conscious activity, what is going on in parallel with the inputs themselves, and other active neurons or groups of neurons already activated within the brain. This constantly active complex of reflexively monitored inputs is what plays some part in producing the epiphenomenon of consciousness.

Phenomenal (P) consciousness supplies the raw sensory and associated material but Access consciousness supplies the conversion, and interpretation, using all the modalities the brain has accumulated in a lifetime, of neural activities into those other neural activities we call experience. In other words, the brain itself by drawing together, moment to moment, and making comparisons between memories, between sensations, verbalisations, emotions and the overall perceived situation and neural patterning of the past seconds and microseconds gives a context to present inputs sufficiently coherent with the previous few milli- or microseconds to afford what we designate as the flow or stream of consciousness. It would not surprise me if some of the interpretive/associative neural functions contributing to this process were to be found in different cerebral hemispheres. However, we may need further evolution of the human brain both for us to understand how it works and for it to show morphological changes of significance over many generations. The wonder I felt from dissecting the corpus callosum-like a strange, large, white, inverted caterpillar—has never been forgotten. These 200 millions of myelin-sheathed neurons, which keep the two hemispheres 'in step', have always kept some secrets to themselves.

Several times in the course of writing this chapter, I, like many other authors, have vainly attempted to design a schematic representation of the brain's substructures and the flexibility, plasticity and almost mystifying versatility of the trillions of neural cells containing not only memories (long and short term), but recording, encoding and evaluating every single signal, exogenous or endogenous, that will extend, or diminish, our awareness of events both within our bodies, conscious experience and the environment. Making schematic representations risks oversimplification, as does our tendency to use mathematical and other models which are simpler than the brain deserves. Several researches in the field are moving toward the kind of understanding we need from neuroscience, biology, psychology and pharmacology toward a conceptual space in which all of these interact with quantum mechanics and the uncertainty principle. I personally share the view that that approach may in due course increase our understanding of brain functioning in particular, but it may have to wait long enough for our best human brains to evolve favourably. I hesitate to specify what conditions of our and other species on this planet might conduce to such an evolution, but not at the idea that it might be fulfilled.

Although the extreme complexity of brain activity enables us to value conscious experience, it is not too hard to see that if one's sensory input and motor outputs were progressively cut down, as they are in general anaesthesia, illness or injury, then what we call unconsciousness ensues. Deeper levels of reduced input, when only vegetative rather than sensory/associative activities are present, we call coma, and when even these processes maintaining the conditions in the body which allow sensory activity to occur are cut off, death occurs. The cycle is complete: the void which was there before our conception is again just a void.

It has always seemed curious to me that, with the possible exception of the Buddhists, those who struggle to invent, define and populate an afterlife appear to have much less enthusiasm for doing the same for a pre-life. Neither, of course, makes any sense to the scientist. Those who cannot live comfortably with ignorance but are too lazy or impatient to diminish that ignorance by learning more and adding more bits to the great jigsaw of knowledge, often rely on beliefs and other fantasies to fill the gaps in their understanding.

After death, the cell structure of the body deteriorates as it decomposes, and the chemical changes produce a residue of molecules which then are engaged in the general ongoing exchanges of energy and chemical structures that are characteristic of other end states occurring in our earthly environment. The identity of the person can be said to have been lost at death, although to all intents and purposes it is often lost before that point is reached—when the individual is no longer capable of processing sensory input or of acting or communicating verbally or motorically in his or her characteristic ways. This is often the tragic condition of individuals who have suffered from the ravages of severe cerebral trauma, dementia or Alzheimer's disease. Death may be thought preferable to that state by the sufferer and by the close relatives or carers of the patient. In advanced societies, pet horses, dogs and cats are gently and humanely put to death to relieve them of the pain and misery of an incurable terminal illness or injury. Sane and sentient humans suffering in the same way, however, are, in many countries, not allowed to end their lives decently and with dignity even when, in those cases where they are fully aware and mentally unimpaired, they wish to do so.

Wars between nations are described, some as just (usually by the victors) and others as unjust (usually by the losers) even when both kinds result in the premature death and destruction of thousands and sometimes, millions of human beings. One might have thought that the evolution and enactment of modern laws such as the Bill of Human Rights might be beginning to express a developing sense of morality tempered by insight and kindness for all, but it is obvious that there is no consensus among nations, or even smaller groups within nations, about the observation and enforcement of the Bill, nor is there much discussion of a complementary Bill of Human Obligations which might lay down a minimum set or moral commitments for individuals and nations—something which should be taught to all ages in all schools. Reasonably close scrutiny of both legal and moral codes throughout the world shows that a huge proportion of moral conflicts that can give rise to killings, cruel and unjust punishments and even major wars are brought about by the inflexible adherence to specific moral precepts endorsed, sometimes in completely different eras, by different faiths and religions and the political urgings of their leaders. This is a major reason why humanists and many others are now detaching themselves from formal membership of several religions in favour of a secular and scientifically-based view of the world and mankind. Personal responsibility for moral decision-making is one of the keystones of the humanist standpoint. Kindly concern for and support of others at all points of the life-cycle is the humanist way.

Apart from the need for humans to explain their beginnings, the emergence of morality, and, for many, an apparent need to create gods, many seem to have difficulty either in reconciling themselves to or understanding death. Even talking about death and about feelings associated with its inevitable arrival is something that many otherwise sensible people shy away from. People will often put off making a will too long because that would be 'tempting fate' just as, they believe, gratuitously talking about death in a family conversation would be. This shows how very close many are, in spite of protestations to the contrary in other situations, to slipping over the edge of rationality into the abyss of superstition.

For many, the end of life is a mystery and they crave to go on living in some disembodied sort of way after they die. Hundreds, if not thousands, of conceptualisations of an afterlife have been formulated. Often these have been structured and their content specified by various religious leaders, including Mohammed, prophet of Allah and the Christians' Jesus Christ. They tend to specify some sort of supernatural, disembodied afterlife in a heaven or hell. Both of these, rather suspiciously, are defined by very human parameters. For instance, in the Muslim afterlife they would be ageless, while the men would be comforted by up to 72 virgins, even though there must be some uncertainty about how they would go about their duties, including defining virginity, in a disembodied state outside space/time. For

Christians, there is heavenly bliss and 'a land of milk and honey': presumably, being already dead and disembodied, they will not have to watch out for their glucose sugar and calcium levels. (OK, OK, I do realise it's a metaphor, as I am sure Michael Shermer and other sceptical friends would say!)

So far as I and other scientifically trained people are concerned, death is seen simply as the end point of a gradual—in most cases—running down of the biological systems that sustained our bodies and brains in good working order. In cases other than traumatic deaths, one or more of these systems breaks down irremediably and the failure of other systems follows at varying speeds and intervals. The brain, one of those systems, and, importantly, the organ which sustains our sense of identity, also fails. Religious people have said to me, "But what happens after death? What happens to the soul?" I tell them that when I die, the body that was me will begin to decompose and will be burned or otherwise disposed of. Had I been of the Jain religion in India or an American Indian in the 19th century, my body would have been laid out on a tall rock or slung between two trees high on a mountain side, for the vultures or eagles to dispose of me. My body and the energy and atoms that comprised it will redistribute themselves about the universe according to the laws of physics, chemistry and, in particular, thermodynamics. The physical principle of the conservation of energy specifies this. My identity, formerly maintained and stored by my brain and, to a lesser extent, in the brains of others who knew me, in the form of the activity of neural cells and circuits we describe as memories, billions of them, will then be sustained, not by my own decomposed or probably burned brain but by the brains of living others who will possibly have their memories, good or bad, of my identity as they construed it, even if that is bound to be only a partial, fragmentary and 'edited' memory particular to the person remembering me.

Since even simple folk, in long bygone days, observed what appeared to be the terminal nature of death, the concept of 'the soul' was invented (though never observed) by religious leaders and some philosophers, as the vehicle which might represent the dead person in any afterlife. Such a solution to disembodied life is not encouraging and makes one wonder what might be so great 'living' outside space/time as some sort of non-space occupying ghost with no brain and therefore no sensations, no memories, no identity, no desires, loves, fears, intentions or social interactions—for the latter demand a sense of identity to drive them—and for that state to be eternal! No biological organisms other than man appear to hanker after 'eternal life' and few, if any, animals other than man deliberately commit suicide to achieve it. All living things, however, do 'strive officiously to keep alive' as long as they can, not because their lives have been particularly enjoyable or fulfilling, but simply because they are unconsciously driven to perpetuate their genes and therefore the continuance of their species.

Any questions that I have in my time put to religious pundits about the nature of heaven or hell have usually been responded to in a declarative but almost incredibly naïve fashion, with no attempt to present a rational understanding, possibly through metaphor, either of the nature of the soul (wave form or particles?) or of heaven, hell, Nirvana, Elysium or whatever. Indeed, some of the more recent pronouncements of the Church of England appear to come close to discarding totally the traditional notions of either hell or heaven—anything to stem the apparent advance of secularism and humanism!

Both conditions (heaven or hell) are 'places' idealised in terms either of their pleasures or of their terrors and punishments—the rewards for having lived on this earth lives considered by religious authorities as good or bad in human terms. It is easy to see how such promises might be enticing for peoples whose lives on earth had been characterised by poverty, deprivation, illness and a variety of other hardships (many of them man-made, and some self-inflicted). It is also easy to see how the concepts of heaven and hell would be strong reinforcers of pro-social or other conforming behaviour among faith populations whom the religious leaders had, for large parts of their lives, primed with the thought that their god or gods were ever-watchful, wakeful, fair, all-powerful and omniscient of every (mainly errant) little bit of less than, in their eyes, perfect behaviour. Again, unfortunately, there is absolutely no observable evidence that can be verified in the field or in the laboratory or even in the chapel or public domain for any such afterlife, other than the evidence-free pronouncements of various holy men—the authorised transmitters and interpreters of the given word, together with some odd spiritualists and their mediums! One of the great and persisting attractions of 'the given word' is that it supplies a ready-made set of values to guide moral behaviour. If the priest or the imam says it, then there is no need to work out for yourself what is moral. The fact that many of those values derive from Asian or Mesopotamian peasant cultures of one or two millennia ago does not stimulate the masses to further thought about how to live a good life in developed nations in the 21st century. As Bertrand Russell put it, "Most people would rather die than think, and most people do!"

One of the most damaging effects of a belief in an afterlife, and the notion of heaven in particular, is that it misleads various religious fanatics (suicide bombers, beheading executioners and the like) that, since heaven awaits in the afterlife, according to their god, they need not work too hard to make the known world a better place. Humanists, by contrast, live and work on the basis that each of us has but one life, even those that believe otherwise, and that if our species is to survive and progress, in saving and protecting our earth, we need to do all we can to be kind, thoughtful, supportive, generous, tolerant and understanding of all our fellow men, including the deprived, misled and uneducated, and care for all the resources of our wonderful planet and universe. Man must seek his own salvation. "Carpe diem!" ("Seize the day!") cried the more sensible Romans. The guiding rules should be rationally based, so that they are open to modification when required; they must also be the result of wide observation and experience, specialised knowledge and the wisdom of the best of men. The philosopher A C Grayling puts it neatly in his book, 'The God Argument' (2013): "The key point about humanism is that it is an attitude to ethics based on observation and the responsible use of reason both together informing our conversation about human realities, seeking the best and most constructive way of living in accordance with them."

As I noted in the previous chapters, the rules of moral behaviour will need constant revision—more updating than Windows 10—as we and our planet change and evolve. The law tends to follow morality rather than create it. While every human being will make some contribution, philosophers, politicians, economists, biologists, neuroscientists and psychologists all need to instigate and sustain regular discussion of ethical matters so that both the law and the populace may be influenced and the latter guided about the best way to resolve new dilemmas and lead a good life. Up till now, that has been a role almost wholly assumed by religious and theological leaders, but with several scores of religions practised around the world, it is inevitable, because of their social histories, that inherent contradictions and ambiguities of principle abound. That mattered less when communication encompassing the globe was less available than it now is, but it does matter more in the Facebook- and Twitter-influenced world of the internet. It is, of course, very important to acknowledge the fact that much of the development of moral ideas up to now has been massively influenced by, in the Western world particularly, Christian moral teaching. Many humanist principles already derive from this and the earlier Stoic traditions, quite apart from the fact that it would be unrealistic as well as unnecessary to discard many of those long-established principles. The humanist would, however, see their underpinning not by the authority of a god or from holy books but by rationally and empirically based observation leading to those principles which would be likely to survive because of their pragmatism and evolutionary value to mankind. In other words, the humanist would be sensible to take all the rationally, and sometimes traditionally, established moral principles from any or all religions that have stood the test of time. These can all be scrutinised and the most valuable and rational principles encouraged or endorsed, while the humanist may add more modern insights while justifying all—not by reference to any supernatural influences like gods, but by endorsing all the teachings and moral principles thus distilled. Men and women of all races, levels of wealth and power, education and experience would all be equal participants in exercising the most humanly valuable of those principles that fit with their setting.

It is not without significance that religious fervour and concern for an afterlife is usually strongest and most widespread amongst those populations which have a rigorous and/or deprived lifestyle. The afterlife assumes less importance as the present life becomes richer in experience and security, and more satisfying, comfortable, and happy. For many people, regardless of their economic and social background, the keen awareness of their own consciousness and all the unspoken functions and aspects of it that they are privately aware of (but the rest of the world never sees), make it easy to accept the notion of a 'spirit' or 'soul'. For them, the idea is a stepping stone to eternity. The humanist urges all to work hard to improve the present lives and circumstances of all living things.

At the end of the day, there is no hard evidence for the existence of souls, however they are constituted. It is a poetic idea which must give some comfort to many. But there is little point in giving the idea intellectual houseroom. It gives no further meaning to any knowledge or experience I have ever had. Persons, with all the characteristics we value in them, and some we don't, exist because their bodies and brains exist. When persons sleep, are unconscious or are generally anaesthetised, they function without full use of their memory. When they are seriously ill or are in the process of dying, their memories will be reduced, distorted or irretrievable. Accordingly, when we die, we have none. There is no evidence of persons (or souls, however these may be construed or described) that can be recognised scientifically without a body and brain in working order. The soul is a concept which is of little or no use to scientists. Dictionaries describe it, rather oxymoronically, as a 'supernatural phenomenon'. Scientists, who used in the great and ancient universities to be called 'natural philosophers', reckon that all phenomena that are perceived, studied, measured, described and manipulated by themselves—or by any human being for that matter—are natural. Anything which is alleged to exist but has no known properties, defining characteristics, which cannot be observed, studied, tested and manipulated, may well be casually described as 'supernatural', but in all probability does not exist at all and is therefore irrelevant to our understanding of ourselves and the universe(s).

Many religious people of several faiths (Muslim, Christian, Hindu and Jewish) with whom I have at various times tried to discuss such matters tend to shy away from too much involvement, falling back on the principle that they have 'the advantage of faith'. Let us remind ourselves of the dictionary definition of faith. It is "a belief sustained out of conviction rather than proof, a belief which is even held in the face of contrary evidence, a belief held simply because it is a matter of religious dogma." This is therefore an irrational position entirely irreconcilable with a science-based viewpoint. The notion of a 'soul' or 'spirit' as some other epiphenomenon of past consciousness or as some sort of transcendent entity which can exist apart from the body which is said to have originated and 'housed it' in the past, is one which has been posited by many religions. In times past when life was, as Hobbes put it (and rather like my golf swing), "nasty, brutish and short", it is easy to see how attractive might be the notion that, even if one's earthly life were hellish, some sort of afterlife which might, if one behaved appropriately on earth, compensate by offering a better existence.

The word 'soul' is not one to which I can, or have ever, been able to attach any meaning. So far as I understand other people's use of the word, it seems to refer to what are sometimes called 'spiritual' aspects of the (dead) person's style or personality. Otherwise it seems to be construed as some kind of supernatural 'ghost in the machine' which can exist independently of the body. It does not seem to be an entity which can be definitively described, observed or measured either after the body has gone or while that body still lives.

The notion that somehow 'the soul' is the mediator of 'spirituality' in humans seems to have survived closer scrutiny because it is just an easier way to classify and describe human situations and experiences which are subjectively valuable and sometimes mysterious but which, in the end, still represent patterns of neuro-electro-chemical activity of the central and autonomic nervous systems. It is the latter which determine oxytocin levels and warm feelings when we are in love, when we are moved by unexpected good news, music, visual art or the sight of wonderful skies or scenery. Our in-built chemical factory in the brain synapses and elsewhere in our bodies has the capacity to synthesise more or reduce, as required, by the second, the tiny amounts of neurotransmitter and other chemicals which determine how our bodies and brains may work and make us feel from moment to moment. Serotonin, dopamine, adrenochrome, acetylcholine, endorphins and oxytocin are but some of the critical organic substances that determine how we vary the emotional context within which we think and feel from moment to moment. Certainly, for all these to be generated and activated there has to be a particular, and valued, stimulus, be that music, visual art, special human interaction, beautiful scenery or the like, but our subjective feelings and experience depend, in the end, on the chemistry. Recent studies show that the chemistry acts even faster than we are aware of the subjective emotional response. It is not entirely fortuitous that lovers declare that there is 'chemistry' between them!

A lack of apparent spirituality in humans is seen by some as a lack of sensitivity. It is well recognised that emotional sensitivity, like such phenomena as pain thresholds, fine tonal difference perception in music, or resting anxiety levels, can vary considerably both between persons and within persons at different times and under different stimulus conditions. So, too, what people describe as spirituality, because it is determined by the same mechanisms, will show wide variations but no positive signs that it is anything other than another subtle combination of cortical, subcortical and autonomic bodily processes, many coordinated into working algorithms by millennia of quiet evolution. Nevertheless, normal emotional sensitivity as commonly demonstrated by empathy and sympathy, perceived by other people in the appropriate human situations, is seen as an admirable quality—and by humanists too.

It is important, and I have touched on this topic several times already, to realise that without memory, we are nothing. When Alzheimer's disease, a cerebral embolism, haemorrhage or tumour or the effects of some other illness damage our capacity to store and recall experiences, to play golf, enjoy an argument, buy the right things in a shop, store information and events, multiply 19 by 5 and so on, we are seriously diminished as persons, as is our role amongst others. From birth it is our memory which stores information about what our bodies are like, what is us and what is not us, that is, what we call the environment. It is our memory which retains intellectual and physical skills, and which enables us to store and retrieve information about ourselves, the emotions we have experienced, other people, the world and the universe. Our memory stores the mechanisms of movement, speech and communication as well as the data we use and pass to others. Harari (2016) attributes the enormous success of humans over all other living creatures to the combination of cooperativeness and communication by language. All of that depends on a healthy and intact central nervous system and in particular the integrity of certain brain structures which afford us some understanding of ourselves, our world and the known universe.

Sceptics like me are often asked whether we do not feel much pleasure in living just the one life with nothing further to live for. My response, and what turns out to be the humanist response, is that we all have it within ourselves and our relationships with others to live a rich, fulfilling life in the course of which we can achieve a considerable variety of personal and communitarian goals. It is up to us to adopt roles in which we can try to do as little harm as possible to our fellow creatures and as much good as we can to enhance their lives, even in small ways. Each of us has the capacity to discover what we reckon to be a good life which we can lead freely, capably and in a thoughtful and considerate way. That is something that each of us can work out rationally and through a deep understanding of ourselves and the human condition without any recourse whatsoever to any supernatural or other self-styled superior being or god. It does, however, require us to make constant revaluations of what seem to be the most well-informed and valued moral principles adopted by other significantly well adapted and successful persons and groups in our own or other cultures.

Many have, on their own initiative and often in accordance with some, possibly even religious, aspects of their upbringing, reached their own understanding of what it means to live a good life without being religious. They may not be practised in articulating the key principles they adopt in traversing the moral maze with which everyday 21st-century life presents them; however, many quite ordinary folk pride themselves in knowing 'right from wrong', and, mostly, they do. I think it was A C Grayling again who remarked that many thousands of people are probably humanists without their ever having realised it.

It is easy for me to appreciate that the somewhat rigorous and ascetic view of life and personal experience that I have here outlined is not for everyone. The psychologist in me recognises that everyone, if they hold any beliefs at all, hold the beliefs they will need if they are to succeed in facing up to life's vicissitudes, tribulations and trials. In other words, people hang on to beliefs not because they are necessarily true, but because holding on to them supports their psychological adjustment. For those who are reluctant to acknowledge that they will always be ignorant about quite a lot of things, beliefs fill the gaps in knowledge. For me, and many humanists, ignorance (which everyone shares in to some degree) is a challenge. More pieces of the great jigsaw of knowledge must be found to diminish it. Because I don't happen to need any beliefs does not blind me to the fact that the satisfactory social and psychological adjustment of many requires that they cleave to some. Beliefs are often retained because they have been taught to the holders by parents, politicians, religious leaders, writers, poets, managers and others or because they find it just too taxing to work out a detailed rationale for their own existence themselves. Only a developed, and perhaps protracted, education of a scientific and intellectually disciplined nature can help to chip away at the primitivism of the irrational or of beliefs by replacing them with knowledge.

The notion of any continuity after death of particular lives such as yours or mine is hardly sustainable. So far as my own views go, it seems that the chemical breakdown of bodies after death (the return to the inorganic from the organic and beyond, to entropy) allows a reversion to the pool of molecules available for other fusions and interactions, not necessarily affecting any human or even necessarily biological involvement in the earthly environment. There may be a kind of immortality in that others who have known us will carry, for a time, memories of us in their brains. Similarly, we leave traces of our identities in the gene pool through our children and grandchildren. I think Bill Bryson (2004) has more recently suggested that any of us might be carrying around a molecule or two that have already comprised part of Lord Nelson, Robert Burns or Judas Iscariot, of a pine tree in Rothiemurchus forest or of a humble little tree frog, molecules that got mixed into new roles between the time of their original owners' deaths and our lives. Because of the conservation of energy, not much is wasted.

As Edward Fitzgerald has it in the *Rubaiyat of Omar Khayyam*:

> "Ah, make the most of what we yet may spend,
> Before we too into the Dust descend;
> Dust into Dust, and under Dust, to lie,
> Sans Wine, sans Song, sans Singer, and—sans End!"

The 'immortals' of literature, science and the arts are, in these terms, those individuals whose lives, products or ideas have triggered certain specific memories/actions in the brains of an unusually large number of people, cerebral activities which may also have high persistence if they are, in evolutionary terms, relevant and useful for enrichment and survival of the species, or even just the genes of individual members.

The notion of a heavenly/hellish after-life, probably more talked about than death itself, is especially hard to sustain empirically as well as being fairly useless except as a kind of incentive programme for those deprived and disappointed within this life. Indeed, the positing of some other existence temporally and spatially succeeding the known existence seems to me a singularly aimless process. The parameters determining the kind of life to be experienced in that afterlife are never fully specified, the dimensionality in terms of space/time is unknown and the nature and locus of such 'life' is open neither to observation nor to experimental examination. That anyone should wish to pick up such an intellectual burden at any time for so little effect on present life activities seems to suggest that they have intellectual energy to spare which might be more productively used in solving the current problems of living humanity.

Worst of all, the perpetuation of notions of an afterlife would seem to distract those persuaded of its existence from the proper business of fully exploring and enhancing the kind of life conditions we now enjoy on this planet. The latter would seem to be much more a worthwhile activity for the sake of our species and in particular for the sake of those closest to ourselves, those in whom our immortality really resides, who carry our genes—our immediate descendants. The notions of 'salvation' or 'eternal life' bandied about by religions of various sorts I am unable to find appealing in any way.

First, it is hard to see from what one is to be 'saved' that could attract more attention than the various hazards from which any alert human would wish to save him or herself or many others on this earth now. Second, considering the difficulties many humans have in simply managing themselves through this life—or even just through something like early retirement or redundancy—how they could cope with 'eternal life' causes me more than minuscule concern. In short, living in eternity must be a bore! Perhaps its best value for our species is that the exploration of the concept of eternal life can be an intellectual exercise which extends our brain capacity, rather like the notion of infinity or nothing. Rather than live in it then, we may serve the species better by trying to define it, look at its analogues or use it in metaphor as a way of increasing the flexibility of thought, an approach which does seem to have worked well for the evolution of our species. But we should do all this from the firm base of our present lives and experience—something of which we and those around us, who behave as if we were alive, can be convinced of without too much difficulty.

Finally, while the behaviours which have typed these words are a product of a sensate human organism, so far as those around me can tell, these behaviours allow the inference that certain molecular cerebral activities underlie them. From the point of view of a physicist rather than a biologist, however, there are only arbitrary barriers or boundaries between atoms or objects, including human bodies, dead or alive, which we find it convenient to recognise in understanding our world and relating to each other. In quantum mechanical terms, the whole of existence, animate and inanimate, has to be seen as a never-ending maelstrom of subatomic particles or wave forms of energy. In subatomic terms there is no substantial boundary at any time between parts of ourselves, other people and the rest of the environment as we move toward entropy. But I am not a physicist, only an eavesdropper on those who are.

Just as the gasses whirling in preparation for the formation of new stars and planets are understandable in terms of subatomic interactions, so also are the very cells of our brains and other parts of our bodies built up by the activity of the same subatomic particles or radiant energy. At that level, there can be little distinction between the life and death of organisms, other than a transfer of subatomic energy. No more can there be a distinction in energy or particle physics between a process such as oxidisation or compression—all are transformations within the permanent flux of 'being'.

If one reflects on it, the duality of 'self' and 'the environment' is little more than a useful convention, a conceit deriving from habitual perceptions of our own body images. In infancy, when we are but part of William James's "blooming, buzzing confusion", we learn to separate our bodies from what is not our body. It is a convenience which has evolutionary value in that it allows us to relate to other organisms and to form different levels of perception and subsequently, understanding of the world in which we live. The curiously reflexive nature of knowledge is such, however, that certain of these processes and transformations are part of cellular biological activity which in turn allows what we call consciousness, perception and thought. And these last three are what leads to our understanding of our own status through perceptual processes which make that outside world accessible to us and interpretable in terms of energy, matter and space/time.

For all we know, it may be that one evolutionary route for the further development of our species will depend on a progressively less clear distinction between microbiology and quantum physics. There has been since the nineteenth century a kind of scientific preoccupation with understanding the human condition in bio-social terms. The preoccupation with the biological and the organic/inorganic distinction may have blinded us to the enormous continuities available through the unity of existence (of energy and matter, if not of organisms) at the subatomic/wave form level where concepts of time may be more complex and flexible and where other modes of understanding and even of existence may emerge. The parallelism—between, say electro-physiological energy as exemplified by the transmission of neural impulses, and electro-mechanical energy, as exemplified by the transmission through semiconductors—that we have accepted as useful, even habitual, may in due course be discarded in favour of a more all-embracing theory of energy. So-called thought transference or even just the more commonly experienced thought convergence between persons may be more easily understood in terms of quantum physics than of associationist psychology.

Perhaps the vision of an existential condition expressed in terms of matter, time and energy transfer is what some humans are hankering after in their construction of religious ideas involving a 'higher being' or 'god'. Such ideas certainly allow for a comparison with or even a contrast to the socio-biological understanding of the human condition which is so habitual for many. However, the notion of space/time is perhaps the crucial one. Other dimensions like size are easier to conceptualise and we happily construe our present world in terms of the very large (e.g. the universe or cosmos) and the very small (e.g. protons and neutrons). These can be reconciled by our understanding fairly usefully and with empirically verifiable results. It is less easy for many to construe the directionality of time in more than the usual two directions of forward and back, or future and past. In physics, however, there is no absolute need for time to be construed in terms only of these two directions. Just as graphs can be drawn to express three directions on two-dimensional paper, so also may time be construed as travelling in several directions—even in a circle. In any event, the contemporary view of cosmological physicists, including Stephen Hawking (2010), is that time can only be properly construed as a composite, space/time, rather than as two separate dimensions. We need to construct several models to guide our struggle towards understanding. Religion and humanism, intuitive and artistic insights and the purely scientific understanding are some of these models. Thus the wide-ranging human mind shuffles ever closer to infinity. We cast about the world of ideas until we find an understanding of ourselves and our world which satisfies our inner experience as much as it does our interactions with our environment and other people. We all travel different routes on this journey and reach different destinations. The concepts we use change and diversify until we are no longer able or motivated to use them or to modify them. These differences in people and ideas are what allow the great evolutionary process to continue. From variety and individual differences comes the possibility of change, adaptation and development in what, we hope, will be a better world.

We sharpen up the interest in the journey by the experience of pain and pleasure, love and hate, wisdom and stupidity. Sometimes we are joined by others during the quest for understanding but at the end of the day it is for each to consider whether the journey has been worthwhile. What more could be asked than that one should, at any point along the route, and better still, at the end of the road, consider it to have been so? Perhaps the only other thing that could be asked is that one might have done something to have made the journey worthwhile for someone else. By now it is probably apparent that, since the days when I sat at the feet of Professors Rex and Margaret Knight and Professor Donald McKinnon, I have long considered myself to be a 'scientific humanist'. In my work as a clinical psychologist and in my habits of enquiry and understanding, I have tried to be both rational, humane, and a scientist. Others will have to judge whether, in living, I have succeeded in the rather harder task of being human!

"Because I have loved life, I shall have no sorrow to die."

('A Song of Living', Amelia Josephine Burr)

Chapter 11
A Humanist Glance at the Wider World

The background literature on Humanism offers several definitions of what the term means. All are helpful to the newcomer to this philosophy; however, a popular one runs as follows: "Humanism is a philosophical and ethical stance that emphasises the value and agency of human beings, individually and collectively, and generally prefers critical thinking and evidence (rationalism and empiricism) over acceptance of dogma or superstition." There will be more on this topic in Chapter 12.

This definition provides one of the reasons why humanists prefer to concentrate on the present life of people and encourage them to make the most of the life we know, both for themselves and others, rather than being preoccupied, even if only occasionally, by some fantasy afterlife that is no more than a wish or an illusion. Humanists have seen the evolutionary value of habits that respect the rest of humanity. They see it as a matter of their personal responsibility to foster tolerance, gentleness, and kindness, cooperation, sharing knowledge, offering help and doing no harm to one's fellow men. They repeatedly advocate the continuance of such qualities in humankind as honesty, fairness and an even distribution of the world's goods and resources. They fail to see where the interjection or intervention of a god or gods might have any place in this process or relevance to it.

The moral principles outlined in the previous pages, many of which have also been supported by some religions—though for reasons other than their evolutionary value—should ease the transition of, for example, many wavering Christians toward humanism as their guiding philosophic stance. Nor should it surprise any thinking person that a significant number of moral and ethical principles first enunciated and later established by religious leaders, mainly Christian, require little or no modification to be wholly acceptable to humanists. In the case of the latter, however, these principles are supported and evaluated by close observation of how they can best operate in the contemporary world and by rational, evidence-based thinking, especially about their evolutionary value for our species, not by the 'authority' of holy writ. Such principles as have been adopted with little change, however, are those that, after close scrutiny of purely human needs and purposes, are demonstrably founded on reason and can be adapted to modern times and activities. Humanists prefer to work for the good and wellbeing of all who are currently alive in the world, regardless of nationality or race.

The whole point of a sound morality and ethical awareness of the true nature of our world, its exigencies and its resources, is to enhance the wellbeing and development of our species in a world which, we hope, will continue to sustain itself and its populations, human and animal. Humanists see no role for a god or the trappings of religion in this, and indeed, when they look around at the history of our planet, there is more evidence of strife and conflict occasioned by the worshiping of different gods than any impartial observer might think likely, especially if there were to be omnipotent, omnipresent and wholly benevolent gods presiding over what their adherents say that they themselves created.

There is much discussion in the literature about intelligent design on the part of some creator. There is, of course, no need for a creator if, as I have proposed in previous chapters, the universe, like space/time, has no beginning and no end. In any event, how do the religious even know there was only one creator? There could have been the rather boastful and self-absorbed one we always hear about, but how do those who claim to know about such things know there was not a more modest and introverted second creator who played his/her/its part in proceedings? I might offer the thought that many contemporary designers, in creative institutions often work, on bigger jobs, in teams, rather than as individuals, yet the possibility that one designer's work might be compromised by the interference (or help) of another contemporaneous, or more or less intelligent, designer seems never to have been seriously considered by theologians. Presumably if the head man in the office is omnipotent, etc., then he will have fired all his rivals before getting down to business—even just for a week's work! In any event, the achieved design was second-rate compared to evolution's step by step design, based on the principle of natural selection, fitness for purpose—and survival!

Amid this evolving scene, man has survived and developed using a variety of what we call ethical systems—morality in one form or another—the better to organise his coexistence with others who crowd around in his camps, settlements, cities or countries. But for an early recognition of and elaboration by pre-Christian Greek philosophers of the Golden Rule, "Do as you would be done by!" such coexistence would have succumbed to the self-seeking drives to achieve personal as against family or larger group survival. Archaeological and historical evidence suggests that the beginnings of such an arrangement may well have been in the form of simple small group or family alliances to facilitate hunting, the control of food, fire and shelter, or mutual protection from both human and other predators. As has been already pointed out, gorillas, chimpanzees, bonobos, African hunting dogs and several other species did the same and continue to do so. Their simple moralities have not crumbled in spite of their failing to worship any gods. With the development of the species, more complex needs would have to be met by a more complex and developed set of socially-based moral principles.

The first human groups were small, perhaps a few extended families of about 20 to 50 people, and the group's possessions, initially, would have been very restricted in quality and number. Later, these groups merged, became tribes, clans, and, in due course, small nations. As that happened, then rules about ownership—of tools, weapons, wives and, later, land and gold or money—had to be adopted and agreed if the social integrity of the group was to survive. With cooperation and social cohesion came the strength and ability to survive against groups which had failed to work out and agree among themselves ways of solving problems inherent in sustaining food supplies, protection and an atmosphere relaxed enough to allow novelty and origination of all the elements of living. These included safe and stable patterns of family rearing, the emergence of art forms such as painting, carving wood, bone and stone, and greater control of the surrounding flora and fauna so that the group's hunter/gatherer habits, originally the only option, could be supplanted, if that's the right word, at least in part, by cultivation in small plots and the rearing of domesticated birds and animals.

The few and simple rules that governed these earliest stages of civilised man, like the rules that were also evident in some of the other species—like primates grooming each other to ensure some later food sharing, protection and so on—worked because they contributed to cooperation and sharing of necessary duties. These were the early precursors of a morality which worked for the benefit and survival of those who, wittingly or involuntarily, collaborated in it, as against the failure to survive of those who failed either to formulate or follow such pro-social forms of behaviour. Such behavioural patterns, of course, arose from existing behaviour and subsequently guided it in successful species other than man, all without any reference to supernatural agencies. Later, when it became clear, due to the size and complexity of the new societies, that many more rules of moral behaviour were needed. Allegedly wise but self-seeking Egyptian and other Asian and European kings, philosophers, teachers and other potentates discovered that they could bolster their personal power by claiming to be the messengers of various gods and often the sole interpreters of these gods' instructions.

The previous paragraphs have contained a brief recapitulation of the content of earlier chapters largely because they describe how the exponents of religions tended to see many aspects of human affairs, natural phenomena and perceived mysteries as demonstrating the interference or other involvement of gods and the supernatural. In general, the latter were the agencies seeming to make good or bad things happen to people. Under such conditions, it was clear that prophets could turn profits—a perception that has been shared by the cleverer, though less scrupulous, members of modern society ever since. (Bookmakers, bankers and stock market dealers spring to mind.) As human groups, large and small, learned the value of principles of cooperation and mutual support, they became less nomadic and established more permanent homes in small settlements. This laid a foundation which, over time, allowed them to enjoy the opportunities to indulge spare energies in mercantile, agricultural, artistic and sometimes, regrettably, even warlike behaviours. Hunters castrated bulls to tame them enough to haul ploughs; gatherers discovered that they could grow suitable fruits and vegetables by saving some of what they had grown as food to replant as seed. Thus the beginnings of the agrarian revolution were born. This would transform enormous areas within man's ambit to the extent that, now, for example, only two percent of the population of USA work in agriculture but nevertheless can supply hundreds of millions of the population there with all the produce they need and still have enough to send elsewhere.

Researching some of the information above, I have been much entertained and informed by a recent book to which I have referred several times already. It is a book of substantial erudition and conceptual range, though at the same time the reader may be struck occasionally, as I was, by what at first seems to be a kind of naivety. The book is *Sapiens, A Brief History of Humankind* by Yuval Noah Harari, Professor of History at the Hebrew University of Jerusalem. Without ever querying the validity of the concept of a god or gods, he delivers a sweeping history of the many variants of religious beliefs of the past three millennia. Indeed, as he unfolds his understanding of the religions of the world (which is detailed and compendious), he comes to the conclusion that the three most powerful forces or principles that have held a previously disorganised *Homo Sapiens* together have been Money, Empires and Religion. To many, this would seem to be an unusual, even strange position to take simply because an alternative (and, to me, more accurate) representation of these three principles would seem to indicate that these have, during the last three millennia, been the sources of more dissension, wars, human misery and destruction than otherwise. The first encouraged and developed trade but brought avarice, greed and, latterly, the maldistribution of the world's goods and wealth. At the beginning of the twenty-first century, selfish and secretive bankers, financial dealers and international market traders brought a large part of the developed Western world to its financial knees and thousands of individuals to bankruptcy. As I write this (in 2018), a slow recovery continues.

The second element, Empires, whether Aztec, Roman or British—or others—brought massive human inequalities through the exploitation of lands and peoples from which those subjugated either never recovered at all or took centuries to do so. Harari does point out that, to its credit, the British Empire probably did a better job both of creating its empire and of ceding it back to its proper inhabitants than did any others. Like other historians, Harari has remarked on how it could be that the British Empire, which at its height coloured almost three-quarters of the globe in its traditional pink on schoolroom world maps, increased its dominance as much by introducing such cultural elements as transport, education and law as it did by military superiority. India is a case in point. An English judge called Wilson was appointed to the Calcutta Judiciary but soon became interested in the several languages of the country, became a researcher into philology and history of languages, expanded education for the many and encouraged the building of railways, some of which remain today. Twenty original miles of track soon became twenty thousand. The same was tried a little later in China, but the Ming Dynasty was not in favour and had the few hundred miles of track which had been laid down destroyed.

One of the crucial differences between the British Imperialists and others such as the Spanish, Portuguese, and Dutch that Harari describes was that whereas the latter usually explored with a view to conquest and appropriation of wealth and assets by carrying soldiers in their ships, the British exploratory ventures tended to use single ships or small flotillas, each of which invariably, whether Darwin's voyage in the 'Beagle' or Captain James Cook's journey in H M barque 'Endeavour' to Asia and Australia in the 18th century, carried a number of soldiers for self-defence if required, but also a miscellany of almost equal numbers of scientists such as geographers, geologists, cartographers and draughtsmen, naturalists and so on. This meant that while other imperialists kept clear of unmapped areas ('Here be dragons!') where they landed, the British explorers were intent on discovery, dragons or no dragons, mapping the topography, recording the flora and fauna and finding out the characteristics of the indigenous peoples they encountered. The British were not by any means free of moral stain in this. For example, they ruthlessly wiped out the total indigenous population of Tasmania and are still failing towards the aboriginal population in Australia. The integration of settlers and the native Maoris in New Zealand was handled much better but still has some way to go.

What is significant for humanists about all this is that a scientific ethos was by now well established in the UK where the Enlightenment was already getting up to speed and a more thoughtful view of what the rest of the world might hold was prevailing. The evolutionary effect of that would not have been in any way apparent at the time simply because the effects were compounded from a set of many smaller influences, such as changes in social values and behaviour, as well as habits of enquiry sufficient to satisfy the growing curiosity of the increasingly educated in northern Europe in particular. Compared to the less constructive and exploratory styles of other imperialist cultures of the time, that of Great Britain bore the stamp of favourable evolutionary change through the mechanism of generating social memes which would be elaborated by individuals who carried genes likely to produce further generations of a similar stamp.

In the case of Harari's third principle, Religions, although I have already quoted many examples, even Harari seems to have been able to shrug off recurrent inter-faith wars and other horrors such as the persecution of Christians by the Romans over the three hundred years between the death of Christ and of the Roman Emperor Constantine (which, compared to many other episodes of wanton killing of religious cadres, was probably far from being the most heinous). Throughout the sixteenth and seventeenth centuries, disputes about theological differences became so progressively more violent that not thousands, but hundreds of thousands of Christian believers were slaughtered by fellow Christian believers—all in the name of the same God. On 23rd August 1572, French Catholics, who stressed the importance of good deeds, attacked communities of French Protestants who highlighted God's love for humankind. This was the St Bartholomew's Eve massacre in which between five thousand and ten thousand (some report 70,000) Protestants were slaughtered in less than twenty-four hours. Harari goes on to describe how the Pope in Rome was so overwhelmed by joy on hearing this news that he ordered festive prayers to celebrate the occasion and instructed the artist, Vasari, to decorate one of the Vatican's rooms with a fresco of the massacre. Harari remarks that that room was off limits to visitors. It is important to note that formally declared and reported wars, while many religious believers of many faiths are killed in them, many killings of religious populations occur quite apart from war casualties. For example, there was never a declared war between Protestants and Roman Catholics in Northern Ireland, but that religious enmity was interwoven with historical grudges to fuel the reported and secret killings of many of both religious sects. In the same way, the two million Muslim Burmese who were forced by a Buddhist majority to flee recently to Bangladesh or India will not be reported as casualties of a religious war—though that is, in effect, what it has been. International opinion still manages to describe it as 'ethnic cleansing.' There have been many 'official wars' in the course of which tens of thousands, even millions of members of one religion have been both deliberately and unintentionally massacred. The Nazi-originated Holocaust against all Jews was against their religious beliefs but was embedded within another World War between states which itself was not about religions so much as the sovereignty of several nations. More recently, religiously determined mass murder mainly of Bosnian Muslims by their ethnically Serb neighbours (in alliance with Serbian forces), following the fragmentation of the former Jugoslavia, will not be described by historians as a religious war—although the fact of war made it an excuse to massacre large numbers of a resented religious group.

However, my minor irritations on reading Harari's book soon evaporated in my huge enthusiasm for the great sweep of Harari's vision and the engaging fluency and cogency of his writing and analysis, especially in the second half of an outstanding and memorable volume to which I shall often be returning. There is no way of knowing that if all modern populations within or across states consisted of humanists, there would be no occasional aggressive episodes between smaller groups. However, large-scale slaughtering over points of religious doctrine would not occur.

Sapiens is not explicitly about evolution, but from start to finish it lays out a detailed and deeply engaging history of mankind which, when I review it in the light of my own thoughts, supplies an historical structure from Neanderthal man to the cyborgs, brain implants and robots of our future. It illuminates how, unnoticed except by a few historians and life scientists, evolutionary changes in all living creatures have been effecting changes so slow and subtle that hindsight alone can let us afford them the scrutiny they deserve. Many of these changes do *Homo sapiens* little credit. One such example of the ecological prodigality of exploratory imperialists is that almost all the expeditions of mankind into new lands have led inexorably, it seems, to the predation, to the point of extinction, within about two hundred years of occupation, of all the larger species of other animals found as settlement proceeded. This process can be seen to be repeated in the present day as we struggle to save the rhinos, elephants, tigers and great apes from the shrill but fashionable demands for 'bush meat'. Now several nations are having to provide game wardens and troops to combat not only that demand but also that being met by rhino horn and ivory poachers who roam central Africa only to ravage a great resource by wantonly killing hundreds, even thousands, of great animals to meet the irrational and superstitious demands of ill-informed populations, mainly in the Far East. It is estimated that the number of all currently existing living things on earth equals the number that have already become totally extinct so far. The causes of so much destruction of life over the millions of years of the past are, of course, partly due to natural hazards rather than man (so much for 'intelligent design'!), but the latter is clearly the agent of destruction now. Man is now littering the oceans with discarded plastics which, unless stopped very soon, will kill thousands more species including the next most intelligent mammals, whales.

At last, humanists are beginning to see that their formerly almost exclusive preoccupation with the human condition had obscured the wider evolutionary picture of how important it is to maintain diversity of species, not just diversity within species. We, as the most advanced animals on earth, now realise we have a duty of care towards, as well as a vested interest in, all living things and the many special environments they require. That should compel us to be watchful about the ecological complexity and inter-relatedness of all creatures and to give some thought to the general welfare and freedom from unnecessary harm and suffering for all living things. Scientists from the World Wildlife Fund and the Zoological Society of London have found that the number of wild animals on earth has halved in the past forty years alone. Mike Barratt, director of science and policy at WWF said, "We have lost one half of the animal population and knowing this is driven by human consumption, this is clearly a call to arms and we must act now." He said more of the Earth must be protected from development and deforestation while, in parallel, food and energy have to be produced sustainably.

The steep decline of animal, fish and bird numbers was calculated by analysing 10,000 different populations, covering 3,000 species in total. This data was then, for the first time, used to create a representative 'Living Planet Index' (LPI), reflecting the state of all 45,000 known vertebrates. Today's average global rate of consumption would need 1.5 planet Earths to sustain it. But 4 planets would be required to sustain US levels of consumption, or 2.5 Earths to match UK consumption. Barratt went on to say that while many people were daily aware of the levels of the FTSE Index, hardly any were aware of the steadily falling trend of ecosystems and animal populations all over the world. Many authorities can foresee major conflicts being generated if we fail to develop and sustain all provisions for the continuing survival and wellbeing of all species, as well as forestation and water supplies for every living creature on earth.

At the time of writing, there is a new awareness of the near desperate situation for the life, in all its diversity of forms, in the oceans of the world. While ecologists and other scientists are doing their best to instigate both governmental and other organisations to attempt to combat the damage caused by the dumping of many forms of plastic into the sea, one hardly reads or hears any of the so-called great religious leaders across the world making any supportive declarations or endorsing plans to reduce the hazards that will, if not massively reduced, rob our planet of a great proportion of its vital resources. The present Archbishop of Canterbury is an exception.

Biodiversity is so critically necessary for the wellbeing of mankind, but yet is overlooked, often because so few are cognizant of how important even microbes, insects, worms and rare mosses and plants are for the development of research into, for example, new vaccines and drugs. Steven Pinker (2018) usefully devotes Chapter 6 of his book *Enlightenment Now* to a fascinating and informative catalogue of the many drugs, vaccines and associated procedures that, in the past couple of centuries, have both saved and enhanced the lives of millions all over the world. Biodiversity allows the often-subtle relationships and interactions even of tiny organisms to present us with clues about incompatibilities which might be harnessed in exploring still newer medicines or vaccines.

Calm Highland lochs, tumbling, sparkling waterfalls and rapids anywhere in the world have always fascinated travellers. It was surprising therefore to discover from Dave Tickner, WWF's chief freshwater adviser, that the fastest decline among the animal populations was found in fresh water ecosystems, where numbers have plummeted by 75% since 1970. Whatever happens on the land, it all ends up in the rivers and then the sea. For example, tens of billions of tonnes of effluent are dumped in the Ganges in India every year. Many devout Indian Hindus not only bathe in that daily but also float funeral pyres out on it as tourists watch.

As well as intense pollution, both in advanced industrial and isolated rural areas, the natural cleansing effects of fast flowing rivers and streams are often seriously reduced by the building of dams for irrigation or power generating purposes. Some 45,000 dams around the world are 15 or more metres high. They slow up the water flow, cause migration and other difficulties for fish and other animals and make for easy water extraction by humans from the rivers and lakes the dams create.

While human population has risen fourfold in the last century, water use has gone up sevenfold. That simple two-element molecule is so fundamentally necessary to sustain all life but is also so much used in manufacturing and thousands of other ways that we tend to think of it as an inexhaustible environmental resource. It does not seem to be easy to find on other planets and it is now apparent that global warming is likely to make it progressively more precious on this one as the next couple of decades roll by. With increasing global warming, whether man-made or otherwise, over some years to come, fresh, clean water is likely to become increasingly precious. Means of collecting and storing it have to be constructed near different kinds of sources, for humans often find that water comes either in massive quantities or is at other times too scarce to the point of drought. Water supplies have been a source of dissention in many parts of the world both in the recent and distant past. It is clear that the secure protection from both sabotage, terrorist attacks and deliberate or even unintentional contamination will shortly become imperative.

The close relationships between man, animals, afforestation and water supply is well known to ecologists and geographers. Forests are necessary living environments for man, animals, birds, insects—indeed all kinds of living creatures to survive and thrive. Trees need water as do the animals, insects and so on to grow and prosper—and for more reasons than the more chemically obvious one of carbon dioxide/oxygen conversion. Even the apparently inexhaustible rain forests of the Amazon basin, however, are being decimated by ruthless exploitation by timber companies and local natives seeking more land for cultivation at both domestic and manufacturing levels. Some corrective efforts are succeeding. Nepal, by careful conservation methods, has restored some of its past tiger population; Thailand has done the same with its native elephants.

As part of such programmes there has also to be a regeneration of appropriate habitats. This is true even in European countries such as Scotland where the capercailzie, the wildcat and the adder are, after a period of serious decline, now beginning to increase in number in selected areas following quite modest conservation efforts. Because of the lower scale of conservation required, smaller countries may offer opportunities for individual humanists and humanist organisations to involve themselves and even run conservation projects of greater or smaller scale.

There are several points in this rather depressing narrative where opportunities arise for humanists to involve themselves more actively than they appear to have done in the past. There are occasional academic papers exploring what we might mean by the terms 'humanism' and 'the ecological perspective' using a new kind of systems model. It is argued that humanism represents an uncritical acceptance of boundaries in the course of analyses that always prioritise individual human beings, human societies and/or human communicative systems. The contention is that this can no longer be considered legitimate. If an uncritically prioritised boundary is always placed around the human element, then that which is seen as lying beyond the human boundary (our 'environment') will inevitably be marginalised. Because we now realise that there is no real separation between 'us' (human beings) and 'it' (the environment), we, as humanists, can no longer be solely concerned to establish our philosophic stance as more rational and evidence-based *vis à vis* religious and other philosophic systems of thought if we do not extend our duty of care beyond other human beings to all other living creatures on our planet. Recognition of the world's biodiversity, which includes ourselves, and support of all the means to sustain it needs to feature more in the humanists' Weltanschauung than it has done so far. Humanists therefore need to align themselves with political parties and agencies which support an environmentally conservative approach and can mobilise governmental resources to promote it. For some parts of our world it may be already too late. There may well be, and probably are, many tacit humanists who are already actively engaged in various forms of environmental and wildlife protection activities, but we must now all become more explicit about the integration with humankind of all other species and the mutual wellbeing of these.

That is but one reason why the rules guiding what we now describe as moral behaviour had necessarily to become not only more varied but also more numerous to take account of new human and environmental circumstances, events and attitudes. This process continues to this day as we contend with the new moral problems associated with, for example, the conflict between conserving the habitats and needs of other animals and those of humans who press for a greater share of the same habitat.

At the time of writing, there are reported to be only just over 120 declared MP humanists in the English Parliament. There are all too few occasions when they can escape from the Whips and Party leaders to express themselves more pointedly and fully on environmental and other issues. Progress to a more enlightened debate is, in consequence, bound to be slow. When we have USA's President Trump on the other side of the Atlantic refusing, in spite of the scientific evidence, to believe that climate change, man-made or otherwise, is occurring at all, and when there are still enormous swathes of the world, for instance in Siberia, China, central and west Africa and Brazil, where for much of the population such matters remain on the edge of folklore or fantasy, the next generation or two of scientifically informed humanists have their work cut out. The debate about global warming and its non-acceptance, even today, by President Trump, the President of Brazil and others has the potential to destroy much of our world's resources. Perhaps if religious leaders throughout the globe were to raise their voices in support of efforts to minimise global warming—and not just in the occasional oblique reference to it in (ineffectual) prayer, they might focus the attention of millions more sharply. For myself, I have always been left of centre politically without feeling committed to any party. Now, however, the policies of The Greens have my support more than any others.

In passing, it occurs to me that omniscience must have come easier to a god simply because the sum of knowledge, among humans anyway, was, two or three thousand years ago, relatively tiny. From the sayings and writings of most reported gods it appears that none of them, or their interpreters, had mastered the calculus or logs and none, if tasked with taking exams in Scotland, would have passed mathematics or physics. If they did know more than it seems, it's a bit surprising that they failed ever to show off what they knew about black holes, tectonic subluxation or the Higgs boson particle. The occasional alleged miracle was all they could pull off to impress the laity. One has to wonder when their omniscience was last checked. The best they seemed to manage was the occasional storm or tempest, plague of locusts, flood or feeding thousands of refugees with two small fishes and some loaves. Even UNHCR or Save the Children can do better than that! None of the gods seem to have rated very highly on modesty so it's also hard to believe they would not have shown off some of their omnipotence rather more spectacularly than they have ever been reported as doing. Nor has there been much of it about during the past couple of millennia. Over the last four billion years of the earth's existence there have certainly been plenty of occasions when a bit of benevolence might have mitigated the awful effects of earthquakes, tsunamis, plagues, volcanoes and millions of evil specimens of all species—some human, some other animals (viruses and microbes, to start with).

Philosophers and theologians frequently incorporate such examples under the rubric of 'the problem of evil'. That the latter exists at all does not say much for what many religious people describe as 'Intelligent Design'. Of course, it may be the 'Intelligent Design' idea applies to the whole universe as well as previous and future universes rather than just to our little blue planet and the rest of our currently observed universe. In that case, the 'Intelligent' bit of the design may well include the end of our planet and species before or during the predicted collision of the Andromeda nebula and Milky Way galaxies. The 'problem of evil' for many not versed in the convoluted thinking of theologians seems to be a problem largely because 'evil' is a word representing an abstract concept which is awkward to use constructively because it is too over-inclusive to be usefully descriptive. Humans may do evil things—and in the case of these there is a huge variety of slightly evil, averagely evil and terribly evil behaviours. But how does one class tsunamis, earthquakes, erupting volcanoes or violent storms which kill or maim thousands of innocent men, women, children and other creatures? These, presumably, are all part of the great intelligent design. Is the Ebola virus an 'evil' creature, or is it only evil when a person infected with it deliberately passes it on to another human? Or is it just the person infecting another who is evil? If the god of the religions was genuinely omniscient and benevolent, why would he/she/it create a world containing all the recurrent nasty natural hazards, especially when there had been more than four billion years to try out the workings of the planet before man ever appeared on it? The humanist simply declares that all the allegedly evil natural phenomena I have described are simply as natural as the wind or clouds and morally neutral—even if they demonstrate a far from benevolent and omniscient god, carelessly operating outside his pay scale! Evil actions by groups or individuals are, however, a different kettle of fish. The problem, if such there be, does not lie anywhere other than in the behaviour of those inflicting harm, directly or indirectly, on others. That is in the hands of humans to deal with justly. It requires no god or gods to be the judge and wield the appropriate sanctions in present life rather than to promise heaven or hell in some supernatural afterlife. There's little point in the theologians saying that the problem of evil is not god's doing, but man's, when it was god who is said to have created man in the first place, and in his image!

Such debate may fascinate in the classrooms of those lucky enough to have benefited from higher education, with the result that the more scientifically educated sections of the populace progressively reject religions as failing to offer constructive and rational systems of thought. On the other hand, the uneducated or poorly educated masses of earthlings still hang on to one or another religion because of the simplified and apparently supportive understanding it affords. They are, of course, strongly reinforced in their superstitious and irrational thinking by institutionalised indoctrination from early childhood in churches, mosques, madrassas, synagogues and many schools. Both Professors Daniel Dennett and Sam Harris—American philosophers who know more than a little neuroscience—are well aware of this and foresee that for all that atheists and humanists support and defend a scientific and humane intellectual curriculum and Weltanschauung, any erosion of belief in the supernatural, and religion in particular, is likely to take many decades, maybe more than a century, to purge superstition and irrationality from the thinking and behaviour of the majority of religious communities.

It is a simple fact that many humans have found religions, with their gods, prophets, disciples, angels, devils and, for many, certainty, a source of succour and comfort in times of stress and for them to be helpful and satisfying in their understanding of their existence and of the human condition generally. Various cultures create their gods in their own image to make dependence on and worship of their gods easier. Many of the more self-confident religious humans claim again that their god states that (s)he made humans in her/his image. Like so many human assertions which fail to qualify as knowledge in the scientific sense, that is an empirically unprovable (unfalsifiable) assertion. Moreover, to those for whom the God-concept has no meaning, it is wholly irrelevant to a coherent understanding of human behaviour, experience and the environment. It may be historically interesting to future historians of philosophy, religions and social change, even if there is no way of checking human DNA against the supernatural. The humanist hypothesis is that man has generally made his gods in man's image. The fact that the extant and man-made statues of gods are pretty well like the statues of humans testifies to this. It's easy to see why gods were not at all keen on "graven images"!

None of the surviving civilisations in man's history is without some formal and ancient code of behaviour which, where the rules allow some tolerance of periodical reviews and adjustments, finally amounts to little more than a complex elaboration of "Do as you would be done by!". When a principle like that breaks down under the influence of another such as the primacy of personal gain usually disguised as 'private enterprise' or 'the demands of the marketplace' and the principle of the pursuit of personal gain at the expense of others less physically, economically, or educationally strong is promoted by governments, gangsters, advertisers or religious groups, then a morality supportive of the majority of the species will crumble and the survival of the species will again come under threat.

Some might aver that such an evolution of ethical thought in man is but an expression of a 'god's will' and an endorsement of the notion of divine purpose. It is a possible, improbable, but not a necessary explanation. It is much more likely, in the light of how it can be demonstrated by contemporary psychology that humans are manipulated by their environment, including what others have taught them and their innate constitutional characteristics, that existence within an ethically (and eventually, legally) regulated society offers more and better reinforcers of continuing ethical behaviour than otherwise. Such a Skinnerian explanation of continuing moral behaviour is usefully parsimonious, i.e. it fits with our explanation of many other human and animal behaviours and it draws upon concepts the validity of which has been tested and which have value in other contexts. (See below for more on the canon of parsimony.) The introduction of some supernatural presiding genius is redundant and unnecessary.

A humanistic view also allows for some accommodation to the notion of a changing ethic. Not only is it obvious from both history and anthropology that there can, in the foreseeable future, be few or even no absolute rules of human moral behaviour for every human alive (except by the scientifically unsupported assertions of various religious or political pundits), but it is also clear that each passing day brings forward new ethical issues which had never previously been considered until the expansion of knowledge and technique made them relevant. For example, if a domestic robot goes wrong and sets off electrical switches with the result that there is a fire in that home which kills a sleeping baby, is the robot, the control person or its constructor to be blamed or is the householder to be blamed for not being at home to supervise the machine's actions? At another level, what is ethical in terms of premarital sexual behaviour or in the legal transmission of property in Polynesia may not fit comfortably with what is endorsed in the Vatican, western China, or in suburban San Francisco. The ethical rules for in vitro fertilisation of childless mothers using ova from dead women arose only when the technique and knowledge for so doing became available. The possibility of removing for ever from some families or individuals the risk of suffering in the future from some damaging genetically determined disease such as Huntingdon's chorea, can now be avoided by very subtle genetic engineering. The humane exercise of such knowledge and skill is not uncommonly delayed, if not wholly prevented, by quaint, irrational and sometimes incoherent objections from the religions like "It's playing God" (so what, God's not been doing much for humanity recently anyway), or "It's putting us on a slippery slope"—towards what? Since well over 90% of scientists don't believe in any god or even understand the concept (see Stenger, (2009), it seems unlikely that any will bother with 'playing god', whatever that means. As for the 'slippery slope' argument, mankind has been placing himself on all manner of 'slippery slopes' since he invented skates, the wheel, the bow and arrow, atomic energy or took up animal husbandry and the controlled breeding of cattle, horses and sheep.

It is demonstrable that early man had quickly discovered the benefits of cooperation with other, and usefully, stronger groups both in the hunt and later in agrarian pursuits. The benefits of such continuing cooperation lay in the form of assurances on the part of the stronger allies regarding the protection of personal property and the sustaining of relationships such as marriage or parenthood. However, such delayed, longer term and less immediate kinds of protection, more diffuse in their effects, depend on a particular human characteristic, one which has had a lasting evolutionary benefit for the species. That characteristic is the capacity to behave in anticipation of delayed reward, on the understanding that the delay is not overlong. We flatter the boss the better to influence favourable attitudes to our work or promotion prospects and we happily pay premiums for years in order to reap the benefit of a handsome endowment payment in later life. Pro-social behaviour can of course have both immediate rewards in the form of happy companionship or acceptance in a team as well as longer term and delayed benefits in the mutual acceptance of forms of social regulation which smooth out the organisation of behaviours as diverse as queuing for a train ticket or signing an international non-aggression pact between nations. Similarly, the misbehaviour of a toddler at table can be modified by the promptly delivered and obvious temporary loss of love and affection. If short-lived, withdrawal of love is effective in children who misbehave, then more serious felonies in adults may be punished by loss of liberty or payment of a fine. All of these day to day motivating impulses now come easily to most as the coarse, broad-brush motivations of early man are overlaid by the refinements of millennia of modifications through learning.

It is easy to become beguiled by the habitual analytic stance of science at this point and to forget that there will also be consideration of the value system within a culture. The average man in the pub, family or workplace will almost always revert in discussion of good ethical behaviour and will draw upon past daily experience to help clarify how he has come to value certain ideas above others and his behaviour in relation to them. That does not prevent analysis of all these processes, using the scientific principles available to advanced cultures. It simply enriches decision-making for many in a way which is enlightened by personal experience—often more useful to the non-scientifically trained person who will still have to evaluate an ethical stance for himself about so many modern issues as they arise. In the absence of such experimental and knowledge-based analytical methods, it is easy to see how earlier civilisations and cultures might have rationalised their ethics by calling upon an omniscient god or similar prepotent force to be the ultimate arbiter of personal values, social rules, sanctions and (often posthumous) rewards. The more that is learned about the range, determinants and nature of human behaviour, however, the less is it necessary to use the 'God' hypothesis. The rationalist's concession to the Armageddon fantasy would be simply that if mankind fails to maintain a morality which can control and modify its own destructive forces, then the species will indubitably destroy itself long before its habitat on this earth has been exhausted by 'natural' processes either of climate change or of careless depletion of resources such as minerals, water and food.

Theologians and religious apologists will often declare that science (behavioural or otherwise) has nothing to say in response to the question 'Why?' One assumes that the question is about such issues as why the universe or gods exist and not about why young Johnny likes playing football. The latter seems to be a reasonable question because it is about human motivation, whereas there can be no question of motivation in the case of a non-human phenomenon. The question 'why?' is about the reason, whereas the question 'how?' is about the means, cause or process. Only the answer to the 'how' question is relevant to the advance of knowledge by means of the hypothetico-deductive method. The 'why' question might be answerable too by that means, but it is a question about human motivation and intention, not about the nature and effects of natural phenomena and processes. That is why scientists do not spend time with the question of 'why' unless they are neuroscientists or psychologists studying motivation and intention in humans and other animals. Why carbon exists or why water is a compound of two elements simply doesn't matter so long as we can discover how carbon and water are constructed, what are their properties and what are the necessary consequences of finding that out. There is little point in knowing why so long as one aims to pursue the 'how' question subsequently.

The religious apologists will often assert that science cannot 'explain' phenomena such as beauty in music, a poem or painting, or love in a living organism. If my understanding of their position on this is correct, they will say that while one may analyse in scrupulous detail the elements such as the disposition of the various pigments on a canvas or the meanings and connotations of words in a poem, or the sequence of notes in music, this does not explain the sense of satisfaction, wonder and sometimes awe that may be experienced in the face of great art. They tend to forget, however, that an individual's response to a person, picture, music or a poem is not a function only of the stimulus object. It is also a function of a whole gamut of learned preferences and previous patterns of perception in the person participating. What are the determinants of these preferences constitute another extension of the same story, though the model of explanation may be switched from time to time – psychological rather than neuro-physiological. It would still be scientific. All the sciences adopt the best models of understanding while ensuring their mutual compatibility.

How individuals will respond to different kinds of art, paintings, music, personal relationships or literature can be effectively predicted (explained) following a full prior analysis of that individual's existing artistic and other personal preferences, perceptual style and habits confirmed, if necessary, by brain scanning, record of habits, personal psychological condition, education, current physiological arousal and the secretion of brain enzymes, such as dopamine, serotonin and especially oxytocin. The more relevant parameters that can be isolated and measured, the more accurate the prediction. The intensity of an individual's response to a poem, a painting, a mathematical equation, a piece of music or a lover has also to be inferred from that person's behaviour, i.e. spoken words, motor behaviour, exclamations and physiological change, including specific blood flow patterns in particular cortical, sub-cortical and hypothalamic areas (Damasio, 1994), if we want to measure it at all! Anyone who has undertaken experimental work of this sort will, of course, be well aware of the technical problems of separating 'between person' differences from 'within person' differences. More recently, fMRI and CAT scanning have allowed more detailed analyses of how our brains are activated in these situations.

The fact that we indulge in such complex experimentation relatively infrequently does not mean that it cannot be done at all. Similar techniques are of course applicable to what is called 'religious experience'. The subject of the experiment does of course 'enjoy' the subjective awareness of what (s)he is going through in a way that is lost to the experimenter. That simply takes one back to the truism that consciousness is normally always private to the individual. Given that all other measures and observations available, including recording and considering the content of his/her speech are taken account of, however, an individual's conscious experience as elicited by another is only a relatively small element in the prediction and control of her/his behaviour. That of course does not mean that what a person says in describing his conscious experience is either veridical or irrelevant. Speech is behaviour, and everybody draws inferences from what a person says to him/her. What is said of course is not necessarily a fair reproduction of or even accurate description of that person's conscious experience. As I have often said to my students, "If, at all times, you simply sit still with your eyes open and your mouths closed, I will never know whether you are an imbecile or a genius!" Happily, most rose to the challenge. Perhaps I should also have said: "... and I may never find out if you do not allow me to use various pieces of apparatus, apply certain tests or administer certain drugs."

Poets, mystics, religious converts, shamans, some ill people, anoxic patients having 'near death' experiences and drug addicts can have personal experiences of an entirely subjective nature which may convince them, certainly at the time, that they have been vouchsafed some earth-shattering truth or special awareness which means much to them and which they may be convinced will be valuable to others who have not shared in them. There is a syndrome related to temporal lobe epilepsy, Geschwind syndrome, in which the patient will become, among other things, hyper religious and compelled to write down, in a slavish fashion, all his thoughts and activities to the exclusion of attending to normal life. There remains a need for further research to clarify the condition, though some have suggested this as underlying St Paul's epiphany on the road to Damascus described in the New Testament.

The writer himself has had one such experience as an undergraduate when he was administered mescaline in controlled conditions in the course of doing the experimental work for a degree thesis on the psychology of mysticism and religious experience. Subjectively, he felt that a great truth was given to him, that his perception, even of the laboratory desk beside him, was a heightened perception of a strange, valuable and mystic beauty. Objectively, he was tape-recorded as repeating *ad nauseam*, "The world is round, the world is round!", while wearing a smile of either imbecilic or beatific vacuousness. He had also read Aldous Huxley and several science fiction writers! The point is, however, that my conscious experience, while subjectively bland and perhaps valuable seeming, was totally unreliable as a veridical insight into my close environment at the time.

A religious person therefore may, in some cases, set great store by subjectively important experiences of this kind, but while these may appear to validate her/his own point of view, they do nothing to validate the truth or falsity of that point of view for others who have not had that particular experience in a similar setting. The so-called 'out of body' experiences which are reported sometimes in the course of operative surgery are all found later to be caused by cerebral anoxia. Other religions will abhor such 'personal revelations', preferring a more reasoned approach to validation of a personal truth derived from scripture such as the Bible, Koran or Talmud. Few scientists demur with either approach to religion and/or morality for those who find them acceptable. The difficulties arrive when the 'revealed truths' fly in the face either of each other or of empirically observable fact or when they lead to behaviour in masses of the world's populations which can be shown rationally to be damaging to or destructive of others or of civilisation itself. That is when a rationally and evolutionarily appropriate morality needs to be insisted on. Religious leaders of several major religions will dispute this insistence because the rational, scientific humanist view allows, following the canon of parsimony, a wide understanding of everything in the natural world, including the religions. The canon of parsimony states that if one principle or hypothesis is sufficient to explain what is under scrutiny, then it holds primacy over the case where two or more principles or hypotheses are necessary to satisfy the same level of explanation. A slightly more brutal affirmation of the canon states that this canon excludes from scientific affirmation all statements that are unverified and, still more so, all that are unverifiable, or unfalsifiable, as it is more commonly put. As I indicated above, it is a principle according to which an explanation of a thing or event is made with the fewest possible assumptions.

Many are well aware of trends in the world today which exemplify all too well the potential conflicts which derive from entirely different frames of reference. The humanist looks to the scientific, rational understanding of what we know and what we do not know. The religious, on the other hand, also set some store by the unverified words of soothsayers and prophets. Many religious may accept the scientific, empiricist intellectual habits to a greater or lesser degree, but still do not apply that rigour or style of thinking to the whole of their experience.

The attitude of traditional Islam to the role of women conflicts with the modern Christian view but both claim to be right. The Roman Catholic view of contraception flies in the face of data about overpopulation in some parts of the world (and the use of condoms as a protection against sexually transmitted diseases) as well as causing conflict with the Protestant views of the family and personal rights to freedom of choice, especially in regard to rights concerning marriage, abortion and child-rearing practices. In lieu of exact experimentation or social engineering, observation of the effects of each of these philosophic positions in particular cultures, using agreed criteria, could, in the course of, say, two or three generations, resolve the relative evolutionary value for humankind of each principle.

Should man be unable to resolve some or all of those conflicts of belief, as distinct from knowledge, then his survival in the long term will be prejudiced to the point of extinction. Unfortunately, beliefs, like faiths, are what the lazy, the poorly informed and the intellectually challenged use to fill the gaps in their knowledge. They seem to be unable to say, "That is uncertain" or "I don't know—yet!" There is no shame in not knowing something, provided that one strives to keep on learning. Because of the very evolution of the human brain itself, there will always be more remaining to be discovered and used than any of us can know now. But the evolving brain offers no structured plan of further development of knowledge nor does it in itself suggest new hypotheses to be tested or observations to be made. Each human brain has to construct and express novel and searching ideas for the necessary new neural circuits to be generated and assimilated. Simply to say that what mankind does not at this point know is 'in the mind of god' is meaningless because if all that is unknown is 'in the mind of god', then the mind of god is also full of the unknown (or, at best, knowledge that this god is unwilling to share) and it is not at all clear why we should sustain such a selfish, useless and unexaminable concept.

Should man eventually do away with himself, then any further evolution of life forms will be left to species which will need to have the properties which will allow them to survive, breed and develop in the devastated world we leave. In due course, some of those new species will probably have to survive, thrive and socially organise themselves by some behavioural and socially regulative processes recapitulating or cognate with at least some such as I have been describing.

Writing just over fifty years ago, Julian Huxley (1964) was impressed by the way man, arriving on the scene a million years ago, and as a socially organised being very much later (about ten thousand years ago). Huxley saw this as a mere second of cosmic time in which to make so many and diverse achievements. It is the case that some of the latter have been destructive and misguided. For all that, Huxley sets man's activities, good and bad, against the wide context of evolution (a notably slow worker!). We are reminded that man has had to develop all manner of political, industrial and belief systems, many of which continue to evolve often in critical and unexpected ways. At the time of his writing, Huxley adumbrated continuing crises involving dominant systems of thought and belief which any careful contemporary observer can see will modify present economic, political, ideological, humanist and religious systems at a cost not yet evaluated by those with the power and motivation to disturb, modify or prevent them.

Even then, perhaps, Huxley had some inkling of the new complexities involved in moral and social decision-making. He was, nevertheless, confident that these complexities were well within the capacities of man to resolve in due course without resort to supernatural reference points or religious dogma. Humanism therefore sets out a system of thought and behaviour which puts the responsibility for the continued wellbeing of ourselves, our friends and families and indeed all those of our species in our own hands. It encourages the view that there are more similarities among all humans than differences, especially in many of the goals we set ourselves in life, our aims for what sort of a world would be good for our children and would be good for the extension of all human happiness, prosperity, health and understanding among all races, nationalities and creeds.

Chapter 12
Humanism for All Humanity:
A Background

It is one of the main purposes of the British Humanist Association (now Humanists UK) and the Scottish Humanist Society to increase public awareness of what Humanism is, and to let the many millions of non-religious people in this country and elsewhere know that, far from being somehow deficient in their personal qualities and values, they have an outlook on life which is coherent and widely shared, which has inspired some of the world's greatest thinkers, artists, writers, scientists, philosophers and social reformers, and which has a two-thousand-year-old tradition worldwide. These organisations also aim to consolidate the confidence of people whose guiding habits of thought are humanist by style and content. It can offer resources here and elsewhere that can develop their knowledge of humanist approaches to some of the big ethical, philosophical and existential questions in life all over our world.

Although the British Humanist Association originated in 1896, it became more active only in the early 1950s and now has over 65,000 members. Humanism, if not as an organisation but as a philosophical stance, has roots that go very deep indeed. Let us take a brief look at great forerunners of humanism, from whom many later humanists have drawn inspiration.

Marcus Tullius Cicero (106BC-43BC), Roman lawyer, orator, political commentator and philosopher, was arguing, during that late pre-Christian era, that 'humanitas' (his Latin term) should imply a capacity for humankind to order and manage life in a balanced and sensible way, affording all others their rights and responsibilities to further the wellbeing of all. Cicero, either in his treatises, speeches or other recorded conversations, was a highly productive philosopher to the extent that his wide-ranging views on many political and philosophic matters would change as he learned more or discovered new perspectives on a topic. He was a sceptic and in some ways his attitude to learning was that of a modern scientist. If what he was now learning differed from what he had previously learned because of valid new experience, then he would modify his former position. This was why he could be critical of the gods and their status, doubtful about divination based on signs following the disembowelling of animals, and yet, for a time, he was considered a champion of the gods in spite of doubting their alleged powers. Julius Caesar thought that Cicero could 'enhance the spirit' of Rome, though he could not 'extend the frontiers of Rome'. Marcus Tullius Cicero might well have been accepted today as a humanist. I like to think of him as one of the great freethinkers of all time, a sceptic who advocated the primacy of reason and who was unafraid to change his mind in the face of new evidence. Would that we had more politicians of that stamp today! It is no surprise to find his ideas being referred to by philosophers right into the Age of Enlightenment seventeen centuries later and beyond.

Down the years since, there have always been some, bolder spirits of independent thought: mostly men, because the emancipation of women, even in the Western world, came late. Those sturdy souls were to a greater or lesser extent non-conformists to the predominant, often religious, systems of thought and belief prevailing at the time. Caught up in the sweep of history and frequently unsupported by appropriate power brokers, some, both men and women, even lost their lives because they dared to challenge religious or political orthodoxy. There are echoes of that threat even in the world of today.

Before Caxton and the printing press, the only media available to dissidents and freethinkers which might allow them to indulge in open discussion were manuscript letters or pamphlets and even the production of these demanded the ability to write, read and spell. Since monks, priests and a few others with that sort of learning held a near-monopoly in literacy skills until at least the Age of Enlightenment of the 17th, 18th and 19th centuries, it is no surprise that we see little written material or evidence of protracted open discussion of the case against religion, gods, angels or demons before that. Generally, however, it is clear that throughout recorded history there have been non-religious people other than Cicero, who have taken the view that this life is the only life we have, that the universe is a natural phenomenon, constantly regenerating itself with no supernatural component, and that we, men and women alike, can live ethical and fulfilling lives on the basis of reason, kindness, gentleness, empathy and humanity. They have trusted the scientific method, evidence, and reason to discover a full and growing understanding of the universe and have placed human development, welfare and happiness at the centre of their ethical decision-making.

Significant influences which jointly emerged to determine how humanism would develop and mature included the works of such as Jeremy Bentham, David Hume, Thomas Paine, John Stuart Mill, and of course Charles Darwin, who added a more scientific rather than philosophical approach to understanding. Evolutionary theory represented a massive change in the frames of reference on which earlier thinkers had been dependent and added many new pieces to the jigsaw of knowledge.

David (later Sir David) Hume (1711-1776) was an Edinburgh Scot, the younger son of Joseph Hume, who, whilst being the modestly financially endowed laird of Ninewells, near Chirnside, south-east of Edinburgh, on the Scottish side of the border, was not unduly rich and sometimes doubted how young David would turn out. David's mother, Catherine, a daughter of Sir David Falconer, president of the Scottish Court of Session, was in Edinburgh when David was born. He was only three when his father died. Nine years later, when he was no more than 12 years old, he entered Edinburgh University and left it at 14 or 15, as was then usual. Because it was in the family tradition on both sides, David was encouraged to study law. He was not enthused by this and instead read voraciously in the wider sphere of letters. Because of the intensity and excitement of his intellectual development at this time, and perhaps too because of some deeper unstable or cycloid personality traits, he had in 1729 a 'nervous breakdown' from which he recovered only after a few years of rest.

Sir David Hume was to become a scion of the Scottish Enlightenment, philosopher, historian, economist, and essayist, known especially for his philosophical empiricism and scepticism. He was as prolific a writer as was

Cicero, to whom, in spite of the many centuries between them, he occasionally referred. The subtitle of his great *Treatise on Human Nature* was bold and ambitious— "An Attempt to introduce the Experimental Method of Reasoning into Moral Subjects." Hume conceived of philosophy as the inductive, experimental science of human nature. He took the scientific method of the English physicist Sir Isaac Newton as his model and built on the epistemology of the English philosopher John Locke. Hume tried to describe how the mind works in acquiring knowledge. He concluded that no theory of reality is possible; there can be no knowledge of anything beyond experience. This is, remarkably, an adumbration of my earlier stated view that all perceptions of phenomena and all ideas depend on the efficient working of a healthy human brain. Subjective experience, on which Hume depended for the raw material of his own reasoning, is part of that. Despite the enduring impact of his theory of knowledge, Hume seems to have considered himself chiefly as a moralist. Nevertheless, the great, almost naive ambition of his *Treatise*, his devotion to empiricism, healthy scepticism and attempts to engage with the scientific method all demonstrate the kind of philosophical underpinnings of modern humanism.

If the chronological gap between Cicero and Hume is massive, due to my largely arbitrary selection of philosophic figureheads, the 18th century saw a veritable rush of discursively inclined protagonists in the world of ideas. Up till then, the organised religions had had it all their own way in many parts of the world. Educational systems, largely supported by religious factions, were geared to maintaining the irrationally-based doctrines of the various religions and creeds. The social and political structures of the time tended to reinforce the orthodox doctrines. But increasing numbers of more highly educated people in many of the more developed countries were gaining access to books, finding opportunities for active debate and the advantages of the wider spread of knowledge. The Scottish Enlightenment was a significant part of this. Sir David Hume was a sociable man in and out of philosophic discussion in the coffee houses of Edinburgh. Just across the Forth estuary, in Kirkcaldy, a near contemporary and friend, Dr Adam Smith, was writing *The Wealth of Nations*. Prior to 1950, that book was the most cited, second to Karl Marx's *Das Kapital*, and Smith was often available for discussion with Hume and others in Edinburgh. The result was that alternative models of how societies might successfully organise themselves in matters of belief, morality and ethics could be analysed, discussed in depth, and if thought worthy, propagated.

Two more examples of influential thinkers at the roots of modern humanism are worth a mention. Thomas Paine (1737-1809) was an English-American political activist, philosopher, political theorist, and revolutionary. Born in Thetford, Norfolk, Paine emigrated to the British American colonies in 1774 with the help of Benjamin Franklin, and was soon involved in the American Revolution, his writings on the rights of man and his pamphlet *Common Sense* playing a significant part in stirring 'rebel Americans' to move for independence from Great Britain. One of the Founding Fathers of the United States, he authored the two most influential pamphlets at the start of the American revolution, and he inspired the rebels in 1776 to declare independence from Britain. His ideas reflected Enlightenment-era rhetoric of world-wide human rights. He has been called a corset maker by trade, a journalist by profession, and a propagandist by inclination.

Paine lived in France for most of the 1790s, where his thinking became much influenced by the French revolution. He wrote *Rights of Man* (1791), in part a defence of the French Revolution against its critics. His criticisms of Anglo-Irish conservative writer, Edmund Burke, resulted in a trial and conviction in absentia in 1792 for the crime of seditious libel. By contrast, and in spite of his not being able to speak a word of French, in the same year he was elected to the French National Convention. In December 1793, he was arrested and was imprisoned in Paris. While in prison, he continued to work on *The Age of Reason* (1793–94). It is thought that future American President James Monroe used his diplomatic influence to get Paine released in November 1794. Because of the content of his pamphlets in which he advocated deism, promoted reason and free thought, and argued against institutionalised religion in general and Christian doctrine in particular, he became notorious rather than famous. He continued to write further pamphlets on property and other social/economic desiderata and in 1802 he returned to the U.S. where he died on June 8, 1809. It is reported that only six people attended his funeral as he had been ostracised for his ridicule of Christianity.

Early in the next century, John Stuart Mill (1806-1873) would become a philosopher much influenced by Jeremy Bentham, who was enrolled by

John's rather strict academic father to help him educate the young John Stuart Mill. The child was educated at home to the point where he was reading several Latin classics before he reached the age of four and the poor boy was allowed no childhood friends lest they interrupt his studies. One is bound to wonder how, then, John Stuart Mill in his adulthood was equipped to put "the greatest happiness of the greatest number" as a key construct in his work propounding Utilitarianism, the philosophy by which he is probably best known by lay people. Was the wish being father to the thought?

His book, *Utilitarianism* (1863) set out the notion that all should seek to judge behaviours and events by how far they were useful and added to the sum of happiness and wellbeing of the actors and everyone else without causing harm to any. However, in providing yet another of the great historical roots of humanism, in his posthumously published essays (1874) on 'Nature', 'Theism' and 'The Utility of Religion', he proposed a measure of scepticism about traditional religious views, preferring an alternative, designated as the religion of Humanity. Mill was also critical of the intellectual laziness that permitted belief in an omnipotent and benevolent God. He felt, following his father, that the world as we find it could not possibly have come from such a God, given the evils rampant in it; either that his power is limited, or he is not wholly benevolent. Although Mill was tempted somewhat by the 'intelligent design' theory of the earth's and its contents' existence, he acknowledged Charles Darwin's great work *The Origin of Species* (1859) as adding some scientific element to philosophic considerations generally, although he initially reserved judgment on it.

Only on reading the final draft of this book did it occur to me that there may be something in my DNA determining how at least some of my thinking has deep familial roots. My paternal grandfather was born in 1832, was schooled only to the age of 11 and worked as a farm labourer and jobbing gardener near Girvan in Ayrshire. Something of an autodidact, he schooled himself by reading avidly books from the Rationalist Press and Everyman's Library to the extent that he regularly corresponded with Keir Hardie on socialism and George Bernard Shaw on politics and religion. He was a proselytising atheist and became a soap box orator – the scourge of the southern Scottish aristocracy. He died, still working, in his nineties and was buried, at his own request, without ceremony in a field at the farm where he worked. My own copy of John Stuart Mill's "Utilitarianism" is dated 1910 and was my father's but I sometimes wonder whether it might have been originally my venerable grandfather's. My father told me old James Clark was a doughty debater in argument and of course he put my father out of the family house in Girvan for all time when my father gave up a good teaching job in Glasgow to become a Christian minister. I greatly regret that I never knew either of my paternal grandparents.

The 20th century saw British philosophers such as Bertrand Russell, A.J. Ayer and Gilbert Ryle all make significant contributions to the trend toward and further support for the humanist position. Nor can I fail to mention the more recent major contributions of Richard Dawkins' *The God Delusion*, Christopher Hitchens' *God is Not Great* and A.C. Grayling's *The God Argument*. The last of these is not only tightly argued and clearly expressed, but represents a fair and useful advocacy of Humanism today.

Augmenting the philosophic contributions of the above, American clinical psychologists Carl Rogers (1902-1987), Abraham Maslow (1908-1970) and G.A. Kelly (1905-1967) were making humanistic psychology not only a useful tool for helping troubled patients but also securing the importance of self-actualisation, emotional balance and ways of reconstructing relationships with other people. Maslow was actually a member of the American Humanist Association on the strength of his vigorous advocacy of his ideas on understanding people's responses to a hierarchy of human needs and the process of self-fulfilment. Unfortunately, he died suddenly at the age of 62 of a heart attack while jogging in a Californian park.

Maslow's near contemporary Carl Rogers was a humanistic psychologist very closely aligned with Maslow's ideas of self-actualisation or the drive to fulfil one's potential. Only the subject would be fully aware of what that potential might be. Rogers' understanding of people's motivations and psychological growth was less deterministic than that of the Freudian psychoanalysts or the Watsonian or Skinnerian behaviourists. But he added that for a person to 'grow', they need an environment that provides them with genuineness (openness and self-disclosure), acceptance (being viewed with unconditional positive regard), and empathy (being listened to and understood). Without these, relationships and healthy personalities will not develop as they should, much like crops will not grow without sunlight and water.

Rogers believed that every person can achieve their goals, wishes and desires in life. The psychologist's task would be to explore, accurately define and aid the client/patient to achieve these goals with a measure of autonomy and self-confidence. The reader will realise how much this would have appealed to me as a therapist with a troubled or oppressed and unfulfilled patient in my consulting room. When, or rather if, the patient did eventually succeed in working toward these goals, self-actualisation took place. For that to happen the person had to achieve a condition that Rogers described as 'congruence'. In this condition the person's actual self (how that person habitually saw him or herself) and the person's ideal self (how that person would wish to be ideally, and in all respects) merged.

American Professor G. A. Kelly, at the State University of Ohio and subsequently two prominent British clinical psychologists, Drs Don Bannister and Fay Fransella, further elaborated Kelly's ideas and developed the Repertory Grid Test which became a useful tool in clinical and some other branches of applied psychology. Among other things, the technique measured, at various times for any subject/patient, the psychological distance between what they construed as their Ideal and Actual selves. In that sense it supported some of Carl Rogers' notions of 'congruence'. In psychotherapy or cognitive behaviour therapy, for example, the aim would be to effect closer congruence between these notions of self as treatment progressed.

I remember being fascinated by how Bannister and Fransella expounded the Kelly principles and practices at a continuing professional development course I attended at the University of Southampton toward the end of the 20th century. Subsequently, the Repertory Grid Test, or variations of it, became an important part of my clinical armamentarium. If the treatment regime I had worked out for my patient was effective, then there would, as treatment progressed, be increasing measured congruence, toward the ideal, between the ideal and the actual selves of the patient.

George Kelly's theoretical starting point was that people are like 'naive scientists' who see the world from a particular standpoint based on their uniquely organised systems of construction, which they use to anticipate events. Personal Construct Theory explores the individual's understanding of their life experiences based on the main constructs they form by coping with the psychological stresses of their lives. But because people are naive scientists, they sometimes employ systems for construing the world that are distorted by idiosyncratic experiences not applicable to their current social situation. Constructs are not concepts; rather, they are personalised but fairly consistent ways in which persons classify and construe people, their personal attributes and events. This is a system of construction that chronically fails to characterise and/or predict events and is not appropriately revised to comprehend and predict one's changing social world, is considered to underlie psychopathology or mental disturbance or illness.

Kelly believed that each person had their own idea of what a word meant, beyond the dictionary definition. If someone were to say their colleague is greedy, the word 'greedy' would be interpreted in different ways depending on the person's personal constructs they had already associated with the word 'greedy' because of previous experiences of greedy people. Kelly wanted to know how the individual made sense of the world based on their constructs. These are built up and refined over the years and often have, in the case of 'greedy' for example, a polar opposite, say, 'generous', or possibly, 'careless' also generated by significant earlier experiences of the person whose constructs are under examination.

Kelly's fundamental view of people as naive scientists emerged in the 1970s and '80s was jammed, as it were, between psychoanalytic (Freudian) drive theories concerned with sex on the one hand and aggression and the behaviourist learning and conditioning theories gradually developing into cognitive behaviour therapy on the other. Because the constructs people developed for construing experience have the potential to change, Kelly's theory of personality is thought to be less deterministic than drive theory or learning theory. People could conceivably change their view of the world and in so doing change the way they interacted with it, felt about it, and even others' reactions to them. For this reason, it is an existential theory, regarding humankind as having a choice to reconstrue themselves, a concept Kelly referred to as 'Constructive Alternativism'.

Constructs provide a certain order, clarity, and prediction to a person's world. Kelly referenced many philosophers in his two-volume work *The Psychology of Personal Constructs* but the theme of new experience being at once novel and familiar (due to the templates placed on it) is closely akin to the notion of the Greek philosopher Heraclitus: "we step and do not step in the same rivers". Experience is new but familiar to the extent that it is construed with historically derived constructs.

The Repertory Grid test was an almost inevitable product of Kelly's theorising. Constructs are bipolar categories, the way two things are alike and different from a third, that people employ to understand the world. Examples of such constructs are 'attractive,' 'intelligent,' 'kind.' A construct always implies contrast. So when an individual categorises others as attractive, or intelligent, or kind, an opposite polarity is implied. This means that such a person may also evaluate the others in terms of the reciprocal constructs 'ugly,' 'stupid,' or 'cruel.' In some cases, when a person has a disordered construct system, the opposite polarity is unexpressed or idiosyncratic. The importance of a particular construct varies among individuals. The adaptiveness of a construct system is measured by how well it applies to the situation at hand and is useful in predicting events. All constructs are not used in every situation because they have a limited range (range of convenience). Adaptive people are continually revising and updating their own constructs to match new information (or data) that they encounter in their experience.

Maslow, Kelly and Rogers all built theoretical structures that could usefully inform both their work in a clinical setting and their wider understanding of ordinary people making their way in a complex world. They would almost certainly have described themselves as humanistic psychologists. They valued a scientific but not overly rigid scientific approach to human problems, the need for and satisfactions deriving from self-fulfilment and balance, tolerance and fairness in their view of others, and their quiet confidence in the abilities and adaptiveness of humankind to overcome difficulties without having to invoke outside agencies, supernatural or otherwise. Professor H.J. Eysenck, one of the outstanding psychologists in Britain just after WW2 once wrote that he could divide all the various schools of psychology into two classes—'Erklärende Psychologie' and 'Verstehende Psychologie'— psychology which explains and psychology which understands. While Eysenck himself would have been placed in the former group, Kelly, Maslow and Rogers clearly fall into the latter classification. They too, however, provided, it seemed to me, further intellectual bases for humanism as a philosophic position and way of life. Many of my values and much of my professional practice has been rooted in the work of those psychologists. The fact that, even if they were not self-proclaimed humanists (with the one exception), they all operated on the basis of empirical, evidence-based science with the aim of helping other human beings, regardless of race, creed or nationality, toward a healthier, richer and self-fulfilling life all seemed to push me further in the direction of the humanist position.

As someone who had been stumbling his own weary way toward humanism through teenage rebellion, then university-induced scepticism and finally a more adult desire to live out my life according to a reasoned and consistent philosophy, I talked with many others of all faiths and none and read (at least until I began to lose my sight because of macular degeneration), I was formulating a philosophy which would support my personal and permanent relationships, my scientific and professional ideals and goals and my parental and other responsibilities. Throughout the busiest years of my life I was gradually firming up the moral and ethical but non-religious ideas that I have tried to express in this book. Accordingly, for many of my earlier years I was indubitably one amongst that not inconsiderable band of people who are really humanists by inclination and habit without knowing it themselves. What I was clear about was that a religious approach to understanding people, events and the phenomena of the whole universe was, for me, utterly untenable for the reasons I have already set out.

Then, out of the blue, I was invited to be one of four 'local notables' to be the central participants in an 'Any Questions' evening for the community in a local hall. The original topic now eludes me but, among other topics, some discussion of religious belief and its alternatives was pursued. Perhaps someone had read a lengthy article, 'The Sceptic's Tale', which I had published (Clark, D. F. Scottish Review (2008) pp 54-98), and may have known that, as a student, I had rejected the Christian or any other faith. Nevertheless, there I was, sitting alongside a rather evangelistically inclined minister from the neighbouring town, and two other bright participants, one of whom turned out to be the first established humanist (celebrant) I had so far met. The occasion was significant for me in that it established my own philosophic stance once and for all. Not many questions had been responded to before I was aware of almost total congruence between the kind of atheistic, but, I hope, wholly humane responses I had made and the somewhat less, but very discursively potent responses given by the humanist lady. Something 'clicked' and at last I began to structure my thinking on such matters—and, in so doing, I formed a lasting friendship with the humanist and her celebrant husband. Those events pushed me into a sharper recognition of what humanism entailed.

There can be no doubt that formal attachment to Humanist groups world-wide is growing but needs to be further supported in any way possible. Engaging with some of the topics in this book, however, has guided me to note some features of Humanist organisations which have led me to compare them with religious organisations.

First, humanists do not seem to proselytise. Although many humanists I have met are model citizens, humanists do not send out missionaries to, say, the isle of Lewis, the state of Alabama, madrassas in Yemen or even to pubs in greater London. By adopting a policy of 'Live and let live' and a general commitment to tolerance, they are more likely to let those who are not yet humanists be persuaded by their own observations of others. Humanists are happy with their own understanding of what life is all about. Other people must find out about it for themselves. Humanists also see tolerance of others' viewpoints (so long as these viewpoints do not lead to any harm to others) as particularly important. The problem about proselytising is that, in addition to trying to persuade others to adopt a new philosophic position, one is almost certainly bound to undermine any existing belief system held by the subject to be converted—that is, assuming that I am right, as a result of my clinical experience, in thinking that all who hold beliefs of any kind do so because they must, because they need them to maintain some sort of psychological equilibrium. The humanist then has to tread carefully and with gentleness. The humane approach therefore is to allow others simply to see that the humanist point of view may not necessarily require too much fundamental change in the convert's lifestyle or view of the human condition. Only a requirement to drop any dependence upon gods or any other supernatural influences in how to live a fulfilling, happy, moral and productive life would be required, as would be maintaining good relations with all other people, indeed with all living things.

Secondly, humanists do not have meeting houses, nor do they worship. They may value highly the efforts of mankind to ease the troubles of the deprived and the afflicted and to advance the achievements of others but, by and large, they do so as individuals for the sake of humanity. The corporate growth of humanism, in the western nations particularly, is now quite significant but it is seldom, if ever, evoked as an expression of social or political power. This does not inhibit 'the establishment', spiritual or temporal, from springing to the defence of unreason on any occasion when humanists seem to be pressing for the pursuit of their own aims. Only recently, as I began to write this, the Scottish Education Department decided that school pupils in the senior classes in schools should not be allowed to opt out of classes in religious education on the grounds that they are humanists. The Scottish Humanist Society is seeking a legal review of this decision (which would seem reasonable as such an option is already available to senior pupils in England and Wales). The outcome is awaited with interest, but it does show the residual touchiness about real freedom of thought in the establishment. It has also recently come to my attention that Officer Cadets at the Royal Military Academy at Sandhurst are not allowed to opt out of religious services on the grounds that they are humanists. How that might interfere with their future abilities as officers in combat or otherwise is far from apparent.

The fact that humanists do not usually meet in congregations as do religious groups suggests that they cannot readily supply a recognised structure of social group support when, for any number of human stressful situations, that might be needed. The intellectual stringency of the humanist philosophical standpoint perhaps dulls the individual humanist's awareness of when emotional support could be needed. I shall refer to this later in the context of what I have called the 'pastoral role' of a humanist.

A third major difference between humanism and the religions is that humanists, because of the demonstrable inefficiency and inefficacy of prayer, do not pray. They may recognise that because, for many religious people, it may give comfort, solace and sometimes hope; it can tide some over periods of personal loss or difficulty, but there are many well researched and effective ways of dealing with such situations psychologically that humanists can call upon to do the same job better. In my own nearly four decades of clinical practice, I have seen many, indeed most, of my patients, through a variety of psychological therapies, come to deal successfully with life crises and emotional disturbances enabling them to benefit from the emotional support of other groups and organisations which had failed them in the past. Prayer had not been found by most to be helpful, but others were able to return to a religious setting (even if they then chose not to pray) or to a supportive secular group. Some may even have become humanists, though my normal follow-up procedures never included any questions about that sort of thing.

Psychological studies of prayer tend to distinguish intercessory prayer—that is, praying for the effects of prayer to work on someone or something else other than the person praying—and private, personal prayer in which the praying person seeks some result which will benefit him or herself. In both cases the objective analysis of what is going on is hugely complicated, not only because it can be hard to know whether a person is really praying or not, what may be the intention of the prayer and we do not know whether some are better at praying than others. In the Roman Catholic church, for example, it is often thought by the laity that a prayer uttered by the Pope or by a senior Cardinal will have more potency than one uttered or stuttered by a village priest. In Islam, much prayer is heavily ritualised, but the observer has no way of knowing whether the prayer uttered by one is anything similar in content to that uttered by the man on the next prayer mat. Muslims seem to have to face toward Mecca when they pray but in spite of such rituals, others have no idea whether their prayers might be more effective because of that.

In many religions the process of prayer is so ritualised that every member of a Christian or Muslim congregation, for example, will be, in some situations, uttering or sub-vocalising the same words, e.g. for Christians, the Lord's prayer. Tibetan Buddhist monks may simply spin some prayer wheels or drums as they pass, each spinning drum representing a prayer.

For these and several other reasons, sound research on intercessory prayer has been found easier to structure into clearer goals, content and practices. Even in that, however, there are huge difficulties. In his carefully researched book, *Adieu to God*, Mick Power (2012) has also remarked on these difficulties which can even be compounded, in some reported researches, with some results which are so unreliable that some witting or unwitting cheating may have occurred. Even in the better controlled researches (see Benson et al. below), there are problems of experimental control caused by the fact that others, not part of the experiment, might be simultaneously praying on behalf of the experimental subjects for outcomes which may or may not be aligned to those the experiment is about. Many atheists, humanists and other sceptics have wondered how a god or gods can sort out priorities for outcomes when praying millions throughout the world may be all praying simultaneously to him, her or them for different outcomes. Is there some scope for omniscience here?

There have never, to my knowledge, been prayer contests, head to head, so to speak, in which two equally devout religious believers and talented prayers, either in each other's company or not, pray for very different outcomes to one critical situation or event. Only the other day did I see on television two football supporters standing next to each other. They devoutly crossed themselves and held their hands, palms together in prayer. However, one wore a Man. U shirt and the other a white "Spurs" scarf. Of course nobody knew what they were praying for, but only the Man. U man was rewarded – maybe neither, if God was at the time supporting Man. U. and omniscience was paying off. For one example from my own clinical experience, one child in a family prays that the father may win the lottery (because she/he is the father's favourite and he will distribute his winnings fairly) while another sibling prays that the father will never win the lottery because he or she believes he will spend it all on drink and others, including the praying person, will be forgotten—or worse. Now statisticians will be well aware that the probability of the second outcome in this little narrative, for reasons other than religious ones, is very much greater, but of course, true believers will hold that the god to whom the prayers are directed can reconstruct probabilities to suit his ends. It is just as well that the gods to whom they all pray are omniscient since there must be tens of millions of prayers uttered daily all clogging up the godly in-tray and many seeking mutually incompatible outcomes. Who would want to be a god, omnipotent or otherwise? Nor do priests, pastors or theologians seem to be at all keen to record the efficacy of all the prayers daily expressed by them in favour of others. No actuaries or target setters appear to have considered whether it is really worthwhile for any prayers to be said at all. Children's messages sent up the chimney to Santa Claus every December 24th are likely to be more productive. It amuses me to observe every week during the soccer season, players of both teams, none of them noted for any regular access of religious fervour, emerging on to the field of play and crossing their chests in hope of heavenly support.

Mick Power would probably agree with me when I suggest that the enduring habit of prayer among most religions lies in the contemplative and relatively relaxed emotional tone that accompanies it. Meditation and its partner, controlled deep relaxation (or what is included in what is now called mindfulness), have, in recent years played a progressively significant part in clinical psychological treatments and it is something that can be effectively used outside the clinic or consulting room. When in the 1970s I was in Sri Lanka as a World Health Organisation consultant, working at Kandy General Hospital and doing a little teaching at the associated University at Peradeniya, I was persuaded by some Buddhist academic colleagues to join them at some meditation sessions after work. Each seemed to adopt his or her own style and technique, but we all sat, cross-legged and silent in a largish ring. We were all instructed to keep our eyes open or closed as we wished and to concentrate on slowing our breathing. There was no chanting of any mantra in that group. There was often, instead, because it was usually just before sundown and we were in central Sri Lanka, the insistent throb of distant drums, but I found the experience pleasant and relaxing. Similar meditation techniques would certainly have a place in Western clinical psychology. But it was not prayer and it did not pretend to be.

Several commentators on the efficacy of prayer have remarked, almost tongue in cheek, that the first attempt at an objective study of the possible efficacy of prayer was reported by the anthropologist and statistician Sir Francis Galton (1872). In one of the first applications of statistics to scientific psychological research, Galton tried to establish whether life expectancies of what he described as 'prayerful people' (e.g. clergy) were greater than those of more hard-nosed scientific or 'materialistic' people (e.g. doctors, scientists and, more curiously, lawyers). He also wondered whether persons frequently prayed for, such as kings, queens and other royalty in general, tended to live longer than other less fortunate mortals. His results led him to the conclusion that (intercessory) prayer did not favourably influence longevity. There are, of course, as we have seen, many difficulties with the assumptions, designs, and conclusions of Galton's retrospective studies. Is longevity, for example, a sufficient reward in itself to make it worth praying for—unless it is prayed for to be illness and dementia-free? However, Galton deserves credit for his view that the efficacy of prayer was amenable to empirical study and for his application of the statistical method to the study of this issue.

It was only after a very long hiatus that other researchers began again to examine prayer's efficacy using more sophisticated methods in well-controlled, prospective studies. We now know that various forms of meditation and of contemplative prayer, developed in the contexts of both Western and Eastern meditative, mystical, traditions, may beneficially influence the health and well-being of those who earnestly practise such disciplines (Benson, 1975; Benson, Greenwood & Klemchuk, (1977). This finding is not wholly unexpected, since it is becoming increasingly acceptable in neuroscience to expect one's own mental activities, which in some cases might include prayer, to affect one's own bodily or psychological condition. Our understanding of what used to be called mind-body interactions has been aided by investigations of placebo effects, stress reduction, suggestion, expectancy, hypnosis, biofeedback, self-regulation, and psycho-neuro-immunological principles. (See: Achterberg, 1985; Ader, 1981; Frank, 1961; Green & Green, 1977; Justice, 1987; Locke & Colligan, 1986; Ornstein & Sobel, 1987; White, Tursky & Schwartz, 1985; Wickramasekera, 1988.)

The best experimental test of prayer is usually considered to be of intercessory prayer in which the praying person is attempting to achieve the favourable intervention of a god or other supernatural force to effect positive therapeutic change in the persons or patients prayed for. In the *American Heart Journal* (2006) Apr, 151(4) 934-942, Dr H Benson et al. of Harvard Medical School reported a 'Study of the Therapeutic Effects of Intercessory Prayer in cardiac bypass surgery patients: a multi-centre randomised trial of uncertainty and certainty of receiving intercessory prayer'. Intercessory prayer is often indulged in by the religious to influence someone's recovery from an illness or injury. Generally, however, claims for the benefits are not supported by well-controlled clinical trials. Earlier studies have not considered whether the outcome might have been produced by prayer itself or by the certain knowledge on the part of the patients that intercessory prayer was being provided on their behalf.

The researchers evaluated first, whether receiving intercessory prayer, or second, being certain of receiving intercessory prayer was associated with uncomplicated recovery after coronary artery bypass graft (CABG) surgery. In the course of the experiment, patients in 6 US hospitals were randomly assigned to 1 of 3 groups: 604 received intercessory prayer after they had been told that they may or may not actually receive prayer; and 597 did not receive intercessory prayer also after being told that they may or may not actually receive prayer; and 601 received intercessory prayer after being informed that they would receive prayer. Intercessory prayer was provided for 14 days and was started the night before the operation.

The primary outcome measure was presence of any complication within 30 days of CABG. Secondary outcomes were any major adverse event and mortality. The results showed that in the two groups uncertain about receiving intercessory prayer, complications occurred in 52% (315/604) of patients who received intercessory prayer versus 51% (304/597) of those who did not (relative risk 1.02, 95% CI 0.92-1.15).

Complications occurred in 59% (352/601) of patients certain of receiving intercessory prayer compared with the 52% (315/604) of those uncertain of receiving intercessory prayer (relative risk 1.14, 95% CI 1.02—1.28). Major adverse events and 30-day mortality were similar across the three groups. The authors concluded that intercessory prayer itself had no effect on complication-free recovery from CABG surgery, but, ironically, certainty of receiving intercessory prayer was associated with a higher incidence of complications. Consequently, if knowing you are being prayed for tends toward a less satisfactory operative outcome and actually being prayed for, whether you know it or not, makes little or no difference to outcome, then why bother with prayer at all? Presumably the prayers would have been directed to a god so either that god is wilfully deaf to such appeals or doesn't care to do much about it.

There is no requirement imposed on humanists to pray. They recognise that some of the tried and tested psychological methods of self-help and stress reduction mentioned earlier are much more likely to be effective and supported by recent and contemporary research.

By their very nature, humanists I have known have been and remain self-sufficient and happy (perhaps at times even a little complacent or smug) with their own life stance. They do not, therefore, seem to feel any need to be members of any sort of congregation or to foregather in any particular kind of building with its own style of architecture to support each other or to worship anything other than the good behaviour and works of brilliant examples of humankind—even when those people may not be or have been humanists. Humanists value thoughtful and caring human behaviour rather than worshipping persons, gods or anything else. I have earlier suggested that this is something that humanists should seek to review in the interests of offering emotional support to others when they need it.

If humanists do not habitually congregate or hold what might be described by the religious as services, humanist celebrants are making themselves publicly accessible to non-religious or otherwise uncommitted persons for naming ceremonies, weddings and funerals. These are events which require some celebratory recognition in a setting shared by humanists and non-humanists alike simply because they mark strongly emotionally loaded human situations in which the support and co-participation of others may be of considerable psychological importance and value. The humanist approach to any ceremonial will, however, concentrate on the lives, past and present, of the individuals for whom the ceremony has been instituted without any direct or even oblique reference to the supernatural such as gods, angels, afterlives and the like. There is always, even in the case of the humblest, enough richness and drama, love, quirkiness and worthwhile relationships and experiences to make any digression into anything outside normal human experience unnecessary, irrelevant or even bizarre. I have personally attended several humanist, as well as Christian, funerals in recent years and much prefer the former. The celebrant will speak warmly and accurately about the personality and past life activities and experiences of the deceased in a way which faces up to the reality of helping the relatives and others to set that dead person's life in a real-world context, enabling all present to remember the real person in the real world as all present knew it. The dead person's life is valued as it was by all who loved him or her. The Christian funerals tend on the other hand to be burdened by liturgy and often too little is said by the priest or minister about the dead person's actual real life in our world and too much about the meaningless (for many, and even some Christians) supernatural and very unreal worlds of heaven and hell and an unknown afterlife. That may be all very well for those who are steeped in religious dogma and the irrational, but I personally leave a humanist funeral buoyed up by the resilience, candour and realism of the event as a good closure to a life well lived. Perhaps those indoctrinated religiously from childhood would find the Christian ceremony supportive in its way, but I often wonder whether they would not themselves prefer to be remembered in the humanist way[1].

Where humanism, in spite of recent developments in this area, may be seen to have still some way to go, by contrast with the organised religions, is in the matter of what is often described by the religious as 'pastoral care'. My late father (1882-1966), a Doctor of Divinity and Scottish Presbyterian minister, to which he came late after having been, until he was thirty, a perfectly respectable school teacher, always considered the church services on Sunday, his sermons (delivered with a touch of the histrionic), Bible classes and so on to be much less important than his duty of pastoral care to his parishioners. Never owning a motor car, he would walk up to 20 miles a day, summer and winter, visiting them all across his rural parish simply to give comfort, practical advice, consolation or encouragement to well or ill, rich or poor, haughty or humble, in all weathers, in war and in peace

---

[1] One strange development which I have noticed at one or two recent funerals is that the "celebrant" will claim to be a humanist (though not on the officially published list of the Scottish Humanist Society or of the Humanists UK) but then goes on to invoke the kingdom of heaven, god and the angels and so on. It then transpires that the "celebrant" is not a humanist at all, in the formal sense, but some sort of local lay preacher who had described himself as a humanist to the bereaved. Many of the less sophisticated of the attenders go away thinking they have been to "a humanist funeral" and because they have never been to an authentic humanist funeral they are being misled. Such misrepresentation offends because it presents a completely false impression of all that humanism stands for. It probably represents a kind of subconscious deference to the increasing acceptance of humanism in society at large. It is hard to imagine a Muslim Imam presenting himself as a putative humanist celebrant in this way!

without stint or hesitation. Were he to be offered a dram of malt whisky, so much the better! As a young lad I admired him for this, just as I admired him for his sometimes having doubts about whether the advice he had given was the best or whether he had really grasped his parishioner's problem. This experience was something I later shared with him from time to time in my own professional life. Similarly, I think I almost shared his small satisfactions when he reported 'a good day'. At home, of course, when I was a student, and for some years subsequently, we would argue vigorously about philosophy and religion into the night, but in the end, he would nearly always retreat into the fact of his faith, which he knew I could not share, but I always did admire in him the qualities that would have made him a cracking good humanist. There are probably a goodly number of Christians who could easily qualify in this way were they simply to live by a traditional Christian morality, simply for the sake of humanity, but eschew the primitive irrationality of their belief in the supernatural. Perhaps, however, humanism does need to consider what equivalent pastoral function its adherents should foster. From what I have read recently, I think they are doing so.

Incidental to the specific functions that any humanist celebrant may bring to the occasion being celebrated, there will be times when those engaging with him or her will perhaps wish for further ongoing support and guidance. Christians, Muslims, Buddhists or Jews I have talked with on these matters almost all find the support of 'a congregation' or 'a pastor', Rabbi or Imam or saffron-robed monk invaluable in times of personal or family crisis. It is a bit too easy for the humanist to be glib about the available help from other secular social, medical and psychological agencies when we all know that these are under-resourced, sometimes hard to contact and may have to be paid for! If modern humanism is to progress beyond a rather rare and self-satisfied loose organisation of individuals, then, as its size and identity firms up and grows, it will have to place its stamp of care, tolerance and kindness much more firmly on the social and political structures of a continent and even world where so many other less generous, less caring and less tolerant systems of thought and religions prevail.

The latter, as the philosopher Daniel Dennett has averred, will not be easily dislodged from the highly institutionalised, though irrationally based, foundations they have laid down over two or more millennia. Humanism makes demands on both heart and head and on the need constantly to be apprised of developments in science and the scientific method. The latter is an important distinguishing feature of humanism from the religions. The latter tend to be characterised by their haughty disdain for scientific scrutiny of their ideas and principles. They make no distinction between the differing validities of knowledge and belief. They are prone to set out a catechism or creed which adherents are bound to be committed to and guided by. Indeed, in some cases, non-acceptance of the creed is defined as apostasy which means they cannot be of that faith and possibly too may be threatened by death for their pains. No humanist needs to be a signatory to any such formal statement of his or her personal philosophic stance. The Amsterdam Declaration, which I shall refer to shortly, is a set of guidelines about humanism, but not anything like a creed which must be punctiliously obeyed.

The religious worship 'the given word', 'God's word', and change comes hard to them. Humanists hold human beings in high regard but do not worship anything because they observe that everything changes (according to natural law) and therefore all knowledge is in constant revision and flux, a flux which depends both on the evolution of the human brain, the whole organism of which it is but one part and representing everything outside it. A healthy and active human brain, evolution's finest achievement, is the simultaneous repository for each of us of our present, our past and our future. Mostly, in health, we succeed in making accurate discriminations between all these although there will be times when there may be some blurring between present and past or between present and future.

By contrast with those systems of thought which rely on the 'given truth', science is characterised as recognising that all scientific knowledge is conditional rather than absolute. It holds matters to be 'true' only so long as no new experiments, or observations do not refute them. Indeed, good scientific work will be presented to other scientists and the world on the understanding that it is open to refutation by sound argument, careful observation and/or experiment at any time. That is why it is in the very nature of science to progress by iteration and by the building of new work on the basis of previous work already tested and found to be sound. Every scientific statement must be open to falsification by experiment or by new findings incompatible with what has gone before. That is why, when one surveys systems of thought over the past five or six centuries, the scientific method has to be seen as having made a greater contribution to the wellbeing of mankind than any other system of thought—including much of philosophy and all the religions.

For example, from the story of Icarus' failure, given its legendary nature, to the first heavier-than-air flight of the Wright brothers took man two millennia, whereas in only the past century we have progressed from the Wrights' faltering start to massive airliners each carrying over 500 persons to almost anywhere in the world in great comfort and in a few hours, and space vehicles have circumnavigated and landed men on the moon. Computers and space satellites allow us, shipping and aircraft navigators and satellite commanders to know our position anywhere in the world to the nearest yard, and to calculate more and more accurately in a split second than a whole team of mathematicians could do with pencil and paper in a month. New drugs and prosthetic devices enable us to defeat pain and to live more satisfying and longer lives and at least some of us have set up social organisations the main function of which is to enhance the lives of others, regardless of creed or religion. Several religions, on the other hand, spend time and resources trying to inhibit scientific advances rather than recognising the massive overall contributions science has made to the wellbeing of the whole human race. The plague, pulmonary TB, smallpox poliomyelitis, malaria and several other formerly fatal diseases are progressively being beaten and, in some cases, eradicated. Steven Pinker (2018) has done us all a great service by detailing much more of the many advances that science has made—all adding to the wellbeing of millions. Dentistry is no longer a terrifying experience for tooth ache sufferers in most developed countries. Other advances in anaesthesia, prosthetic design and genetically based treatment programmes have all added to the life expectation of humans all over the planet. As a senior citizen myself, I cannot help being encouraged by the fact that there are currently over 12,000 centenarians alive in the UK.

It is notable that conflicts, based on differences of doctrine, between systems of thought other than the sciences, have, down the centuries, caused many wars, episodes of ethnic cleansing, other lesser conflicts and a sum of human misery far greater than any disagreements between scientists or humanists. Several of the major religions have, in the past, encouraged and fomented mutual intolerance and strife leading in many cases to disastrous, often futile and sometimes inhumanly cruel conflicts and internecine practises, not always amounting to wars in the technical sense but still killing thousands. Such episodes are scattered like confetti down the centuries: Jews and Arabs against Christians in the early Christian era; Christians against Muslims (The Crusades) in the middle ages (12-13th centuries); Roman Catholics and Protestants in Northern Ireland; 'ethnic cleansing' of Christians and Muslims from Buddhist Myanmar at present; similar ethnic cleansing (murders) of Muslims by Serbians at Srebrenica; the ruthless slaughter of six million Jews by Nazi gentiles during WW2; the killing of Shia Muslims by Sunni Muslims and vice versa in contemporary Syria, Iraq and Afghanistan; religiously-based killings by the Taliban and ISL in the Middle East at present (2018). These, not an inclusive list by any means, are all examples of differences in religious beliefs underpinning serious conflicts which unnecessarily kill thousands.

There is, of course, much in the writings and sayings of the religious which will have given, for long years, comfort, support and encouragement to distressed and deprived people. Many of the so-called 'commandments' of several religions contain soundly-based, well-intended and well-tried advices which have relieved suffering and guided moral behaviour. Many of these, however, remain rooted in the geographic regions of their early beginnings and in the cultural patterns of smaller populations extant at the time of their first formulation. Such ideas and principles can be transferred only with difficulty and tortured philosophical gymnastics to the thinking, conceptual armamentarium and life-styles of the more advanced (mainly Western) communities of the 21st century. One might expect humanists to be in the vanguard of updating and modernising such moral ideas and precepts. A large number of people, especially in more backward and deprived cultures, will find such religious precepts and comforting solutions to their personal and population problems valuable to them mainly because these problems are simple and do not require a high degree of learning and scientific discipline to understand and manage them.

By contrast, science has seen us shrink the world by air transport, defeat, as I've described, many formerly lethal diseases by drugs, vaccines and advanced medical care techniques, expand world-wide information links by various forms of electronic communications and the internet. Increased food production by new fertilisers, pest control and plant breeding and more specific genetic modification will, in coming decades, be the means to prevent millions starving to death. Praying to the gods for rain, larger crop yields or 'manna from heaven' will, I am confident, prove to be less effective or efficient. Surgery and medical science have helped many to live longer, more productive and, importantly, happier, lives. Prosthetic devices of great ingenuity and strength allow amputees and others to win Olympic and other athletics medals. Electricity and hydraulics have transformed so many of our instruments and tools and given us power beyond dreams. All that has come about only because science is evidence-based, open to scrutiny and builds knowledge upon its prior well-founded base and practices, holds nothing as absolutely true and constantly revises and restructures existing knowledge and theories. Scientists know that they will never know everything, but—and this is important—they are happy to live with the fact of their relative ignorance and do not try to fill prematurely the gaps in their present knowledge with beliefs and superstitions, incantations to witches, priests or gods, in the way many humans have done in earlier centuries. Scientists, however, are impelled to push out the boundaries of their knowledge, to place new little pieces in the steadily expanding jigsaw of knowledge. Because of what we already know of the rate of expansion of present universes, it is highly unlikely that human brains will ever evolve far and fast enough to allow knowledge to be totally comprehensive. Scientific truth or knowledge, which is what humanism takes as foundational, will always be partial and subject to revision. Nevertheless, within these limits, science has achieved much more than any other system of thought both to understand the nature of humanity and to further its development as a species. It has struggled to construct a template which may guide the exercise of power, technological, social, political as well as moral, and an awareness that man holds that power in the palm of his hand. It is to this responsibility that humanism draws our attention both as human beings and as humanists by persuasion.

A humanist is expected to live according to a soundly based ethic: to live, in other words, a good life, to help and never harm another and to support the survival and furtherance of humankind through tolerance, respect for others, kindness and generosity of spirit. Having come far enough in my journey through life, in other lands, in war and in peace, in good times and bad, I now feel that my journey toward humanism is complete. It is the right life stance for me.

Perhaps I should now take a look at what the formal position of organised humanism lays out as its governing principles. These are a guide, not a compulsion and lay out what the statement, "I am a Humanist!" entails. These principles have emerged from all the sources I have chosen to explore in this book, and many more from earlier centuries. The many strands of thought and experience which have led to the following outline and which have been woven into a closely textured cloak which can be freely shared with others, even those who might be dissenters. As it wears, new threads may be woven in, but the pattern will be retained.

A great gathering together of all these various philosophic and psychological threads began to form the warp and the woof of humanism in Amsterdam midway through the 20th century. In 1952, humanists gathered there to attempt to declare the nature of their philosophy and to stress its world-wide appeal at a time of some tensions in international affairs such as the 'cold war' between USSR and the Western nations. The document became known as 'The Amsterdam Declaration'. As organised humanism matured as a philosophy—friendly to evolution and hostile to dogma—the statement was updated in 2002. The 50th anniversary World Humanist Congress in 2002, again meeting in the Netherlands, unanimously passed a resolution known, not altogether surprisingly, as 'The Amsterdam Declaration 2002'. Following the Congress, this updated declaration was adopted unanimously by the IHEU General Assembly, and thus became the official defining statement of World Humanism. I am indebted to the Humanism UK for permission to quote the full Declaration.

The 2002 Amsterdam Declaration:

1. Humanism is ethical. It affirms the worth, dignity and autonomy of the individual and the right of every human being to the greatest possible freedom compatible with the rights of others. Humanists have a duty of care to all of humanity including future generations. Humanists believe that morality is an intrinsic part of human nature

based on understanding and a concern for others, needing no external sanction.
2. Humanism is rational. It seeks to use science creatively, not destructively. Humanists believe that the solutions to the world's problems lie in human thought and action rather than divine intervention. Humanism advocates the application of the methods of science and free inquiry to the problems of human welfare. But Humanists also believe that the application of science and technology must be tempered by human values. Science gives us the means, but human values must propose the ends.
3. Humanism supports democracy and human rights. Humanism aims at the fullest possible development of every human being. It holds that democracy and human development are matters of right. The principles of democracy and human rights can be applied to many human relationships and are not restricted to methods of government.
4. Humanism insists that personal liberty must be combined with social responsibility. Humanism ventures to build a world on the idea of the free person responsible to society and recognises our dependence on and responsibility for the natural world. Humanism is undogmatic, imposing no creed upon its adherents. It is thus committed to education free from indoctrination.
5. Humanism is a response to the widespread demand for an alternative to dogmatic religion. The world's major religions claim to be based on revelations fixed for all time, and many seek to impose their world-views on all of humanity. Humanism recognises that reliable knowledge of the world and ourselves arises through a continuing process of observation, evaluation and revision.
6. Humanism values artistic creativity and imagination and recognises the transforming power of art. Humanism affirms the importance of literature, music, and the visual and performing arts for personal development and fulfilment.
7. Humanism is a life stance aiming at the maximum possible fulfilment through the cultivation of ethical and creative living and

offers an ethical and rational means of addressing the challenges of our times. Humanism can be a way of life for everyone everywhere.

These seven affirmations offer a clear and unequivocal template for living a good fulfilling life among one's fellows and other creatures—a life which allows the freedom to act and think with due forethought, to be resilient in the face of stress and change and to be fair and generous to those who differ from us. Are these not guiding statements that are for you too, both aspirational and inspirational? It is my earnest hope that they could be and will be.

Postscript

The day after I typed these last few words and should have felt some slight satisfaction about 'having my say' on humanism, I watched a thin flurry of snowflakes. One or two, uncertain of their destiny, drifted erratically and almost horizontally past my study window. Some lighted hesitantly on the glass—reluctant icy stardust again to remind me of my various inadequacies, tedious repetitions, omissions, frustrations and boring banalities before relieving me of all of these by melting gently, as we all will one day, into the endless void.

Unlike Cardinal Newman from my Preface, I have a family who are quick to spot when the bright and lilting litany of the quotidian round imperceptibly (so far as I am concerned) becomes 'my lecturing voice'—the perfect audience switch-off. I am not entirely free of guilt in this regard, but normal home life tends to act as a natural corrective. One of my main aims when I set out to write this book was to engage the many interested and reasonable people who are really humanists by inclination, or even by persuasion without ever having recognised this or declared themselves as such. If the arguments I have put should have persuaded some others that reason and the weighing of evidence rather than a frustrated dependence on superstition and the supernatural can support a scientific understanding of our natural world and personal lives, the pursuit of a rational, flexible and adaptive system of morality and ethics should define how best to live a good and fulfilling life, then I shall take some satisfaction from my efforts.

The snowflakes silently dissolving on my window panes had become a lesser intrusion into my consciousness. My reverie cut short, I slipped back half a century or so to when I would strum my guitar and sing popular folksongs and some verses of my own—(nearly) the Tom Lehrer of lower Aberdeenshire! An admirer of Scottish poet, Professor Douglas Dunn's poem, "Thursday", because of how well it encapsulated my feelings at the conclusion of writing the book, I had originally thought of quoting it as a valedictory summary. Instead, because its less subtle content in relation to my theme, I decided to use some lines of my own:

I'M DONE!

The snow falls gently down—last chapter scrawled,
I can bore for Scotland—and my wife's appalled
That the likes of me who's getting old and bald,
Whose web of life has been well spun,
Should not capitulate now and gasp, relieved,
"I'm done!"

I know of ten thousand gods of wood, stone or brass
And of the son of one who just sat quietly on his ass
To offer his simple homilies to many lesser men,
Who knew nothing of astrophysics or the root of minus ten,
But reason and science now know what are the odds
Of knowledge being interfered with by any ghosts or gods
We know now how the thread of life is spun,
And now can tell the gods, "You're done!"

Sagan and Cox have unlocked the box
Holding the cosmic secrets of endless time
And space, for books and theories yet to come.
Even in our hubris we know our half-spent sun
In five billion years will die—no light, no heat, no fun—
and then, I fear, we'll all be done!

"I find it shocking," said a piqued Steve Hawking
"That the writer's made no mention of my favourite tenth dimension!"
But Einstein had muttered, "A stitch in Time should save nine!"
While in such learned halls as Trinity or Merton,
Young Heisenberg, in principle, remained uncertain.
"The improbability of gods has clearly won—
So just for now, I'm done!"

Now godless man must save this earthly sphere,
By science, goodwill, respect and free from fear,
So my children's children can happily become
Aware of what reason and tolerance have won
To let the light clear clouds of ignorance and strife
And let reason, science and justice illuminate all life
As all species still evolve, our human brains will grow and solve
More problems yet, before we ever say to anyone,
"This time, we're really, really done!"

About the Author

Perhaps unsurprisingly, in the light of what he has written here, Dr Clark is rather ambivalent about his early history of having been a son of the manse, caught between religious orthodoxy and his natural inclinations. Brought up in the north of Scotland and educated at Banff Academy and Aberdeen University, he retired as a Consultant Clinical Psychologist after nearly 40 years in the NHS and followed that in 1990 with six years in part-time private practice and writing his other books. Now, after several years more than his sell-by date, he looks back on a varied but intereting and reasonably successful career.

After a period of National Service in the RAF (from AC2 to Fying Officer) which provided the material for his 2006 book *Stand by your Beds!,* he worked first as an industrial psychologist at Leicester Industrial Rehabilitation Unit before becoming a clinical psychologist in the NHS, also in Leicester. He has taught and researched at the universities of Leicester and Aberdeen in the course of his work within a number of large NHS hospitals. He returned to Scotland in 1966 to take up a Consultant post in the Grampian Regional Hospital Board, eventually retiring as the Director of Grampian Health Board's Area Clinical Psychology Services and Hon. Clinical Senior Lecturer in the Dept. of Mental Health at Aberdeen University Medical School.

For his work in that context he was honoured with the OBE in 1990, and having been active in one or another form of public service formost of his life, was appointed by the Queen as a Deputy Lieutenant of Banffshire in 1992.

He was appointed as an Hon. Sheriff of Grampian and Highlands and Islands Sheriffdom and has sat on the bench at Banff for more than thirty-five years. In parallel with that he has been both a Children's Panel member and a Safeguarder in the Scottish juvenile justice system for 30 years.

In his earlier life he has been a Town and County Councillor of Banff and Banffshire for nine years as an Independent. He has been a short term Consultant for the WHO in Sri Lanka and has also been invited to lecture on his research in India, Canada and twice to the USA. He is the author of a small collection of occasional papers and several more substantial chapters (at least one of over 100 pages) in academic texts as well as over 30 published professional articles in peer reviewed journals.

Latterly he took to writing magazine articles and books—somewhat more hectically—as he is having to cope with increasing blindness which has already put paid to his painting and drawing, photography, playing music and, of course, reading. He depends more and more on his Kindle, computer and audiobooks.

He lives with his wife of 65 years and has two daughters, two sons in law, four grandchildren and one great grand daughter, all of whom have afforded him his greatest pride and pleasure.

Bibliography

Ayer, A.J. (2002) *Language, Truth and Logic*, Dover Books on Western Philosophy.

Baron-Cohen, Simon (1995) *Mindblindness: An Essay on Autism and Theory of Mind*, MIT Press/Bradford Books.

Benson, H. (2006) "A Study of the Therapeutic Effects of Intercessory Prayer in Cardiac Bypass patients: a multi-centre randomised trial of uncertainty and certainty of receiving intercessory prayer", *American Heart Journal,* April 151 (4*) 934-942.*

Blakemore, Colin (1994) *The Mind Machine*, BBC, London.

Block, Ned (1997) *The Nature of Consciousness*, Philosophical Debates, Cambridge, MA.

Briffault, Robert (1937) *Reasons for Anger*, Robert Hale Ltd, London.

Bryson, Bill (2003) *A Short History of nearly Everything*, Doubleday, Transworld, London.

Cave, Peter, (2009) *Humanism*, One World, Oxford.

Chalmers, David (1997) *The Conscious Mind: in search of a Fundamental Theory*, Oxford University Press, Oxford.

Cicero, Marcus Tullius (106BC-43BC) "Humanitas".

Clark, D. F., (1974) PhD thesis, "Body Image and Motor Skill in Normal and Subnormal subjects", Aberdeen University.

Clark, D. F. (2008) "The Sceptic's Tale", *Scottish Review*, pp 54-98. ICS Books, Glasgow.

Damasio, Antonio (2006) *Descartes' Error: Emotion, Reason and the Human Brain*, Vintage Books.

Darwin, Sir Charles (2009) *The Origin of Species*, Vintage Books, London.

Davidson, et al. (1999) *Principles and Practice of Medicine*, 18th edition, Churchill Livingstone, London.

Dawkins, Richard (1989) *The Selfish Gene*, Oxford University Press, Oxford.

Dawkins, Richard "(2006) *The God Delusion*, Bantam Press, London.

Dennett, Daniel (1991) *Consciousness Explained*, Little, Brown and Co. New York.

Dennett, Daniel (2007) *Breaking the Spell*, Allen Lane, London.

De Waal, Frans, (2013) *The Bonobo and the Atheist*, W. W. Norton and Company, New York.

Eagleman, David, (2015) *The Brain*, Canongate Books, Edinburgh.

Eysenck, H. J. (1947) *The Dimensions of Personality*, Routledge and Kegan Paul, London.

Galton, Sir Francis, (1872) "Statistical Inquiries into the Efficacy of Prayer" *Fortnightly Review*, Vol.12, pp125-135. London.

Grayling, A. C. (2013) *The God Argument*, Bloomsbury Press, London.

Grayling, A. C. (2001) *The Meaning of Things*, Phoenix Books, London.

Greene, Joshua (2014) *Moral Tribes*, Penguin, Random House, London.

Gribbin, John, (2000) *Stardust*, Allen Lane, Penguin Books, London.

Gribbin, John, (1999) *Almost Everyone's Guide to Science*, Phoenix Press, London.

Haidt, Jonathan (2012) *The Righteous Mind*, Allen Lane, Penguin Books, London.

Harari, etc, (2017) *Sapiens: A Brief History of Humankind*, Audiobooks, Penguin London

Harris, Sam (2005) *The End of Faith*, The Free Press, London.

Hawking, Stephen (2016) *A Brief History of Time*, Random House Audiobooks, London.

Hitchens, Christopher (2007) *God is not Great*, Atlantic Books Grove Atlantic, London.

Hume, Sir David (1739) *Treatise on Human Nature*, Edinburgh.

Huxley, Julian (1964) "The New Divinity", in *Essays of a Humanist*, Pelican Books, London.

James, William, (1890) *Principles of Psychology*, Henry Holt, New York.

Kelly, G. A. (1991) *The Psychology of Personal Construct*, Vols. 1 and 2, (2nd printing), Routledge, London, New York.

King, Barbara J. (1994) *The Information Continuum*, SAR Press.

Le Fanu, James (2010) "Science's Dead End", *Prospect Magazine*, July 21, 2010.

Maslow, Abraham (1954) *Motivation and Personality*, Harper & Brothers, New York.

McEwan, Ian (2005) *Saturday*, Jonathon Cape, London.

Mill, John Stuart (1910) *Utilitarianism, Liberty and Representative Government*, J M Dent and Sons, London.

Miller, Stanley and Urey, H.C. (1959) "Organic Compound Synthesis on the Primitive Earth", *Science 130, 245-251.*

Paine, Thomas (1791) *The Rights of Man*, J. S. Jordan, London.

Pinker, Steven (1998) *How the Mind Works*, Allen Lane, Penguin Books, London.

Pinker, Steven (2015) *The Language Instinct: The New Science*, Penguin Books, London.

Pinker, Steven (2018) *Enlightenment Now*, Penguin Books, London.

Power, Mick (2012) *Adieu to God: Why Psychology Leads to Atheism*, Wiley Blackwell, Chichester.

Ridley, M. (1996) *The Origins of Virtue*, Penguin Science, London.

Rogers, Carl (1951) *Client Centred Therapy*, Houghton Mifflin, New York.

Russell, Sir Bertrand, (1910) *The Problems of Philosophy*, Williams and Norgate, London.

Ryle, Gilbert (1949) *The Concept of Mind*, Hutchinson University library, London.

Shermer, Michael (2011) *The Believing Brain*, Times Books, New York.

Shermer, Michael (2015) *The Moral Arc*, Henry Holt and Co. New York.

Skinner, B. F. (1953) *Science and Human Behavior*, Macmillan, The Free Press, New York.

Stenger, Victor J. (2009) *The New Atheism*, Prometheus Books, Amherst, New York.

Stenger, Victor J. (2008) *God, The Failed Hypothesis*, Prometheus Books, Amherst, New York.

Tomasello, M. and Call, J. (1997) *Primate Cognition*, Oxford Univ. Press, New York.

Washington and Lee Law Review (1961) Volume 18 | Issue 2 Article 20 9-1-1961 Act of God.